THE
'X' CHRONICLES NEWSPAPER

Where Fact Is Fiction and Fiction Is Reality - Publishing Since 1990

| Vol 28, No 08 | A REL-MAR McConnell Media Company Publication | Digital Version - Aug/Sep 2018 |

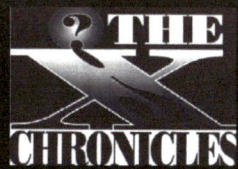

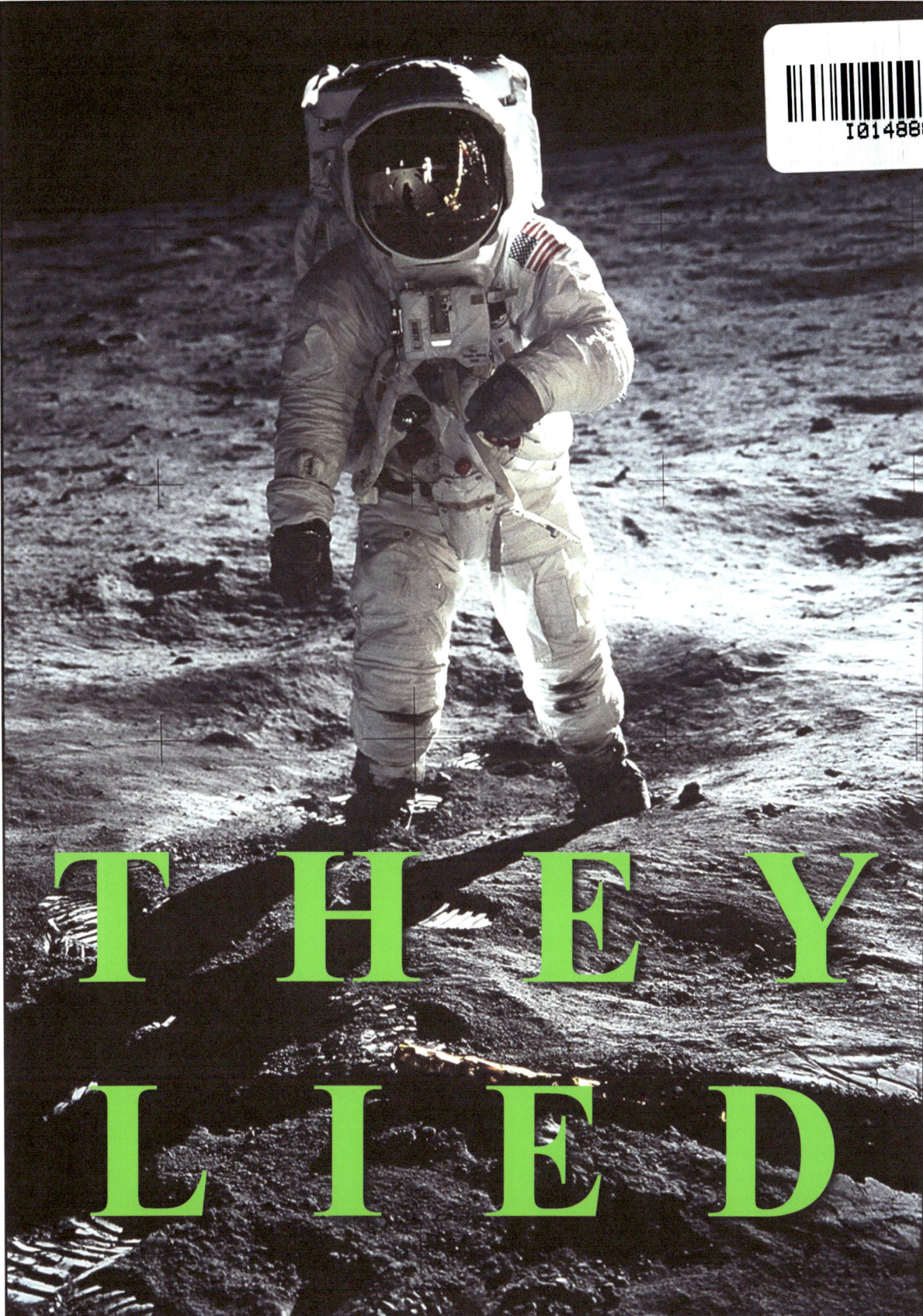

I0148880

THEY
LIED

The 'X' Chronicles Newspaper

August / September 2018

92 Pages

Digital: ISBN: 978-1-927758-73-1
E-Book: ISBN: 978-1-927758-74-8
Paperback: 978-1-927758-75-5

These are just **SOME** of the stories and articles in this edition of
THE 'X' CHRONICLES NEWSPAPER

The 'X' Zone TV Channel and The 'X' Zone Radio Channel, divisions of REL-MAR McConnell Media Company are now available on SimulTV. For subscription information on SimulTV, visit www.SimulTV.com

Coming December 2018 - The 'X' Zone Learning Channel on SimulTV - more information will be in the next edition of The 'X' Chronicles Newspaper.

Current Statistics

REL-MAR Investigations 365 - Buzz Aldrin on Moon Landings "We Didn't Go There"

Astronaut Buzz Aldrin
"We Didn't Go There"

Buzz Aldrin reveals 'we DIDN'T go to the moon' in bombshell clip

BUZZ Aldrin has sent conspiracy theorists into meltdown after video footage emerged of him saying "we didn't go to the moon".

The 88-year-old American is well-known for being one of the first men to step on the lunar surface, during his Apollo 11 mission with Neil Armstrong in 1969.

But now video footage apparently proves that never happened.

The clip, captured during the 2015 National Book Fest at the Walter E. Washington Convention Centre, shows the pensioner speaking to a young girl.

The youngster asks: "Why has nobody been to the moon in such a long time?"

And Buzz replied: "That's not an eight-year-old's question – that's my question.

"I want to know, but I think I know – because we didn't go there – that's the way it happened.

"And if it didn't happen it's nice to know why it didn't happen so in the future if we want to keep doing something we need to know why something stopped in the past if we want to keep it going."

And conspiracists have been quick to share their opinions.

"Oh my gosh, Buzz has spilt the beans," one viewer claimed.

Another added: "This is priceless, Buzz admitting they faked it to beat the Russians."

And a third speculated: "They are going to kill him for this."

But the retired astronaut's bizarre answer did come to a reasonable ending.

He eventually went on to explain that money was the main issue, proving his original answer was the result of confusion.

He revealed: "If you want to buy new things, new rockets, instead of keep doing the same thing over and over, then it's going to cost more money."

And there may be an answer for his bizarre fumbling answer, too.

His children believe the space traveller is suffering with mental health issues, The Blast reports.

Back in April Daily Star Online revealed he passed a lie detector after claiming to have seen a UFO during his moon landing mission.

Here is a transcript of the video which can be seen on The 'X' Zone TV Channel YouTube Channel https://youtu.be/a9tcP_4S1gE.

Little Girl: Why has nobody been to the moon in such a long time?

Buzz Aldrin: That's not an eight-year-olds question. That's my question. I want to know, or I think I know, 'cause we didn't go there and that's the way it happened. And if it didn't happen it's nice to know why it didn't happen so in the future if we want to keep doing something we need to know why something stopped in the past that we wanted to keep it going. uh, money is a good thing if you want to buy new things, new rockets, instead of keep doing the same thing over and it's going to cost more money, other things need more money too, so in order to achieve what the president wanted us to do, and then what thousands, millions of people in America, and millions of people around the world. You know when we toured around the world after we came back, the most fascinating observation was signs that said, "We Did It," not just us, not just America, but we, the world, the different country. They felt like they were part of what we were able to do, and that made us feel very good.

Was this the confession of a man who has had to hide the truth for so many years who finally had enough? Time will tell. []

The 'X' Zone Radio/TV Show Top Picks From Current Shows
by Rob McConnell

Dan Valkos:
- https://youtu.be/e77lWserkNg

Mary Rodwell:
- https://youtu.be/udyOxLA3-iA

Carl Lehburger:
- https://youtu.be/1qsOYXN8jUo

Jim Keopke:
- https://youtu.be/skq5eJhk8Io

Denise Stoner:
- https://youtu.be/vNsy6JyyYEw

Professor Stephen Braude:
- https://youtu.be/tdzTZZPKNxs

Josh Heard:
- https://youtu.be/2DxjGAV9f4Q

Christopher Balzano:
- https://youtu.be/iOx1JgAhpbE

Dr. David Gruder:
- https://youtu.be/L86eHSj4ezw

Sandi Athey:
- https://youtu.be/67RHaXtaBYg

Pattie Freeman:
- https://youtu.be/bY60aMzYXVI

Matt Ralston:
- https://youtu.be/2DMDI0UjRes

Benjamin Radford:
- https://youtu.be/vRw2E2L7wLU

UFO Myths: A Special Investigation into Stephenville and Other Major Sightings

By Phil Patton, with additional reporting by Davin Coburn, Erin McCarthy, Joe Pappalardo and Erik Sofge

What were the speed-shifting, color-morphing UFOs that mystified hundreds of eyewitnesses around Stephenville, Texas, on January8, 2008? Optical Illusions? Secret Military Operations? Alien Spaceships? Despite months of "investigations" by UFO enthusiasts investigating as well as UFO conspiracy theories, the mystery remains.

It was Jan. 8, 2008, and the trucking entrepreneur was sitting around a fire outside the Selden, Texas, home of Mike Odom, his friend since first grade. Then he saw the lights--orbs that glowed at first, then began to flash. "There was no regular pattern to the flashing," he says. "They lined up horizontally, seven of them, then changed into an arch. They lined up vertically, and I saw two rectangles of bright flame.That's when I knew it was a life-changing experience." He watched the lights drift north toward Stephenville, the seat of Erath County. "They came back a few minutes later," Allen says, "this time followed by two jets--F-16s, I think." Allen, who owns and flies a Cessna, has seen plenty of military planes over the years. "The jets looked like they were chasing the lights, and the lights seemed to be toying with them. It was like a 100-hp car trying to keep up with a 1000-hp one."

Odom also saw the lights and called to his wife, Claudette, who came outside in time to see the second display.When Allen returned home, he phoned friends at the local airport who checked with the Fort Worth airport tower. "Both said nothing was flying," Allen says.

That night, James Huse, a former Air Force navigation specialist, was in downtown Stephenville saying good-night to a couple of friends. "Out of the corner of my eye I saw two red orbs moving overhead," he says, "the reddest things I'd ever seen in the sky. They came right in front of me at 2000 ft about half a mile away. They weren't going that fast, maybe 60 mph. They didn't make any noise."

Outside Dublin, about 15 miles southwest of Stephenville, Constable Lee Roy Gaitan finished eating a slice of his wife's birthday cake, then headed out to his patrol car to get his wallet so his family could watch Mr. Bean on pay per view. That's when he saw the lights. "First, I saw a yellow-red orb the color of lava in a volcano," he says. "Then, instead of the red orbs, there were nine or 10 flashing lights maybe 3000 ft in the air, bouncing and very bright. They hovered there, strobing for 2 or 3 minutes, bright like German auto headlights. Then they shot off at blazing speed like a school of fish, you know, when it's frightened." Later, Gaitan says, two jets flew over.

The next day Allen called Angelia Joiner, a reporter at the Stephenville Empire-Tribune, and told his story. The paper published Joiner's piece--"Possible UFO Sighting"--on Jan. 10. It was the first of her numerous articles about the lights. On Jan. 11, Joiner called Maj. Karl Lewis, public affairs officer of the 301st Fighter Wing at the Naval Air Station Joint Reserve Base Fort Worth (formerly Carswell Air Force Base and now used by all the services). Lewis said the base had nothing flying the night of the sightings. Other nearby bases issued similar denials.

It all added up to the most dramatic UFO incident in more than a decade. "Texas Town Abuzz Over Dozens of UFO Sightings," wrote Foxnews.com. "Are UFOs Invading Texas?" asked Texas Monthly. "UFOs Put Stephenville in World Spotlight," said the Fort Worth Star-Telegram. CNN showed up, along with ABC, the BBC and other TV crews from as far away as Japan. So did Bill O'Reilly and Larry King. A longtime UFO fan, King devoted a segment to Stephenville and interviewed Gaitan and Joiner. Jake and Dorothy's Café, near the courthouse square, became a favored journalist hangout. "One day I went into Jake and Dorothy's for coffee, the way I always do," Huse says, "and there was a TV crew on one side of me and reporters on the other."

The Stephenville sightings had all the elements of a classic UFO incident--first reports, official denials, independent witnesses stepping forward. The Texas dairy town of 17,000 with the statue of a cow in the main square had joined Roswell, Area 51 and other small places as an iconic name in the annals of UFOs.

On the December night I drive from Dallas to Stephenville, the moon is in congruence with Venus and Jupiter: The two planets and crescent suggest a flag's heraldic pattern. By the end of the evening, the sinking moon is huge and orange, like a Ferris-wheel-size slice of cantaloupe hung in the trees.

The illusion that the moon is bigger near the horizon is just one of the tricks our eyes play on us when we observe objects in the heavens. Humanity has long infused these mysterious shapes and lights with portents and meanings interpreted according to the cultural notions of the day. The star-related deities of the Egyptians, the godlike comets of the Greeks, the mysterious shapes in the skies of Renaissance frescoes--all were forerunners of flying saucers. "The tendency to believe in the paranormal appears to be there from the beginning," Christopher Bader, a Baylor University sociologist, told LiveScience. "What changes is the content. Few people believe in fairies and elves these days. But as belief in fairies faded, other beliefs, such as belief in UFOs, emerged to take its place."

(Continued on Page 5)

UFO Myths: A Special Investigation into Stephenville and Other Major Sightings

Continued from Page 4

There is no dispute that UFOs exist--that is, objects flying through the sky that are unidentified. (In fact, one in seven Americans say they have seen UFOs.) But that, of course, does not mean they are ships from a distant galaxy. We humans tend to leap to conclusions, imagining alien spacecraft while discounting more likely explanations.

Over the centuries, the technology to record UFOs has evolved from marks on clay to video clips, and the causes of sightings may have changed from comets to secret aircraft, but the psychological pattern endures: It is the story of people projecting hopes and fears onto objects in the sky.

The Mutual UFO Network (MUFON), which is probably the most influential organization within the highly combative and suspicious UFO community, received so many reports about the Stephenville lights that the Colorado-based group set up an open hearing in nearby Dublin, Texas, birthplace of Dr Pepper and golfer Ben Hogan. On Sat., Jan. 19, some 500 people streamed into the 1909 brick building that is home to the local Rotary Club. "Everywhere I turned there were TV tripods," says Steve Hudgeons, a Fort Worth construction project manager and chief of MUFON's investigations in Texas.

Many people in attendance were simply curious. A few wore tinfoil caps. But more than 200 people came forward to tell their stories, with some sightings going back 30 years. Hutcheons and other MUFON investigators considered about 20 reports to be substantive and relevant to the Jan. 8 incident and promised to publish a report.

On Jan. 23, 12 days after denying it had planes in the air, the military reversed itself. According to a carefully worded press release issued by Air Force Reserve Command Public Affairs, "Ten F-16s from the 457th Fighter Squadron were performing training operations from 6 to 8 pm on Jan. 8 in the Brownwood Military Operations Area [MOA], which includes the airspace above Erath County."

Why the flip-flop? "It was an internal communications problem that has now been fixed," says 301st Fighter Wing spokesman Lewis. Inconsistent disclosures by the military have often fueled UFO speculation. The military changed its story about Roswell numerous times after 1947, when Air Force officials first claimed to have "captured" a flying saucer, then denied it.

Adding to the atmosphere of mistrust is the military's refusal to release details of operations, including training flights. Lewis declines to give specifics on hardware or tactics used over Erath County. During training, he says, "we fly like we fight."

By mid-February the Empire-Tribune had lost interest in the Stephenville lights; their reporter Joiner had not. She left the paper to run a Web site about the sightings, funded by Allen. The Dublin Citizen, however, continued to pursue the story. Publisher and editor Mac McKinnon, a former Air Force historian whose office is hung with model warplanes from his days in the service, saw some curious lights in January. "I believe the military has all sorts of exotic propulsion systems and other technologies we don't even know about," he says. He assigned the story to reporter Jon Awbrey, who also saw lights--"a triangle with squares at the corners."

Awbrey put me in touch with Dublin police chief Lannie Lee. In January two of his men had taped one of the lights using the dashboard video in their patrol car. He had not made the tape public. "I didn't want any notoriety to be attached to the department," the mild-mannered chief says.

He pulls out a VHS tape and leads me to the back of the station and puts it in the machine. On the screen, a dot appears against a black sky and begins to dance. The camera zooms in on a shimmering, bouncing but otherwise featureless circle of light. "It goes on like that for about an hour," Lee says.

The reports from January reminded another Dublin resident, machinist Ricky Sorrells, of a huge object he says he saw in December when he was deer hunting. "I looked at it through the scope on my deer rifle," Sorrells tells me over burgers at the Dublin Dairy Queen. He is a big man who has just come in from hunting, dressed in full camouflage. He describes what he saw as a "huge gray object," the color of galvanized metal, with no rivets, bolts or seams. "It was about 100 ft tall and about 300 ft up in the air," he says, comparing the height of the object to the grain elevator where he once worked.

t was the first of several sightings for Sorrells. He captured one of them on video. In the Dairy Queen, he unfolded his cellphone and handed it to me. I saw a tiny video of a barely discernable white shape moving through the sky.

After its Dublin open hearing, MUFON filed Freedom of Information Act requests with the military branches and other governmental agencies. Only the Federal Aviation Administration and the National Weather Service acknowledged they had relevant information and forwarded radar data.

In July, the group released its report, which suggests that several fighters as well as an Airborne Warning and Control System (AWACS) plane were in the area. But so, they claim, was a mysterious large object, without the required transponder that identifies and locates aircraft. The report concludes that a very large unidentified craft or object "was tracked on radar for over an hour. Most of the time, the object was either stationary or moving at speeds of less than 60 mph. At 7:32 pm, the object was tracked accelerating to 532 mph in 30 seconds and then slowing to 49 mph only 10 seconds later."

Radar blips would seem to present a positive, nonsubjective way to observe UFOs. Studies from the Condon Report, published in 1968 by the University of Colorado, to the Air Force's Blue Book project to a 1997 evaluation by the Society for Scientific Exploration, however, have found that radar can be "fooled" in simple ways. Anomalous propagation, or false echoes, is most often caused by ground clutter, often a result of low-level temperature inversions that muffle ground radar's electronic pulse and lead to a circular scatter of returns based on hits from buildings and trees.

In extreme examples, called ducting, the temperature inversion can bend the beam all the way back to the Earth's surface, so a surprising radar blip turns out to be a hill or a building. With the introduction of more advanced filtering software over the past decade, the number of UFOs attributed to false returns has decreased significantly.

Former Air Force pilot, astronomer and longtime UFO skeptic James McGaha believes that some such form of radar scatter was responsible for the returns that MUFON interpreted as a solid object. The FAA did not describe any such object, nor was it clear whether it was in the Brownwood MOA. "They had a huge amount of data," McGaha says, "and they just pulled a few bits of information out of it and drew a line."

(Continued on Page 6)

UFO Myths: A Special Investigation into Stephenville and Other Major Sightings

Continued from Page 5

What's in the sky? Some skeptics, like McGaha, believe that the Stephenville, Phoenix and many other sightings can be attributed to military aircraft and evasion or illumination flares.

Flares have a long association with UFO sightings. One night in late February 1942, the sky over Southern California lit up with strange blinking lights near various defense plants. In what has become known as the Battle of Los Angeles, the Navy unloaded four batteries of antiaircraft artillery at what turned out to be a balloon carrying a red flare. A decade ago, mysterious lights seen by thousands of Phoenix residents were actually leftover flares dumped by A-10 pilots with the Maryland Air National Guard.

Some Erath County residents dismiss the flare theory. "I've seen military flares," Allen says. "They are not even the same color as the ones I saw." But evasion-flare technology evolves rapidly, as the military tries to keep one step ahead of the increasingly sophisticated tracking capabilities of antiaircraft missiles. At one time evasive maneuvers consisted of sharp turns against the sun. When missiles got smarter, pilots began dropping bright flares; infrared seekers homed in on the decoys while warplanes fled from the field of view.

But today's missiles can track far more than the heat signatures of engines. They can pick out targets among decoys by discerning a warplane's movement and shape. Spectral sensors on missiles can even detect the color differences between a jet engine and a flare. In response, the military has deployed a variety of flares that can move under their own power and change color.

People in Erath County are certainly familiar with warplanes. During my visit, I get a taste of the 3200-square-mile Brownwood MOA in action. Helicopters and jets fly day and night. One afternoon, while I'm driving to Dublin on Highway 377, a T-38 Talon supersonic jet trainer rips past only a few thousand feet above the road.

The MOA is well-known to the leading civilian authority on Texas airspace, Steve Douglass. The author of Military Monitoring and an expert consulted by Aviation Week, Douglass has been tracking operations from his base in Amarillo for a quarter century. He is part of the so-called interceptors network, the plane spotters caricatured in the film Broken Arrow as "those guys in lawn chairs" staking out runways and bases. "Brownwood is used by Navy, Air Force and Army units," Douglass says, "including Apache helicopters, B-1s, C-130s and F-16s. There are AWACS from Tinker AFB in Oklahoma City and KR-135 tankers from Altus in southwest Oklahoma. The airspace is especially active these days, with the new F-35 tactical fighter being assembled at a factory in Fort Worth and tested in the MOA." Lockheed Martin spokesman John Kent confirms that on

Jan. 8, 2008, the first--and until June 2008, the only--F-35 test plane, the AA-1, was in Fort Worth, but it was not in the air that night. "It's restricted to daytime flight," Kent says, so that chase planes can monitor it.

Stephenville is only the latest in a long list of UFO incidents that are likely based on military operations, starting with the Battle of Los Angeles. Whether the recent Texas sightings were flight exercises involving evasion flares or tests of an existing plane, a new plane or a UAV, any military activity in the area is likely to remain unexplained for awhile. We now know about the secret programs behind the UFO sightings of decades ago. But what of programs that are still secret?

In the past, many projects sponsored by DARPA, which was behind the original Stealth and UAV research, have begun as secret black programs before showing up as public white ones. One example: stratospheric sensors developed for high-altitude airships under the ISIS program, which may have existed for years before it was made public in 2004. (Its funding for 2007 was $24.7 million.) These sensors could be used on huge wing- or boomerang-shaped blimps that can fly at altitudes of more than 60,000 ft and hover unmanned for months. "There have been many sightings of large, slow-moving triangle-shaped airships," says Steve Douglass, "starting with a sighting near Antelope Valley, Calif., in 1990." For many years airliners and ground observers have reported boomerang-shaped craft near Groom Lake.

The tethered "aerostat" lighter-than-air craft, which appeals to many agencies as a so-called poor man's satellite, also may trigger sightings. The Air Force uses these surveillance systems along the U.S.-Mexico border to support antidrug operations. The departments of Defense and Homeland Security are evaluating unmanned inflatables 500 ft long.

The military's secrecy exasperates some Stephenville locals, even veterans. "It's been 30 years since I was in the Air Force," James Huse says, "but I don't understand why they wouldn't

come out and tell the truth. If they have the capability of putting on a show like that all they have to do is tell us. We'd get out our lawn chairs and watch."

But the Air Force's legitimate need for secrecy extends beyond its black programs. It releases information about all domestic flights on a case-by-case basis, says Capt. Rose Richeson, of the USAF Air Education and Training Command. "Usually we don't mind talking about training," she says. "But we would not talk about specifics if it were a matter of national security, or give details about training methods or mission scenarios that could be used by enemies of the United States."

Meantime, Stephenville has settled uneasily into its newfound notoriety as a UFO site. Some locals have become skeptical about the motives of MUFON. "Who funds it?" asks Steve Allen. And a certain amount of backbiting has set in among some of the eyewitnesses. Lee Roy Gaitan worries that some locals who have reported sightings are "just not credible" and cast doubt on his genuine account. "Some people stretch a story," Huse says. Others resent the way they have been depicted. "I made the mistake of saying it was as big as a Wal-Mart," Allen says. "People have been teasing me about it ever since."

"I didn't call them flying saucers or extraterrestrials," Huse says. "All I said was that it was unidentified flying objects, and I'm sticking to that. I couldn't identify them." People in Erath County, Huse says, aren't nuts or hicks. "We are just ordinary people who happened to look up." []

Fact*oids:

- Jelly fish are over 95% water and have no heart, blood, brain, or gills.
- Twenty-five million gallons of water can fall during a 20-minute thunderstorm.
- Quinine, used to cure malaria, comes from the leaves of the cinchona plant.
- Robert Ludlow was the tallest recorded man at 8 ft. 11.1 in (272 cm).

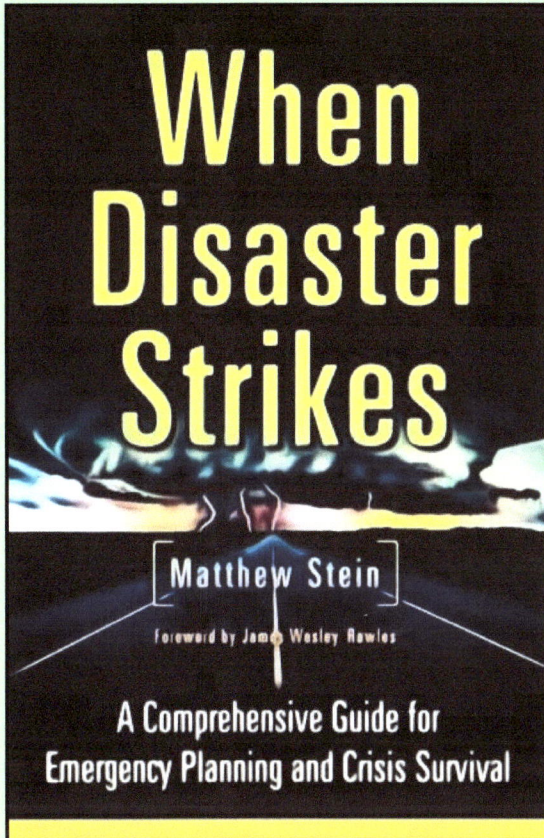

The Stephenville Lights: What Actually
Happened

The Editors
Skeptical Inquirer
www.csicop.org

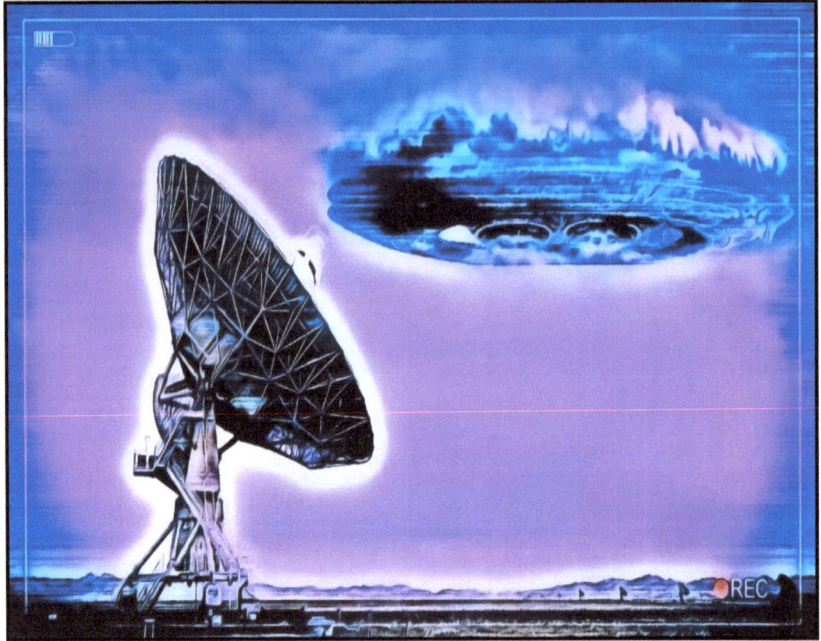

One of the most widely publicized UFO reports of the past few years is the so-called Stephenville Lights of January 8, 2008. Stephenville, Texas, is a small town (population 17,000) one hundred miles southwest of Dallas. Between 6:15 and 7:30 pm local time, forty witnesses reported seeing very bright lights. They made no sound. They were said to be slowly moving, then moved quickly. Many said the lights were pursued by military aircraft. Some said they sped away at 3,000 miles per hour. Some said they saw a single object one mile long. One said it was a life-changing experience.

A local Stephenville newspaper reported the story on January 10, and a public affairs officer for the Naval Air Station, Joint Reserve Base at Carswell Field, sixty nautical miles away, was quoted as saying, "There were no F-16s from this unit operating." (That proved to be wrong.) The national media picked up the story about the lights, and it was featured on Larry King Live on January 18.

Astronomer (and retired Air Force pilot) James McGaha (see the accompanying "The Trained Observer" piece) investigated. On January 17, he contacted the Federal Aviation Administration and asked if any aircraft that night had entered the Brownwood Military Operating Areas (MOAs). These MOAs begin ten miles southwest of Stephenville—a 3,200-square-mile area used for military aviation training. The FAA informed McGaha on January 18 that a group of four F-16s from the 457th Fighter Squadron entered the operating area at 6:17 pm local time. A second group of four F-16s entered the same area at 6:26 pm. They departed at 6:54 and 6:58, respectively. The time the aircraft were flying in the MOA accords with the time of the sightings.

On January 18 McGaha contacted the 301st Fighter Wing Public Affairs Office and asked if they made a mistake in saying their aircraft had not been in the MOA that night. They called him back and informed him of their error. On January 23, they issued a press release publicly acknowledging the error, stating that F-16s had indeed been flying in the MOA that evening.

What were the aircraft doing? McGaha says they were flying training maneuvers that involved dropping extraordinarily bright flares. The LUU/2B/B flare is nothing like the standard flares you might think of. These flares have an illumination of about two million candlepower. They are intended to light up a vast area of the ground for nighttime aerial attack. Once released, they are suspended by parachutes (which often hover and even rise due to the heat of the flares) and light up a circle on the ground greater than one kilometer for four minutes. The flare casing and parachute are eventually consumed by the heat. At a distance of 150 miles, a single flare can still be as bright as the planet Venus.

McGaha also describes the testimony of a medical helicopter pilot, a retired U.S. Army pilot, flying that night, who saw the lights. He said: "I saw multiple military aircraft, with some dropping flares, in the area of the Brownwood 1 MOA."

Much mischief was caused by a Mutual UFO Network (MUFON) report on the incident issued on July 4, 2008. MUFON members tend to promote the idea that UFOs are real and in fact are extraterrestrial spacecraft. The seventy-six-page report is mostly an analysis of FAA "raw" radar returns for the period in question, plus eight eyewitness reports.

These raw data contain 2.5 million points of noise and scatter. MUFON's report selected just 187 of these points to contend that radar had tracked a huge "object" at least 524 feet in size, traveling near the Western White House (the Bush ranch, which is fifty miles southeast of Stephenville). "MUFON's radar analysis is nothing more than cherry picking the 187 targets out of 2.5 million points of noise and scatter to make a track moving forty-nine mph for over one hour," says McGaha. "This analysis is absurd!"

Some MUFON witnesses described "very bright lights similar to the intensity of burning magnesium" and said they saw flares dropped from aircraft. Others said such things as "these were not any known aircraft" and the objects were stationary at times but also "moved at a very high rate of speed." But these witnesses were not trained observers, McGaha says. "How did they know the altitude, velocity, size, and distance of an unknown object?"

There were lights in the sky, McGaha concludes. "There were F-16s flying in the Brownwood MOAs, and they did drop flares. The F-16s did not react to any unknown targets, and radar did not detect any unknown targets."

"The untrained witnesses/observers were seeing nothing more than F-16s and flares. Stephenville is nothing more than connecting 'lights in the sky' to form a very large mysterious object, an object that many that night thought was from another world. But nothing otherworldly happened around Stephenville on January 8, 2008," says McGaha. []

UFO Investigators Flock to Stephenville, Texas

ABC News - January 18, 2008

UFO investigators, flock to Stephenville, Texas!

A team of six investigators from the Mutual UFO Network will be interviewing citizens of Stephenville, Texas, who say they spotted a UFO at sunset on Jan. 8.

The Mutual UFO Network is a nongovernmental group interested in documenting UFOs. State director Ken Cherry says that the network has received calls from 50 citizens who say they witnessed the UFO and that the number and credibility of the people is exceptional.

The rural Texas town has attracted worldwide attention after the sightings. The Stephenville Empire-Tribune, the local newspaper, has received calls from as far away as Finland and Japan as people remain fascinated about the reports of a bright object in the sky that witnesses say was a mile long.

Stephenville prides itself on being the dairy capital of Texas and the shirts that sell for $10 have a picture of a Holstein cow being beamed up to a flying saucer.

Not Just Tabloid News

More than 30 residents of Stephenville, Texas, claim to have seen a UFO, described as a mile-wide, silent object with bright lights, flying low and fast. And now it's actual front-page news. So what was it?

"It was very intense, bright lights," said local newspaper reporter Angela Joyner.

"The lights were like going like this," said Constable Leroy Gateman making hand gestures to describe what he saw when he spotted the UFO.

Rick Sorrells says he saw it while he was hunting deer in the woods.

"You look at the trees, and it was right here," Sorrells told ABC News correspondent Mike Von Fremd as he showed him the location in the woods where he spotted the UFO.

Steve Allen, a 50-year-old pilot, was at a campfire with friends and says the object was a mile long and half a mile wide. "I don't know if it was a biblical experience or somebody from a different universe or whatever but it was definitely not from around these parts," Allen said.

Allen drew a sketch of the object, which he said traveled at amazing speed without making a sound. While drawing, Allen told Von Fremd that he saw "an arch shape converted in a vertical shape, and then it split and made two of them, and then these turned into just fire and it was gone."

A spokesman for the 301st Fighter Wing in Fort Worth says no aircraft from his base was in the area, and says the objects may have been an illusion caused by two commercial airplanes. But those who saw the lights don't buy that explanation.

"It's an unidentified flying object," insisted a former Air Force technician.

"It was so fast I couldn't track it with my binoculars," said Gateman.

Some in Stephenville are a bit embarrassed about all the attention. "It's crazy," said one teenage girl in town.

"A lot of folks aren't used to this kind of thing. They are not UFO nuts or anything like that around here," said City Councilman Mark Murphy.

Like it or not, all eyes are now trained on the sky over Stephenville to see whether any mysterious flying objects return. []

MUFON releases report on UFO sighting in Stephenville, Texas

WikiNews - July 18, 2008

On January 8, 2008 in Stephenville, Texas, one of the larger UFO sightings in the United States occurred. A few days ago the UFO investigative organization Mutual UFO Network (MUFON) released a 77-page report on the sighting. MUFON is a UFO investigative organization in the United States. Founded in 1969, it now has 3,000 members and is headquartered in Fort Collins, Colorado.

The MUFON report, entitled "Special Research Report Stephenville, Texas" was written by Glen Schulze and Ropert Powell. Shulze has radar experience from working at the White Sands Missile Range. Powell has a chemistry degree and has extensive experience with semiconductors from working for Advanced Micro Devices.

The report is an analysis of radar records from the Federal Aviation Administration and the National Weather Service, obtained through several Freedom of Information Act (FOIA) requests, and comparing them to witness accounts.

Shulze/Powell concluded that the radar data confirms the witness observations of an object, as well as the Air Force's statement that said ten aircraft were operating in the area. They say that it is too difficult to say what the witnesses saw, but that there was something there. Twice, they say, radar picked up an object travelling at nearly 2,000 mph, and at other times it showed a slow moving object.

Much media attention has been focused on the report's observation that radar records show one of two objects moving directly toward the Prairie Chapel Ranch in Crawford. This is the home of United States President George W. Bush, which has been nicknamed the Western White House. They did not draw any conclusion as to why such movement was observed.

The authors also concluded that military air activity was heavy at the time, but that the radar records show no overt action toward the unknown object. They express concern about the possibilty that this could have been a terrorist aircraft with no transponder.

Shulze/Powell stated that they felt that they had been stonewalled in some of their FOIA requests by some government agencies. They encouraged the government to more readily provide more information about the incident.

The Stephenville incident on January 8, saw dozens of witnesses reporting a large object in the evening sky that hovered above the community before it took off at high speed. Steve Allen, a pilot, observed the object from the ground and described it as being a half-mile with flashing strobe lights. He also said that it was pursued by two fighter jets, when it disappeared at a speed he estimated to be 3,000 mph.

"I don't know if it was a biblical experience or somebody from a different universe or whatever but it was definitely not from around these parts," Allen said.

Another witness was local law enforcement officer Leroy Gateman who reported it as a red glowing object suspended 3,000 feet in the air. "It was so fast I couldn't track it with my binoculars," said Gateman.

Rick Sorrells says he saw the object while deer hunting in the woods. "You look at the trees, and it was right here," he told ABC News. He estimated it to be the length of "three or four football fields," though he could not be entirely sure due to his vantage point.

Sorrells has later claimed that military helicopters have since overflown his property at low altitude and that he has been getting strange phone calls. He also claims that an unknown man came to his door, even once told him that,"Son we have the same caliber weapons you have, but we have more of them.", after Sorrells grabbed his rifle, and, "You need to shut your mouth about what you saw."

"I'm trying to decide whether or not to open the door," Sorrells said to the Empire-Tribune. "We're just standing there face to face looking at each other. I'm thinking he's dressed for the elements and the dogs are raising such a ruckus he must know he's in danger of being caught. That's when I realized he wanted me to see him." The man then turned away and walked into the woods.

The United States Air Force initially said witnesses must have seen reflections coming from commercial airliners. However, they later clarified that ten F-16 Fighting Falcons had been on a night-time training mission in the area on January 8.

"In the interest of public awareness, Air Force Reserve Command Public Affairs realized an error was made regarding the reported training activity of military aircraft," said the statement.

According to Air Force spokesperson Karl Lewis, the aircraft were from the 457th Fighter Squadron and the error in the initial report was due to an internal communications problem between offices at the base.[]

Fact*oids:

- The stupidest dinosaur was the stegosaurus with an elephant-sized body and a walnut-sized brain.
- Hamsters originated in Syria.
- The quahog clam is the longest-living sea creature: aged 150 years.
- With jaws shut, a crocodile's fourth tooth protrudes but all of an alligator's teeth are hidden.
- The pill bug is one of the few crustaceans that live on land.
- Squids, cuttlefish, and octopuses are carnivores.

Dr. Carl O Helvie

HOLISTC CANCER FOUNDATION

Meet Carl O Helvie, R.N., Dr.P.H., - Carl O Helvie, R.N., Dr.P.H. is a registered nurse with a doctorate in Public Health (Johns Hopkins) and over sixty years' experience as a nurse practitioner, educator, author and researcher. He has published 8 books and chapters in 4 additional ones, and published 40 articles, presented over 55 research papers internationally and 60 papers for lay groups. Some of his books resulted from his development and over 35 years refinement of the Helvie Energy Theory of Nursing and Health that has been used internationally in practice, education and research by 9 countries. Read more about Carl O Helvie at www.HolisticCancerFoundation.com and www.BeatLungCancer.com..

CARL O HELVIE HOLISTIC CANCER FOUNDATION

The Carl O Helvie Holistic Cancer Foundation differs from others because we focus on:

  A holistic approach
  Multiple aspects of education, research, patient care and politics
  Multiple cancer types

A holistic approach consists of combining physical, mental and spiritual modalities as well as considering the environment, relationships and politics because all of these elements influence health and wellness (cancer and recovery) and may need to be assessed and included in any treatment plan.

An important part of any cancer program is education for those who have cancer or want to prevent it as well as lawmakers who influence cancer programs and public access to these programs through the decisions they make. Likewise, because we evolve in a dynamic environment cancer causation changes over time and consequently ongoing research is needed to identify and find solutions to these changing causes. In today's world where harsh invasive drugs and procedures that often compromise the immune system have evolved as the treatment of choice for most medical conditions including cancer, medical coverage is often denied those who wish to find treatment outside the conventional realm. These cancer patients are subsequently often required and frequently unable to pay for their treatment of choice. This gap provides a rationale for both funding patient care and involvement in the political process to bring about necessary changes in cancer care and funding. Please visit and donate today!

www.HolisticCancerFoundation.com

Air Force Alters Texas UFO Explanation

NPR - Jan 24, 2008

The Air Force is changing its story on what happened on a recent night in Stephenville, Texas, when dozens of witnesses say they spotted a UFO.

Two weeks ago, witnesses reported seeing a large aircraft with white lights hovering for about five minutes before being chased away by jet fighters.

The Air Force Reserve in nearby Fort Worth initially scoffed at reports and denied the possibility that it had fighters in the area. Air Force officials reversed course Wednesday, however, and admitted there were nearly a dozen F-16s over Stephenville that night.

Does this new revelation bolster or cast doubt on the witnesses' stories?

The night of the supposed UFO sighting, just after 6 p.m., Claudette Odom, her husband and two other friends, were clearing brush near her house. They were standing on top of a hill with visibility that extended more than 20 miles in every direction. From out of the west, Odom saw an object approach in the darkness.

"I've never seen anything that fast. Maybe a rock or a missile or something," she says.

Odom says they watched in wonder as the aircraft approached Stephenville and then silently hovered outside the outskirts of town. The lights flickered then went solid, shaping into a massive arch, she says, before forming a single bright vertical line that split into two.

"They were extremely, extremely bright. Like an arc on a welder, they were that sharp," Odom says.

As they watched the object hover in place, they were startled by the explosive sound of two F-16s, screaming directly over their hill at low altitude, heading toward the UFO, she recalls.

The Matter of the Jets

Whether there were military jets in the area that night was the first substantive doubt that was cast on the UFO witnesses' credibility.

When contacted, the Air Force at Carswell Field near Fort Worth stated that they definitely didn't have any fighter jets over Stephenville that night. The officials suggested the UFO witnesses might have seen an optical illusion.

When Odom heard the Air Force's response, she says she knew that something was amiss.

"I don't know what they're trying to cover up. We saw what we saw. I knew they were fighter jets," she says.

Now, two weeks later, in a plot line that's out of the X-Files, Air Force officials are saying that there was a communications error. They concede that they had F-16s flying over Stephenville, Texas, on the evening of Jan. 8.

Major Karl Lewis attributes the change in response to an internal communications mistake.

"There was an error that was reported and we corrected that error as soon as possible," he says.

Could Jets Have Been Mistaken for a UFO?

Angelia Joiner, the reporter at the Stephenville Empire-Tribune who broke the story, says that none of the UFO witnesses believe they mistook the F-16s for the massive object that put on a dazzling lights show. The Air Force's belated admission that it did indeed have F-16s there — the exact fighter jet that was described by several of the UFO witnesses as giving chase to the UFO — only bolsters the witnesses' story, she says.

"It just makes it seem like something's going on. The military coming out with this at this point is just going to fuel the fire," Joiner says.

Still unanswered is whether any F-16 pilots saw bright lights and a massive, incredibly fast aircraft. Major Lewis says that as far he knows, nothing unusual was reported. But he also says that he wouldn't want to speculate about what the pilots might have seen that night and that, as far as he knows, the pilots have not been interviewed.

Stephenville residents report an unidentified flying frenzy

**The Houston Chronicles
January 19, 2008**

Days after Stephenville residents reported a mysterious object in the skies, the area has become a hot spot for UFO enthusiasts.

All hype aside, space aliens have not invaded the streets of this rodeo town southwest of Fort Worth — though nearly everyone here is keeping at least a playful eye out for them.

But even if there's been no space invasion of Stephenville, the recent obsession with them has been out of this world in the town of 15,400 — and far beyond.

Ken Cherry, the Texas director of the Colorado-based Mutual UFO Network, or MUFON, which describes itself as devoted to research on the topic, says the multiple sightings of a strobelight-flashing object zipping through the night sky on Jan. 8 could turn Stephenville into a mini-Roswell.

"Dozens of people are coming forward, responsible people, saying they saw something," Cherry said. "We're talking shop owners, ranch owners, oil field workers, just about every demographic imaginable."

Forget being the Cowboy Capital of the World. Folks in town are calling Stephenville the UFO Capital of the World.

Angela Joiner, the only full-time reporter at the Stephenville Empire-Tribune, can hardly put out a paper. Ever since breaking the story last week, she's been swamped with calls and e-mails from around the world — from people who either want to tell her about their UFO sightings or from international media types covering the story.

"I'm not accustomed to this. I don't do

this!" Joiner, who's been on the job 18 months, said with a laugh.

Perhaps the only person who gets less work done these days is the local constable, LeeRoy Gaitan. He's in demand as the only elected official who can corroborate what dozens of others saw: something spooky in the sky over Erath County that evening.

He was on foot approaching his home when in the distance he saw a red glow, not as big as a hot air balloon but big. It didn't appear to be attached to anything. He watched it awhile before it burned itself out. Then it reappeared.

"I knew this wasn't right," he said. So he went inside to summon his family. His wife gave him this "get real" look, Gaitan said, but his young son came running.

Father and son saw what looked like really bright white strobe lights, nine or 10 of them. They flashed as the minutes passed.

"All of a sudden, they shot off, they traveled northeast at a real high rate of speed," Gaitan said.

Though he doesn't believe it was a spaceship, he's had to answer calls from hundreds of people from around the country who do. His solution: "I've started screening my calls," he said.

Military officials have said they had no aircraft in the area at the time of the sightings.

And the military doesn't investigate UFO sightings. So that leaves Cherry's MUFON group. Four or five of its investigators will descend on the area today to begin interviewing witnesses.

It won't be a quick investigation, Cherry cautions. Interviews will be conducted one on one. And even after all the anecdotes have been gathered and sifted through — don't expect physical evidence — the researchers will hedge their bets.

"We could say we eliminated every other possibility. But we never say, 'This is alien technology' or 'This is a spacecraft,' " Cherry said.

For now, people around town are having a ball.

City Secretary Cindy Stafford wore a space alien mask to the City Council this week. It was fun, she said.

Dennis Balthaser, a UFO researcher and former investigator with the International UFO Museum and Research Center in Roswell, N.M., isn't ready to make any educated guesses about what might have crossed the sky in Texas.

But, if the lights were a mile long and half a mile across, as some have suggested, that would be the size of a "mothership," which is much bigger than a flying saucer, he said.

Balthaser, a retired engineer with the Texas Department of Transportation, takes his research seriously and hates when other people don't.

He probably wouldn't appreciate the T-shirts produced by the high school science club here that proclaim: "Erath County: The New Roswell" and depict a spaceship leaving Earth and towing a dairy cow.

By Friday, the club had sold 400 of them.

[]

The Nature Of Evil and Ignorance - Safe or Sorry!

By Jock Brocas

It has always been a common perception within the spiritualistic community to deny the existence of evil - especially when one is communicating through the agency of mediumship. On one side of the fence, there is the medium who will say, "Well in all my years of working and developing da da da da, i have never come across anything evil" Then also following with the recourse that if you just keep your energy high and ask for divine protection, you will be ok.

I am certainly not picking or pointing any fingers out at our spiritual colleagues, but one must consider the nature of evil or everything that is in opposition to the light has of course existed since time immemorial. There are countless examples of nefarious or negative entities that have caused pandemonium, not only to a medium, but within the environment or particular target. Is it not safer to accept, rather than refute the existence and nature of evil within the world and also within our spiritually enhanced energetic environment.

The problem With Denial

You can deny the existence of evil all you want, or bad spirits, but that does not mean they do not exist. All this means is that deep down inside your own consciousness, there is a part of you that will not face the reality and truth of the polar opposite. Think about this; if you did not know dark, you would not know light, if you did not know pain, you would not know health. The reality of our polar opposite is real because it is also a necessary part of our growth. Nevertheless, there is a polar opposite that has its own will, its own law's, which of course are governed by divine law and its own modus operandi. You may never experience this and that's ok, but there are people who do, it is an event or events that are never forgotten.

Personally, I am not supportive of telling someone something does not exist or not to worry about it when there are examples and cases from almost every belief system or spiritual text and from the plethora of communications from the otherside. It is real, it exists and "Knowledge Gives Strength to the arm." It is therefore better, in my opinion, to keep the door of the stable bolted than to let it open and let the horse out.

The individual who is developing or who is beginning to study the mechanics of the otherside are lulled into a false sense of security and though it does not happen so often, things can and will get out of control, should the chink in the armor be weakened. Imagine the responsibility you have on your shoulders and those who look up to you and you tell them something does not exist and not to worry about it. How would you feel if that person's life was turned upside down and all because you never prepared them enough.

That individual may take it upon themselves to delve further and without the proper knowledge or discernment and could find themselves in tremendous hot water. Should they become the interest of a negative spirit, it does not need to be a quick turnaround either, it can simmer and develop over years. The fisherman often has tremendous patience to catch the big catch and that's the same when there is a potential hook on the line for the agency of what is understood as evil.

The Philosophical Argument

The nature of evil is not only a philosophical issue, but also has its roots in folklore and differing belief systems. However, the reality of EVIL can simply be understood as the separation to a greater extent of that which is divine or good, the total opposite. Now, I deliberately make reference to the extent of the division because in reality that which is considered evil was of course created by the same divine essence of all of creation.

Within the Kabbalah, it is understood as the absence of light.
In Christianity, it is that which is in opposition to good.

The argument of whether or not there is a giverning deity of Evil such as the Devil, Satan or its namesake in many other cultures, does not matter. Evil is evil and it hates anything that perpetuates from light.

The Great Spirit guide Silver birch alludes to the presence of Evil within man's perception;

"But do not forget that you are the Great Spirit and the Great Spirit is you. The power which belongs to the Great Spirit, which belongs to you, can raise you triumphant over all matter. It is a power which, properly understood, can enable you to resist all evil, to overcome all sickness and to fight every obstacle. But few of you use it."

In Many seances of the past and even within the psychological work of Carl Wickland, there are a plethora of statements from those communicating spirits that describe the negative and evil spirits that try to gain hold of those spirits trapped within the consciousness of a host.

The philosophy of it all can be argued till the end of time but the reality remains that it still exists, whether manifested in thought, material manifestation or by divine order - It exists. No matter if your perception believes in it or not, the truth of the matter is the existence in multitudinous forms but essentially we can break evil down into three particular sections, that of;

Theological, Logical and of course the Evidential. Consequently, all of these separations are continually argued, but again, I challenge you to prove that Evil does not exist just the same as you will challenge a skeptic to prove the afterlife does not exist. Both exercises are futile and therefore break down further into faith and perception.

(Continued on Page 13)

The Nature Of Evil and Ignorance - Safe or Sorry!

Continued from Page 12

How Can You Be Sure When You Are Not Sure Of Yourself

We as spiritualists have a greater responsibility to not bury our heads and not lead anyone astray. As we look toward the beauty and majesty of a flower and argue the reality for divine order within a chaotic universe, how then can we separate the evil that permeates the universe and claim it is null in void or does not exist and is a mere illusion or creation of man's failures. There is no one here that can be 100 percent sure and though you may not have come across anything of a real diabolical nature in your career, it is foolhardy to claim the non-existence of it. If you think it, it exists, no matter in what energetic form.

Our pioneers of the past within mediumship have warned us about nefarious spirits and negative energy. Think about it, you say a prayer of protection at the beginning of a circle, why? You keep your vibration as high as possible, why? Simply, because there is a negative aspect within that realm, it is clear in all spiritual concepts and in all religious texts.

What If You're Not Ready

Do you think you would be ready to face the challenge should it be presented. It is not enough to run around with woo woo sticks, prayers with no power and an Ignorant mindset of Evil and how to face it. Most of us will never face real diabolical power in our lives and we thank the great spirit for that, but for some the reality is real and often very different from that which is perceived in the real world. The person who takes up the burden of helping others who are experiencing or have experienced, will forever be a target and will forever have to maintain a high vibration in thought, word and deed. There is no adulation for those who serve in this capacity.

It is not enough to have knowledge or even theory for everything we experience in life is within. Nothing exists as an external experience, all is within. I am sure you have heard that statement a million times, but there is a reason the statement keeps permeating our consciousness, and that's because it's true. So the power is within, it is your discernment and your divinity that is the seat of your power and its important to be guarded with it and to continue in its reverence to the divinity within.

The Process Of Discernment

In the previous statement, Silver Birch tells us that most of us don't use it. This is the same within all of our perceptions and the influences around us cause separation from that divine power. So discernment is not about perceiving what is good or bad, it is harnessing the divine power within you that is over and above that which is in opposition to you. It is not something you learn, it is beyond all knowledge, it is something you are. It is better to maintain an

understanding and healthy respect for without yin, there is no yang.

In Conclusion

Evil exists whether or not you believe in it. Even if you don't believe in gravity, it will not stop you falling. []

About Jock Brocas:

Jock Brocas is an evidential Spiritual Medium and spiritual author of several books. Jock writes with passion and in-depth knowledge. The books are written with one common goal, which is to enlighten and teach spiritual lessons of love, compassion and forgiveness. Recognized as an accurate evidential medium, he has dedicated his later years to his own spiritual development and the professional development of his Mediumship.

As a proponent of many different disciplines, these skills have culminated into developing unique perspectives on spirituality and spiritual life. Jock teaches regularly and works tirelessly to help those developing on a spiritual path.

Visit Jock Brocas on line at www.jockbrocas.com

Fact*oids

- The only birds with penises are swans.
- The loudest animal sound is produced by the blue whale - a 188 decibel whistle.
- Dr. Alphonse Rockwell, a dentist, was the inventor of the electric chair.
- Bats always go left upon exiting a cave.
- The first E-mail was sent in 1971.
- The only continent with no tress is Antarctica.
- Women blink more than men and most humans blink 6.2 million times a year.
- Want more Fact*oids? Keep reading!

Did Astronauts Go 1000 Times Farther 49 Years Ago Than They Can Today?

by Bart Sibrel

Ever wonder why they claimed to have walked on the moon, on the very first attempt (even though, right here on earth, Mt. Everest and the South Pole took numerous tries before success), allegedly accomplishing this amazing feat with antiquated 1960's technology (while today a cell phone has one million times more computing power than all of NASA did back then), yet forty-nine years later, the farthest an astronaut can travel from the Earth is only 1/1000th the distance as claimed half a century ago with antique rocket and computer equipment?

Life is not so much a battle between right and wrong, as it is a battle between Truth and Lies, as this generally precedes, and ultimately leads to, good or evil. Truth leads to good. Lies lead to evil. Life is wonderfully simple.

The simple fact is, half of all crimes are "conspiracies". Half are done without forethought, in the heat of the emotion of the moment, and half are plotted out in advance,

thus making them conspiracies. Those who would like the public to ignore half of all the crimes in the world by ridiculing those with an intellect to perceive such forethought frauds are simply those perpetrating the deceptions in the first place.

We have to understand that if a tiny spider, the size of a dime, can meticulously plan and trap its prey weeks in advance, then the human mind, if inclined to evil, can do so much more evil, so much farther in advance. Additionally, a lie, or conspiracy, is the only crime that can exist without tangible evidence. If someone is murdered, there is a dead body. If someone steals, there is the material possession lacking in one place and existing in another. Yet, when someone lies, where is it? A lie is the only crime that you cannot touch, that you cannot see. A lie is purely ethereal. This is why lies are the favorite misdeeds of habitual criminals. After all, out of all of the crimes committed in the world for which people are put in prison, how many of them are there for simply lying?

The origin of crime is the lie, or conspiracy, invented in advance of the iniquity, to cover up the wrongdoing before it is even committed. When crimes are committed on a national and international scale, then national and international lies, or conspiracies, are needed. This is why criminal multibillion-dollar corporations and governments have consolidated all television networks, magazines, and newspapers. It is to control your perception of reality, not to offer you reality. As someone who worked as senior editor in television news for two years, I can testify to this fact. We referred to our broadcast as a "show", not "news", simply because it was completely controlled from the top down like any corporation, where the "anchors" (readers) simply regurgitated the scripted words from unseen superiors. Don't believe me? Simply watch the short, yet very revealing clip below and notice the network logos in the lower part of the screen (left and right) which reveal that ALL of the major networks (ABC, NBC, CBS, FOX,) are receiving the very same scripts from

a CENTRAL authority above them.

"Independent" News? . . . Give me a break!

Highly respected and Pulitzer Prize winning "Watergate" reporter Carl Bernstein had this to say about exactly who it is who has central control over the media (intelligence) . . . The "Central Intelligence Agency" (CIA) of course . . . the very ones who staged the "moon missions" through their favorite manipulative tool . . . Television . . .

"More than 400 American 'journalists' (that we know of) have secretly carried out assignments for the Central Intelligence Agency, according to documents on file at CIA headquarters. In many instances, CIA documents show that 'journalists' were contracted to perform covert missions for the CIA with the consent of the managers of America's leading news organizations. Among the executives (that we know of) who lent their cooperation to the CIA, were the heads of Time Magazine, Newsweek, the New York Times, ABC, NBC, CBS, the Associate Press, United Press International, and Reuters."

(CNN, FOX, MSNBC, and USA Today are not on the list simply because they did not exist at the time of his quote.)

If a President says that their loathing of dishonest information is against the "Media" and not the CIA, they fail to recognize, or at least acknowledge for reasons of personal safety, that they are one and the same thing. The media is controlled by the CIA (as you just read above), whose native language, as spies, is lies. The perhaps once honorable agency, like many others, first initiated to protect American citizens from foreign adversaries, has been turned against them, like a rabid dog on their owner, spending taxpayer's hard earned money to lie to them without their consent, breaking federal law, which forbids domestic propaganda, as well as lying though the medium of television, of which the "moon landings" were the climax thereof.

(Continued on Page 15)

Did Astronauts Go 1000 Times Farther 49 Years Ago Than They Can Today?

Continued from Page 14

If a President is serious about "Ethics Reform", then what better Rallying Cry of the Ages than to inform the citizenry that the corrupt and out of control "Federal Government" took their hard earned money (about $1000 per person in today's dollars) to lie to them about the "moon landings" without their consent. Once every American knows of this outrageous Federal Government fraud, any President will have an Ethics Reform Mandate unlike any in all of American history. If the Truth about the "moon landings" is swept under the rug again and again, like countless Presidential cowards have done before, then America's honorable reputation will be forever sealed with permanent criminality and corruption.

In order to improve America, you have to first tear down decaying infrastructure, methodology, and corruption. This convenient lie of the Nixon administration must be humbly acknowledged by the leaders of America in order for our country to start fresh, otherwise we are just painting over mold that will infest our future. To confess sin is Nobel. It is the very reason why President Kennedy had unprecedentedly high approval ratings, because he acknowledged his and his country's mistakes.

If indeed the "moon landings" during the notoriously unscrupulous Nixon administration were part of a television deception, then you better believe that the CIA played a central role in the endeavor, which was entirely presented by the above media outlets, already proven to be under the CIA's direct control. Furthermore, unlike any other occasion in recorded history, there was absolutely no independent press coverage of such a monumental event. 100% of the television pictures and photographs presented to the public were entirely controlled by the Federal Government, who was assumed to be honest.

Give a thief keys to your house, and see what happens.

When I was a child, believing in Santa Claus was so much fun. Believing that we live in a magical world where men can fly to the moon on their very first attempt with 1960's technology is fun too, even though the feat cannot be repeated fifty years later, by any nation on earth, including the one that allegedly did it first half a century ago, even though all Truth reminds us that the South Pole, and Mt. Everest, and First Flight, and the Light Bulb, was never, ever achieved on the first attempt, and certainly never abandoned once achieved, never to be repeated again. The fact is, when you find out the Truth about Santa Clause, you are glad to know it, even if it hurts a little, realizing that a painful Truth is still better than a sweet lie. All of academia and aerospace needs to know the painful Truth. They will be thankful for it and it will save the future lives of those who wrongfully believe in space travel's falsified ease.

The fact is, if it were so easy to go to the moon with 1960's technology fifty years ago, on the very first attempt, then there would be manned bases there by now and there would have been a man on Mars twenty-five years ago. The fact that there are still not moon bases to this day, with half a century more advancements in rocketry and computers, is proof itself that traveling to the moon still cannot be done, today, much less in the 1960's with 1/millionth the computing power in all of NASA than is found in a modern day cell phone. Claiming that they went 1000 times farther, with five decades older technology, than the farthest astronaut can travel today, with half a century more advancements in rockets and computers, on the very first attempt, simply defies logic. This is like saying Charles Lindbergh flew across the Atlantic in 1927, yet the feat could not be repeated by any nation on earth, including the one who made the original claim, fifty years later, even though, in reality, fifty years later, millions of airplanes, one hundred times larger and one million times more advanced, were flying over the Atlantic. This notion is completely illogical regarding the perpetual advancement of technology, yet this is what we are supposed to believe, through misplaced and manipulated patriotism, regarding the alleged "moon landings" of the 1960's, a feat which is only estimated to be "duplicated" seventy years later . . . at the earliest. Has there ever been a time in recorded history in which such a technological advancement was made yet could not be repeated for seventy years?

This alone should show you the Truth.

Why do so many smart people believe this lie? Because they want to. They want to believe this lie. Believing this lie means that they live in a better world than they actually do. Yet the fact is, they do not. The number one reason I hear from intelligent, yet disbelieving critics of the moon landing fraud, is that, "No one would ever do such a dishonest thing as lying about such an important accomplishment". Really? They forget that they live in a world full of unthinkable child molestation, vicious murder, hateful racism, deplorable rape, and horrific million-man genocide. In a world such as this, what is all of this in minor comparison to merely cheating in a contest, as so many people have done before? In these peoples' longing to be part of a society of pride boosting miraculous science, misguided self-proclaimed "intellectuals" fail to see the plainness of this simple fact:

Technology does not go backwards.

Again, if it were so easy to go to the moon in the 1960's on the very first attempt with 1/millionth less computing power in all of NASA than is found in a modern cell phone, a distance which is 1000 times farther than the most advanced modern manned rocket can travel today, then not only would the feat be easily and routinely repeatable today, there would be lunar bases there by now, nearly five decades later.

Technology does not go backwards!

The South Pole has temperatures that reach below 100 degrees Fahrenheit (-73 C) and nearly continual hurricane force winds, yet there are bases there today. Why? Because it is humanly possible. If it were humanly possible to reach the moon, fifty years ago or today, there too would be bases there right now. The fact that there are not, with half a century more advancements in rockets and computers, is proof itself that it simply cannot be done, not even today, and especially not with fifty years older technology. The problem is, you have to be willing to give up this deep emotional imprinting, in pursuit of Honor and Truth, in order to see the plainness of this harsh and startling reality.

After Columbus arrived in the "New World", within two years, numerous other European nations traveled to the Americas. After Lewis and Clark ventured to the American west, shortly thereafter, citizens everywhere traveled to the American west. After the Wright brothers accomplished powered flight, within two years, numerous others repeated their technological accomplishment.

Charles Lindbergh first flew across the Atlantic in an airplane in 1927. Fifty years later, there were millions of airplanes flying across the Atlantic. In comparison, the 747 aircraft, built after seventy years of successful aviation history and millions of manufactured aircraft, which was developed with a decade newer technology than that of the "moon" spacecraft (the first ever vehicle to allegedly take men to another world), yet the 747 took one year longer to construct than the "moon landing" equipment did to merely fly seven miles above the earth and endured over 160 failed engine attempts before it finally got off of the ground!

When it comes to perceiving the Truth in a world full of lies, historically, the majority has always been deceived, and later proved wrong, by the minority of their contemporaries, whom they persecuted and considered deluded at the time, when in fact, it was the majority who were misled.

Does a person know it when they are deceived?
No, they do not.
You see, you can be sincere . . .
And be sincerely wrong.

The majority of scientists thought the world was flat. The majority of astronomers thought the Earth was the center of the universe. The majority of physicians thought bleeding the sickness out of a person was a cure. The majority of Americans thought Nixon was honest. Likewise, a majority of scientists, astronomers, physicians, and Americans think the moon landings were real, yet their titles and majority do not equal Truth, as history has well proven . . . and will prove again.

(Continued on Page 17)

YOU CAN BEAT LUNG CANCER:
Using Alternative/Integrative Interventions

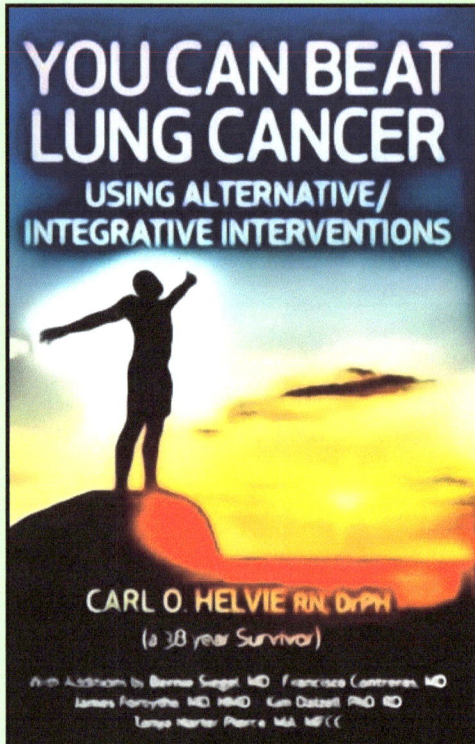

Can you overcome lung cancer without harsh chemicals, surgery and debilitation? Are alternative interventions effective? Why do conventional physicians not use them? Can you prevent cancer recurrences and live into old age without chronic diseases and prescribed medications? This book answers these and other questions.

This is one of the most comprehensive books available on alternative treatments for lung cancer. It explains the treatments used successfully by a health professional/cancer survivor of 36 years and by some of the leading medical and health practitioners currently in the field. G. Edward Griffin, Author of World Without Cancer, The Politics of Cancer Therapy, and other books and films. Recipient of the Telly Award for Excellence in Television Production. President of American Media.

ABOUT THE AUTHOR: Dr Carl O Helvie (1932-) grew up in Gouverneur, New York and functioned as a nurse practitioner, educator, author, and researcher for 60 years. Most of his degrees and practice have been in public health and wellness. During his years in academia he wrote 10 books and book chapters, over 55 articles, gave 57 research papers around the United States and Europe, developed a nursing theory, and received funding for and established a nursing center and provided primary care for homeless and low income individuals and families. He also overcome lung cancer using natural interventions after being given 6 months to live by conventional medicine in 1974. Since retirement he has written two additional books and has been host of the holistic health radio show for the past 4 years. All of his current work since retirement from academia focuses on natural interventions for health problems. Applying these concepts in his own life he is now age 80 and free of chronic illnesses and prescribed medications dispite the average for a 75 year old of 3 chronic illnesses and 5 prescribed medications. In 1999 he received the Distinquised Career Award in Public Health from the American Publc Health Association, and most recently was listed in Wikipedia.

Bart Sibrel: "Did Astronauts Go 1000 Times Farther 49 Years Ago Than They Can Go Today?"

17

Did Astronauts Go 1000 Times Farther 49 Years Ago Than They Can Today?

Continued from Page 15

Does a person know it when they are deceived?
No, they do not.
You see, you can be sincere . . .
And be sincerely wrong.

The majority of scientists thought the world was flat. The majority of astronomers thought the Earth was the center of the universe. The majority of physicians thought bleeding the sickness out of a person was a cure. The majority of Americans thought Nixon was honest. Likewise, a majority of scientists, astronomers, physicians, and Americans think the moon landings were real, yet their titles and majority do not equal Truth, as history has well proven . . . and will prove again.

Why is it so difficult for them to see the Truth?
Very simple . . .
Pride.
"The Pride of your heart has deceived you."
-Obadiah 1:3-

Pride is simply the un-willingness to be wrong, just as humility is the willingness to be wrong. The great thing about being wrong, which is what I had to finally admit about the "moon landings", is that I am learning something new, and I am no longer walking through life in error. The bad thing about being right all the time, is that I cannot learn anything new, and I am living my life in a self-deceived state, which is the very worst form of deception.

When someone else deceives me, if I try hard enough, I can eventually figure it out, after all, I know that other people cannot be trusted all of the time. Yet when I am self-deceived, it is nearly impossible for me to overcome this, because the person I am relying on for "facts" is myself . . . and of course I can trust myself . . . even when I am wrong.

When someone considers themself smart, this is the first step towards their ignorance. They boast about their years of experience and degrees, and thereby pour concrete around their finite knowledge, unknowingly calling their stone mound of limited facts, the entire universe of Truth. If you try to tell them they are wrong, they will defend their post to their emotional and intellectual death at all cost, all the while attempting to defile you with their venomous words for pointing out their error, even though you are right and merely trying to help them.

Just like OJ Simpson's lawyers (who later admitted they knew of his guilt and were only "doing their job"), no matter how plain the evidence, their pride-filled manipulative lawyer-like minds have an explanation for why the Truth is a lie, and why lies are the truth, otherwise they would be forced to admit their error, which their pride will not allow, and

which blinds them from perceiving the unwanted reality. With every evidence submitted to them as to why the moon landings were indeed falsified, no matter how condemning and obvious, there is always a zealous counter-explanation from them to throw away the Truth and institute a lie in its place, in order for them to keep their dying status quo fantasy alive.

Just because someone has an explanation for every piece of condemning evidence, (like OJ Simpson's lawyers and "moon landing" defenders) does not mean that the explanations are True.

Rather than looking for the Truth (at the unacceptable cost of being wrong), the majority of people (because of their blinding pride in the accomplishments of themselves and like-minded others), instead "Gather around them a great number of teachers to tell them what their itching ears want to hear". (2nd Timothy 4:3) In other words, rather than looking for the Truth, they look for people to agree with what they already believe, so as to prove themselves right.

The real question is, if you had cancer, would you want to know? . . . Or would you rather have your doctor lie to you and tell you that everything was just fine . . . even though it really was not? Sometimes you have to cut off a diseased limb to save your life. The same is True of the "moon landings". A costly admission, yet a saving one as well.

If the "moon missions" were real, then they hold a place of prominence in the annals of human history. If they were not real, and One Hundred Fifty Billion Dollars (in today's value) was embezzled from the taxpayers to lie to the very ones who funded the missions, then this would actually be a more *significant moment in history than if they had actually gone!*

Thusly, this Great Truth, the faking of the moon missions out of pride, arrogance, and greed, is being withheld by the minority of government leaders against the vast majority of

citizens.

Why?
Because they think they are better than the rest of us.

It is at this point that I highly recommend you watch the film which I first made on this subject called *"A Funny Thing Happened on the Way to the Moon"*, so that you can not only fully comprehend the historical as well as hidden facts of this event, yet also understand my earnest motives for bringing this sad chapter of American history into the light, for the betterment of future generations, and to prevent such error from forever smearing America's once honorable reputation into once that is permanently criminal.

Until the Truth comes out about the "moon landings", humanity's character, and especially that of America, will be forever stunted from growth and advancement, the very aid of which would come by simply admitting this very mistake with its deplorable dishonesty. Unless we are willing to face and confess the cold hard facts of our errors, much like a disciplined athlete rejecting appealing yet detrimental desserts, we will be under the spell, and complete control of, this diabolical hidden minority of government leaders who represent themselves rather than the people.

The falsified "moon landings" are utter proof that this is the state in which America lives today, the very admission of which would lead to these unscrupulous leaders' demise. This is why there are more than a hundred websites and films in existence today, specifically dedicated to squashing the emerging Truth of the "moon landings" blatant and deplorable falsification.

(Continued on Page 18)

Did Astronauts Go 1000 Times Farther 49 Years Ago Than They Can Today?

Continued from Page 15

The fact is, if the moon landings are so "obviously" real, then anyone who says otherwise is an idiot. Why then are there more than a hundred websites and videos, which took tens of thousands of hours to produce, specifically designed to refute the insane rantings of morons? As Shakespeare so famously said, "Thou does protest too much." Another historical commentator said this . . .

"The likelihood of one individual being right, increases in direct proportion to the intensity with which others are trying to prove him wrong."

Even former president Clinton, once holding the (allegedly) highest office in the land, doubts the authenticity of the moon landings. On Page 156 of his autobiography "My Life" he states:

"Just a month before, Apollo 11 astronauts Buzz Aldrin and Neil Armstrong had left their colleague, Michael Collins, aboard spaceship Columbia and 'walked on the moon', beating by five months President Kennedy's goal of putting a man on the moon before the decade was out. The old carpenter asked me if I really believed it happened. I said sure, I saw it on 'television'. He disagreed; he said that he didn't believe it for a minute, that 'them television fellers' could make things look real that weren't. Back then, I thought he was a crank. During my eight years in Washington, I saw some things on TV that made me wonder if he wasn't ahead of his time."

If a president of the United States is finally admitting his doubts as to the authenticity of the "moon landings" (albeit, after he safely left office) and is calling those who perceive the Truth of the event "ahead of their time", shouldn't you also reconsider your thinking on the matter, if you haven't already?

A year or two after I produced "A Funny Thing happened on the way to the Moon", I suppose influenced by courtroom television programs wherein witnesses take an oath on the Bible as to telling the Truth, I came up with the idea to track down as many "Apollo" astronauts as I could and simply ask them if they would swear on the Bible as to the authenticity of their "moon missions". It was during the production of this follow-up documentary that my infamous encounter with Edwin "Buzz" Aldrin occurred, in which he punched me after I called him "A Liar, a Coward, and a Thief".

I certainly did not wake up that morning intending to say those strong words to Aldrin, neither did he plan earlier that day to sock me in the face. It was just one of those unplanned moments that got heated up and Aldrin, in my opinion, overreacted. Even if he did walk on the moon, as some would like to believe, it would be hard to call him an "American hero" when he will not defend the constitutional right of free speech, instead physically attacking those who utter words of criticism against him, like so many arrogant communist dictators have done in the past. A great thing about America is that presidential candidates can openly call each other "Liars" when debating the facts, yet they do not punch each other in the face for doing so. If they did, I doubt if they would win any elections or be idolized for very long . . . so why is Aldrin? . . . Let me tell you why . . .

I have received so many emails with the similar words, "I am not a violent person, yet I loved seeing you get punched, and I hope it happens again." That is like saying, "I am faithful to my spouse, yet I regularly lust after others." These are violent people in self-denial of their love for violence. When someone reacts with violence, or salivates at the sight of it, simply because I say that the "moon landings" are fraudulent, then like a radical religious sect which kills people for criticizing their prophet, this is irrefutable proof that this "moon landing" event has become a god to them (and a false one at that) whose "prophet" I have insulted. When it comes to false religion, just as it is with the false moon landings, it is this very fanaticism that prevents people from seeing the Truth about their overadored apostatized idol.

The more fanatical people become because I point out that their "moon landing" gods are frauds, the more this very fanatical behavior demonstrates their error on this subject to begin with. I have received uncounted death threats, just for saying that to people that their government lied to them on at least one occasion. I even received a death threat with the words, "I wish I could watch you, your wife, and your children, burn alive before my eyes!" Has anyone on the "Truther" side of this argument ever threatened the slightest violence against those who believe that the moon landings are real? I can firmly answer "no, not ever". This radical defense of something that is supposed to be so "obvious" is proof itself that what is being defended is a lie.

While I do believe the things I said about Aldrin are True, I now feel that it was inappropriate to rebuke an older man so harshly. (See 1st Timothy 5:1) Additionally, I too have been a liar, a coward, and a thief, it is just that I am mindful to be repentant of these things and Aldrin is not yet. If I were to do it all over again, I am not sure I would have made the second film confronting the astronauts, as it even makes me a little uncomfortable to watch it. It is nevertheless, as some supporters of the Truth have noted, a benefit to the historical record when viewed in the future, that these men were given the opportunity to come clean, and they instead, adamantly chose to go to their graves with the poisonous lie they fed lifelong to their misled countrymen.

While I do believe the things I said about Aldrin are True, I now feel that it was inappropriate to rebuke an older man so harshly. (See 1st Timothy 5:1) Additionally, I too have been a liar, a coward, and a thief, it is just that I am mindful to be repentant of these things and Aldrin is not yet. If I were to do it all over again, I am not sure I would have made the second film confronting the astronauts, as it even makes me a little uncomfortable to watch it. It is nevertheless, as some supporters of the Truth have noted, a benefit to the historical record when viewed in the future, that these men were given the opportunity to come clean, and they instead, adamantly chose to go to their graves with the poisonous lie they fed lifelong to their misled countrymen.

(Continued on Page 20)

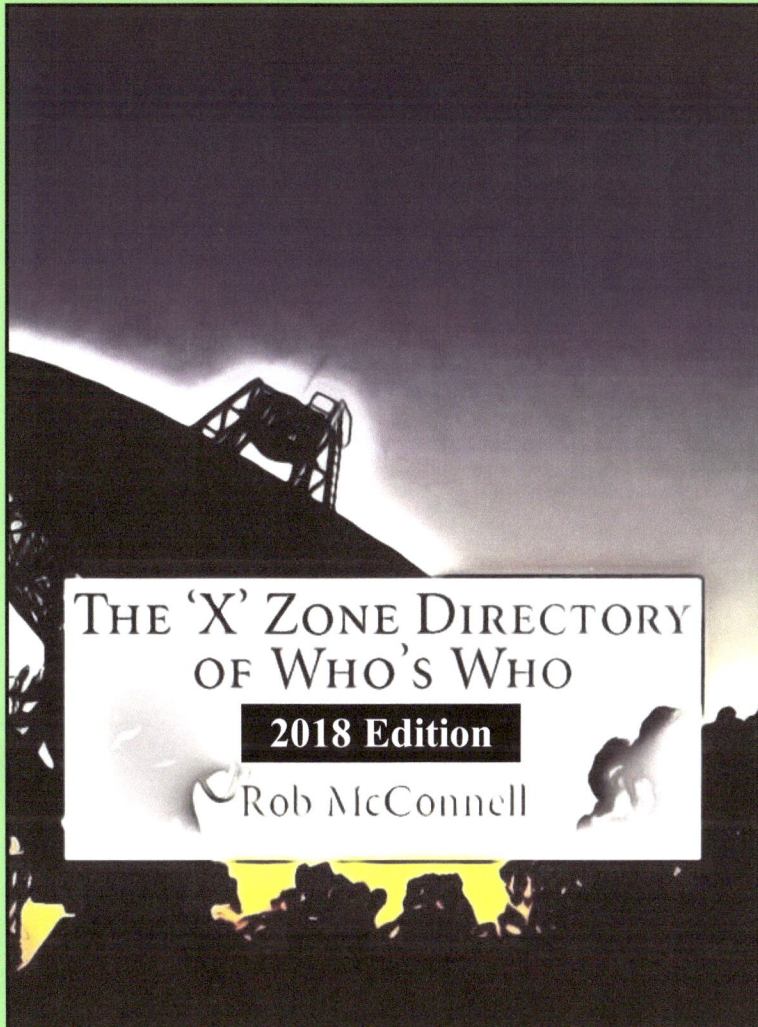

20

Bart Sibrel: "Did Astronauts Go 1000 Times Farther 49 Years Ago Than They Can Go Today?"

Did Astronauts Go 1000 Times Farther 49 Years Ago Than They Can Today?

Continued from Page 18

I later offered Edwin ("Buzz") a sincere apology for my disrespectful words, and he immediately recompensed by purchasing a DVD of *"A Funny Thing Happened on the way to the Moon"* online. With all this said, perhaps a viewing of my second film on this subject, *"Astronauts Gone Wild"*, is advisable at this time, to better understand this predicament I got myself and the astronauts into. Understandably, if people stumble upon *"Astronauts Gone Wild"* first on the internet, having never seen *"A Funny Thing Happened on the Way to the Moon"*, their opinion of the Truth about the "moon landings", as well as my sincere efforts, painstaking diligence, and absolute surety in this Truth so as to make such a film, might be dramatically misunderstood, as this second film does not offer the similar compelling proofs of the fraud as the first film did.

My life story regarding the "moon landings" is a true conversion story, much like an ancient religious leader who previously persecuted the Truth, whom then became the leader of the group he once opposed. My father was in the Air Force. As a result, I grew up around the latest aviation and technology. I loved it! On July 20th, 1969, I was only four years of age, quietly asleep in bed. My father, as a high-ranking military officer, was given a VIP package of commemorative photographs of the event, which he then gave to me as a cherished present. From the age of about four to fourteen, these pictures of the alleged moon landings covered an entire "sacred" wall in my bedroom. It was literally a shrine (like a religion) to the intellectual prowess of mankind. I saw these images, every day, three hundred sixty-five days a year, for ten years. This means I propagated the desired belief in their authenticity, three thousand six hundred fifty times before I even considered the possibility that they were misrepresentations of reality . . . That's a lot of brainwashing!

Fortunately, at the open-minded age of fourteen, I saw an innovative television program featuring an interview with William Kaysing, a NASA contractor during the Apollo "moon missions". He asserted quite confidently, from first hand eyewitness experience, that the impossible Apollo flights were staged to increase the prestige of the United States during the height of the Cold War, and while in the pit of domestic discontentment because of tens of thousands of young American men dying needlessly in an ambiguous foreign war in Vietnam. Nixon himself said at the time that the Vietnam War protests were the number one cause of American strife.

After watching this inaugural program suggesting a moon landing fraud, I went to my bedroom wall shrine of "moon landing" pictures and looked, for the very first time, *with new eyes,* at theses surprisingly telling photographs.

Sure enough, just like Mr. Kaysing had said, stunning evidence of photographic anomalies were hidden in plain sight! (They say that this is the very best place to hide something investigators are looking for!) I just had to have *"eyes that see"*, after all, it had been historically said that most people *"have eyes that do not see, and ears that do not hear".*

This tremendous oversight of mine is likened to a household salt shaker always being placed in the same place for ten years; left kitchen cabinet, on the third shelf, on the left side. If a family member inadvertently moves it to the same left kitchen cabinet, likewise on the third shelf, yet on the *right* side instead of on the left, you do not see it, even though it is right there in front of your eyes! There you stand, with the cabinet door wide open, the salt shaker right in front of you, only inches away (though on the *right* side of the same shelf where you always looked rather than on the left, where you were *conditioned* to *not* look), and you do not see it! Just as such, there I was, looking at the same pictures of the alleged moon landings, over and over again for, a full decade, yet not seeing quite obvious inconsistencies and abnormalities that would quickly give away the deceptive criminality of the event, *if only I would look beyond my programming.*

In a way, like naïve Adam and Eve, you can't blame people for initially being deceived, after all, which is a more pleasant realm in which to live, one in which your country continually lies about history and spending, or one in which your country is honorable and honest? Naturally, most people would prefer to live in the latter, *so they see the latter,* just as we unconsciously overlook the flaws in a new romantic acquaintance with whom we are emotionally infatuated.

Fortunately, ten years after seeing the revealing interview with former NASA contractor William Kaysing at the age of fourteen, then at the age of twenty-four, I had become a filmmaker, and happened to be editing a movie one day for the very producer of the program I had seen ten years earlier which first brought to light the moon landing fraud to

my attention. "Do you remember that man you had on your program who said that the moon landings were fake?" I asked the producer, "What is his name? I'd like to talk with him." The rest is history.

I went from being the biggest fan of the "moon landings", to becoming their most outspoken critic. Why? Because I was *open-minded* and *willing to be wrong* when the evidence presented itself to the contrary of my first opinion, even if that evidence was unpredicted, unprecedented, and quite discouraging.

Hitler, the master of propaganda, said that it was actually easier to get away with a *gigantic* deception rather than a small one, because small lies are commonplace, and therefore anticipated, so that no one would expect or foresee the audacity of a grand deception. This is precisely the psychological tactic that was used by the CIA in precipitating and maintaining the monumental, yet very simple, lie of the "moon landings".

During the domestically injurious riots protesting the Vietnam War, president Nixon decided that a unifying pep rally of a successful "moon landing" was just what the sickly American patient needed. Do you really think that Nixon was going to risk killing three "National Heroes" on live worldwide television, when simply failing to rescue kidnapped hostages would ruin your presidency for life (and especially your potential second term) as it did President Carter a few years later? How then could Nixon absolutely guarantee a successful "moon mission"? . . .

(Continued on Page 21)

Fact*oids

- Humans can see over 10 million colors and smell over 50 thousand aromas.
- The most common dream is of falling, followed by being chased or attacked.
- The fingernail on your middle finger grows faster than the nails on the other fingers do,

Did Astronauts Go 1000 Times Farther 49 Years Ago Than They Can Today?

Continued from Page 20

To stage it . . . just like a skilled poker player's bluff, not to mention that it was technologically impossible at the time to begin with, just as it is today, even with fifty years more advancements in computers and rockets. In fact, according to NASA contractor William Kaysing, who worked for six years on the Apollo program with high security clearance, a classified interdepartmental memo, which he personally read and edited, estimated the likelihood of a successful manned moon mission on the first attempt at a mere one in ten thousand chance. As NASA's own staff at the time readily admitted was their standard motto in such instances, *"If you can't make it, fake it."*

Some *assume* that if the Soviet Union (Russian) or Chinese intelligence agencies found out that the American "moon landings" were fraudulent, they would immediately "spill the beans" (tell the truth) to the rest of the world without giving the highly important matter much deeper thought. This is simply not the case, and again, thinking only one step farther than programmed to do so, reveals the actual Truth. If wars are created for the profiteering of the *"Military Industrial Complex"*, as many forward thinking people including President Eisenhower now realize, then foreign "adversaries" of the United States may only be profitable creations thereof, solely existing in the propagandized minds of Americans, just as the "moon landings" did, brought about through the deceptive CIA's mainstream media outlets, done so to benefit the billionaire military manufacturers, who in turn, help get their like-minded politicians elected, thus perpetuating this endless cycle of lucrative lies which mutually feed corrupted bureaucrats and corporate contractors alike.

Think about it: America has been engaged in a profitable war of some kind for 90% of its short history, yet never with Russia or China. As such, Russia and China are, in fact, allies of the United States, despite mainstream media and CIA fabrications which portray them, for financial gain, as "adversaries", as trillions of dollars in regular annual mutually beneficial trading proves. (Just imagine a fake wrestling match in which both sides are paid by the same party.) This being the case, these overseas entities would not bring the Truth of such an American scandal as the moon landing fraud into the light to injure such an important monetary trading partner toward their own financial loss, not to mention that their own hidden skeletons would then be forced out of the closet in retaliation. Any "bad blood" the United States *appears* to have with these foreign powers is merely staged for the very purpose of keeping their complicity a secret, and the trillions of dollars in profitable military spending flowing.

Even if these two "super-powers" were actual enemies of America (which they are not),

they still would not expose the Truth about the "moon missions". For example, if I had a picture of a famous world leader with a prostitute, would it be more profitable for me to give the picture away to the media for free, or rather to blackmail the entrapped world leader, year after year, with ever increasing tolls? If such countries really were enemies of America and had proof of the moon landing fraud, which I suspect they probably do by now, it would serve their interests *much more* to keep such knowledge to themselves and blackmail the United States with the embarrassing information, year after year, administration after administration, to get the behind-the-scenes negotiations to favor them, whether it regards trade, arms, debt, or anything else they so desire. This is another good reason why the Truth coming out about the moon landing fraud would be beneficial for America. It would put an end to any potential blackmail about this past matter from foreign powers.

The fact is, there were no "independent" tracking stations for the Apollo missions. The only entities that had such capability were the United States' own government agencies (who orchestrated the deception to begin with) and the aforementioned countries, who profited from keeping the secret. Additionally, NASA launched the "Tetra-A" satellite shortly before the Apollo missions, specifically designed to *"simulate transmissions coming from the moon"* so that the ground crews could rehearse the "moon landings" during their many *simulations*. Surreptitiously, it was purported that the Tetra-A satellite "accidentally burned up" in the earth's atmosphere just before the first alleged moon mission, that way the government satellite could secretly still be in service, performing the same *simulation* function during the fake moon missions, convincing even the staff at NASA of their authenticity. In fact, an elderly retired NASA crew member recently acknowledged that . . .

"Our computers could tell no difference whatsoever between a 'real' and a 'simulated' moon mission."

From Wikipedia regarding The Apollo Fraud:

"Some people insist that the Apollo moon landings were a Cold War deception of the Nixon administration. However, 'empirical' evidence is readily available to show that manned moon landings did occur. Anyone on earth with an appropriate laser and telescope system can apparently bounce laser beams off three retro-reflector arrays reported to be left on the moon by Apollo 11, 14, and 15, suggesting deployment of the lunar laser ranging equipment at asserted Apollo moon landing sites, implying equipment constructed on earth was transported to the surface of the moon. In addition, in August 2009, NASA's lunar reconnaissance orbiter claimed to send back high-resolution photos of the estimated Apollo landing sites. These government issued pictures show not only what is reported to be the faint shadows of the descent stages of the lunar landers allegedly left behind, but also apparent tracks of the astronauts' walking paths nearby in the lunar dust."

At first (and only) glance, these appear to be relevant arguments, yet each one is, surprisingly, most easily and unconditionally refuted with only a modicum of further investigation beyond the initial conditioned interpretation. First of all, it has recently come to light through employee "whistling blowing" that United States spy agencies regularly use "Wikipedia", as well as hundreds of other websites, for deceitful misinformation purposes, as they can anonymously post intelligent *sounding* pro-government thesis to the masses, intentionally contradicting and smugly belittling Truthful "conspiracy theories" of very real crimes, of which they themselves have committed, in an attempt to conceal their own wrongdoing through such contrary postings.

The fact that billions of our tax dollars are being spent each year by the government for the very purpose of concealing their own past crimes by investing so many resources toward the perpetual lying to their own citizens, is utterly disgusting.

(Continued On Page 23)

Have an idea for a story?

Here is your chance to get your short story, poem or timely news article published in an international newspaper.

We are looking for writers and budding journalists who want to submit their stories for publication.
(Your submission must be original work and it must not have been published elsewhere)
Submit to: The 'X' Chronicles Newspaper
586 Rexford Drive, Hamilton, Ontario, Canada
Fax: (905) 575-1222
e-mail: publisher@xchroniclesnewspaper.com

Did Astronauts Go 1000 Times Farther 49 Years Ago Than They Can Today?

Continued from Page 21

What high-ranking brave soul in their midst will come forward to save their fellow citizens with this simple Truth about the "moon landings", in order to usher in the much needed governmental reform before our country sinks into oblivion?

When they use statements like *"empirical evidence"* (Because the Emperor says so?) is readily available to show that the manned moon landings did occur", it not only shows their arrogance (which, in and of itself, demonstrates their blindness to the facts), it also exemplifies their desperation to make an argument, that is so much losing ground, that they have to resort to the tactic of claiming that if you don't agree with them, you are somehow deficient in intelligence. Again, if the "moon landings" are so obviously real (even though they cannot be repeated today with fifty years more advanced technology, and the farthest a man can travel from the earth to the moon today is only 1/1000th as far as they allegedly did half a century ago with antiquated equipment on the very first attempt), and there is no robust proof whatsoever of the missions deliberate falsification, then there would be no need whatsoever for the hundred plus films and websites, which took tens of thousands of hours to produce, solely dedicated to reassure the public of the "moon landings" genuineness! The fact that there are, is proof itself that mounting *evidence does* exist which *proves* the "moon missions" to be a CIA forgery, otherwise the deceptively claimed "obviousness" of their authenticity would speak for itself, without the repeated need of hundreds of websites and films to defend them. When a structure needs such continual precarious support and maintenance, this alone is evidence that the structure itself is not sound to begin with.

First of all, it was proven in 1962 that a laser can be bounced and calibrated off of the moon *without a man-made reflector thereon,* simply due to the reflectivity of the lunar surface. NASA just cleverly designated these reflective locations as "landing sites" for the very purpose of contriving this evidence. Furthermore, Russia put a man-made mirror on the moon's surface during the same time of the "Apollo" missions, using instead an *un-manned* probe that would not have to suffer the biological ravages of lethal space radiation en route, one of the main reasons NASA was, and still is, unable to send humans to the moon. Don't believe me? *CLICK ON THIS LINK* to read the March 1959 issue, Volume 200, Number 3, of the magazine "Scientific American", article entitled **"Radiation Belts Around the Earth"**, to see how deadly and impenetrable space radiation is beyond the safety of low earth orbit where the space station currently resides (at an altitude of merely 250 miles above the earth, the moon being about 239,000 miles away, or roughly 1000 Times

farther). Additionally, seeing how all of these lasers have their data computer controlled, it would only take one computer hacker to manipulate the information shown on a viewing screen, making even the employees of NASA ignorant of the actual facts. (This was precisely the case at "mission control" during the "moon missions", where dozens of computer "operators", actually just read the contrived preprogrammed data on their screens like news anchors, who do not write their own words, openly admitting afterwards that they could tell no difference whatsoever between a "real" flight and a *"simulation".*)

Secondly, to say that additional "new" photographs from the criminal NASA are evidence that "prove" the alleged moon landings were real . . . is laughable. NASA already faked high resolution, full body pictures, of an astronaut supposedly standing right on the "moon's surface" nearly fifty years ago, so what is it to fake additional pictures now, with almost five decades better "Photoshop" technology, of such simple things as alleged tiny shadows of lunar landers or supposed faint footpaths, from miles above the moon's surface, allegedly taken from untrustworthy NASA's orbiting satellites? These diehard believers are just seeing what they want to see, like a naïve spouse of a cheating partner, accepting the fox's evidence that they didn't steal a chicken.

Additional arguments against the fraud are reported to be the hundreds of thousands of people throughout the industry who contributed to the "moon missions", who *allegedly* would have been informed of the fraud and kept it a secret. Again, *seemingly* a reasonable argument, yet it is not with only a little extra thought. Do you really think the CIA would be so careless as to tell hundreds of thousands of low-level contractors the goings-on of a top-top-secret project? Would the CIA really be so inept as to tell the person making the rocket's door handle, or the glove or the boot of the spacesuit, that they were secretly faking the moon landings and to be sure not to tell anyone?! Do we really think the CIA is stupid enough to tell hundreds of thousands of low-level workers something they wanted to keep as a strict secret?! *Furthermore, to say that "because my uncle worked at NASA and believed the 'moon landings' were real is proof that they were real",* is like saying that because my uncle worked as a vender at the Super Bowl and believed that the game was honest, that this is proof that the

football players didn't cheat in their game.

Just like a pyramid of power in any business, what the employee, the manager, and the regional manager knows about the business' *actual* agenda, is *completely* different than what the CEO at the very top knows. Remember, there were only *three* people ("trusted" government employees) who were *actually there at the time* of the "moon missions", with *no independent press* coverage whatsoever. As demonstrated in my film **"A Funny Thing Happened on the Way to the Moon"**, the three crew members were indeed on the rocket, they did launch into earth orbit on July 16th, 1969 (to attain realistic "zero gravity" flight photography within the spacecraft), they did splash down in the ocean eight days later (to establish the authenticity), yet the rest of the mission, everything beyond earth orbit *(which is only as far as astronauts can go today with fifty years more advanced technology)*, was completely contrived, like a masterful illusionist, by satellite data manipulation, complete media control, and professional movie sets. After all, what is easier to do, to actually build a rocket and travel to another planet with 1960's technology on the very first attempt, or to simply make a movie set about it? The age-old argument *"The simplest explanation is the True one",* which many Apollo proponents deceptively use to suggest the "moon missions" were real, *actually proves the fraud instead!*

The simple fact is, it is easier to *fake* a moon mission than to actually do one . . . the exact reason why the recent film *"The Martian"* was filmed in an *earthly simulated television studio,* rather than on Mars.

Another overlooked fact is that, according to their own "Scientific Method", a "Scientific" claim, such as the "manned moon landings" of the 1960's, in order to be considered authentic, must be *Independently Verified and Duplicated by a Third Party,* which has never been done regarding the "Apollo" missions, as only the corrupt United States government, alone, has claimed that this feat was possible, on the very first attempt, with antiquated 1960's technology, even though no nation on earth can repeat the claim, even with *fifty years* more advancements in rockets and computers.

(Continued on Page 24)

Did Astronauts Go 1000 Times Farther 49 Years Ago Than They Can Today?

Continued from Page 23

This is precisely why, if someone today made the claim of perfecting "cold fusion", yet said that they could not repeat their successful experiment for another *fifty years,* they would be laughed off of the planet . . . Yet . . . This is not the *standard* for the "manned moon landing" claims of America in the 1960's, which cannot be repeated by any nation on earth, *even fifty years later,* when today the farthest NASA can send an astronaut is only 1/1000th the *distance* as they claimed to have done on the *first* try *half a century ago!* This "event" has become a god of America's greatness, causing even "scientific intellectuals" to intentionally overlook highly valid criticism thereof, because it insults their *self-aggrandized narcissistic idol.*

Some of the best evidence proving the fraud is the fact that in 1998, when the space shuttle flew to its highest altitude ever, 365 miles, one third higher than they normally flew, mission control asked the crew to descend to a lower altitude due to lethal space radiation they encountered, by approaching too close to the "Van Allen Radiation Belts", which don't even begin until one thousand miles altitude (and continue for an additional 25,000 miles). That is to say, they were 635 miles away from radiation that was so intense, that the crew reported they could see the radiation with their eyes closed as sparks of light hitting the retinas of their closed eyes, and were subsequently told to descend away from it. When this happened, CNN inadvertently and unknowingly, reported the moon landing fraud by stating . . .

"The radiation belt surrounding earth is more dangerous than previously believed."

Apparently, not a single journalist on the entire planet figured out, except for myself, that this statement totally contradicts the authenticity of the "moon landings" . . . Here's why . . .

The only time in world history when human beings have *claimed* to have traveled through the 25,000 mile thick radiation field called the "Van Allen Radiation Belts" (which, unbeknownst to most, surrounds the Earth starting at an altitude of one thousand miles and extends 25,000 miles beyond that) is during the alleged Apollo "moon missions", as all other manned missions, from every country on earth, including the United States (such as Gemini, Mercury, Soyuz, Skylab, the Space Shuttle, and the current International Space Station), all orbited about 750 miles below this dangerous radiation field (merely 250 miles above the Earth's surface), *specifically out of safety concerns for the lethal radiation above them.* Even airline crews, 240 miles below this orbital altitude, are subject to health concerns from this hazardous radiation, *so all the more for astronauts, twenty times higher than they at merely 250 miles above the earth in the space shuttle and space station.*

Why is it then that Space Shuttle

WIDESCREEN

Tense, taut and terrifying— it could be true.

CAPRICORN ONE

THE GREATEST ADVENTURE ON EARTH

astronauts, some 635 miles away from this intense radiation, *twenty-nine years after the first alleged moon mission,* knew more about this radiation than the Apollo astronauts who claimed they were in the middle of it to the moon and back? Remember, the Space Shuttle crew's recent discovery proves that this large *radiation field is "more dangerous than previously believed".* What is *"previously believed"* if not based on the previous reports from the "experts" of the *radiation field, the Apollo crews,* who were allegedly the only ones in all of world history to have ever traveled through this radiation, with no ill health effects of any kind and no reports of the visible sparks of radiation being seen, as were later reported by the Shuttle crew from 635 miles away from the radiation!

Of course, this is simply not possible if the "moon missions" were real. What does this mean?

It means that the "moon mission" astronauts, who previously claimed to have been inside of this large radiation field lied about being there! Of course, if the "Apollo" crews never went through the Van Allen Radiation Belt, as this contradictory report reveals, then they certainly could not have gone to the moon either, which the traversing of this radiation would require. This is precisely why, nearly fifty years later, all that astronauts from any nation on earth can do, *including the United States,* is orbit the earth at about 250 miles altitude. Seeing how the Space shuttle has killed fourteen people just orbiting at 250 miles above the Earth, and that with well proven, three decades newer technology than the "Apollo" program had, it is quite a conundrum that thirty years earlier, with antiquated untried machinery, NASA claims to have gone *1000 Times farther,*

six times, without any fatalities or radiation problems whatsoever, and that with inaugural equipment.

According to the highly esteemed "National Research Council", a private nonprofit scientific think-tank which submits recommendations to NASA based on the latest scientific findings, radiation beyond Earth orbit is so dangerous that "*returning* to the moon" is deemed *impossible* until better ways are found to protect astronauts from this lethal radiation. The question is, if the NRC says that "*returning*" to the moon is *impossible today until better ways are found to protect astronauts from lethal space radiation beyond earth orbit* (such as the Van Allen Radiation Belts), then how did men reach the moon on their very first attempt with 1960's technology, or better still, why not simply use the same outstanding methodology and equipment that the supposed first moon crews had to protect themselves from the lethal space radiation rather than reinventing the wheel? (You can read their report by clicking HERE.)

Likewise, when Bush Jr. was president, he went on national television and proclaimed that *"The United States will return to the moon as a logical first step to Mars and beyond".* Did no one besides me notice that if they already really went to the moon six times, why would they need to do a "*first*" step over again for the *seventh* time? He was even so bold as to go on to say that *"First we will need to learn how to protect astronauts from lethal space radiation."* Am I the only one curious enough to ask, "Why not do it the same way that worked so well the first time they went to the moon in 1969?"

(Continue on Page 25)

Bart Sibrel: "Did Astronauts Go 1000 Times Farther 49 Years Ago Than They Can Go Today?"

25

Did Astronauts Go 1000 Times Farther 49 Years Ago Than They Can Today?

Continued from Page 24

Why does no journalist, *except me*, connect the obvious dots with this very revealing information? *Because the dots lead to a horrific Truth that would appall the entire American nation, demanding that their government be re-formed.* It is simply because "journalists" are part of the CIA's media empire that they do not report anything that would cause their very own undoing.

In December of 2014, NASA sent their brand new "Orion" spacecraft, *un-manned*, directly into the Van Allen Radiation Belt, to a 3,600 mile altitude, and then promptly u-turned it for a return to earth.

What is worth studying at 3,600 miles? The Van Allen Radiation Belts.

According to NASA, the purpose of the "Orion" mission was to . . . *"to test the instruments"*. What *"instruments"* were on-board the Orion spacecraft? *Two Geiger Counters to measure the radiation inside of the radiation belts that are necessary to traverse to reach the moon.*

Didn't NASA already have these measurements decades ago from the Apollo moon missions, if indeed men *actually* went through the radiation belts to the moon and back? Why is it so important to *"test the instruments"* at a 3,600 mile altitude inside of the radiation belts? . . .

To see if humans can survive transversing it . . . for the very first time!

Apparently today's new generation of NASA engineers, some in their twenty's, have stumbled upon this significant NASA contradiction. Though they were probably led into the space exploration field by the motivation of the seemingly easy "moon missions" of the 1960's, the fact that such an acclaimed feat cannot be repeated today, with five decades more advanced technology, and that aside from theses alleged "moon missions" of the Nixon administration, no one has ever gone more than 400 miles away from the earth in the nearly fifty years since, the trip to the moon being 1000 Times farther than the space station is today, must make their positions with this newly discovered Truth quite precarious.

Kelly Smith, one of these twenty-ish engineers, was selected as the official "Orion" mission spokesperson in the following NASA video press release. Notice that at 43 seconds into the film, Smith confirms that the radiation belts are made up of "Extreme Radiation". At time 3:06 he again refers to the belts as "Dangerous Radiation". Finally at time 3:36, for the third time, Smith plainly states . . .

"We must solves these (radiation) challenges before we send people through this region of space."

The question is, if the solution to the dangerous radiation belt problem has *yet to be invented* ("We must solves these challenges before we send people through this region of space."), then how is it that the Apollo crews during their alleged "moon missions" went through this *dangerous* and *extreme* radiation nearly fifty years ago when the necessary equipment to survive doing so has *yet to be invented?!* ("We *must* solves these challenges before we send *people* through this region of space.")

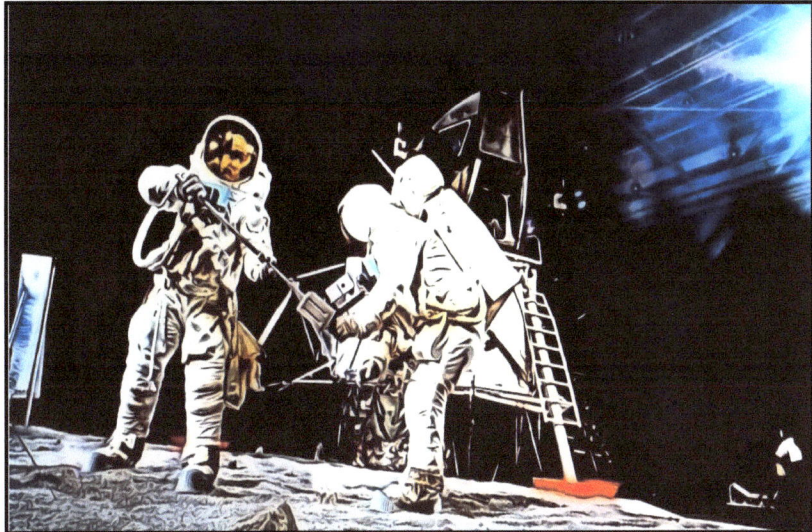

Click **HERE** to view these most revealing remarks.

Did Kelly Smith reveal this contradiction accidentally . . .or intentionally?

When I asked NASA's press office if I could interview Kelly Smith about this matter, they refused to grant him permission to talk with me. When I emailed a list of mostly harmless questions about the Orion mission, NASA politely answered all of them. When I submitted a more difficult inquiry about Kelly Smith's three statements about the dangerous radiation of the Van Allen Belts and how the radiation problem must be solved *before* NASA can send astronauts through them, NASA refused to reply to these questions, *as if I had never asked them*. When I asked for the radiation readings of the Orion spacecraft's two on-board Geiger Counters, NASA said that such measurements were "a secret" and that I would have to file a *"Freedom of Information Act"* request to attain the information. When I asked why such ordinary data about the radiation belt's strength is a secret, NASA refused to answer and then terminated all further communication with me. (Just 1 REM of radiation per hour is *five times* a lethal dose. As you will read later below, the radiation belts contain up to 100 REM per hour.)

When NASA sent publicly funded probes and spacecraft to measure the temperature of the sun and the amount of hydrogen in Jupiter's atmosphere, this information was readily available to scientists and to the public, after all, why would a measurement of a part of nature be a secret? Likewise, the amount radiation in the Van Allen Radiation Belts which surround the Earth is simply a part of nature, and as such, there is no reason whatsoever why such elementary measurements of nature should be a government secret . . . *unless disclosing such measurements would reveal the impossibility of the Apollo crews having gone through them and surviving with decades older technology,* especially seeing how NASA just acknowledged, accidentally or otherwise, that such protection from this "Dangerous" and "Extreme" radiation has yet to be invented by the space agency and *"must"* be invented *"before* we send people through this region of space."

Quite interesting . . . Yes?

James Van Allen, the discoverer of the radiation *belts, originally said that they were "100-1000 times more radioactive than a lethal dose"*! Under pressure from NASA, he dramatically recanted his original findings in order to make it appear as if the moon landings were possible. Don't believe me? Below is the link to his original published findings in the respected national journal "Scientific American", in which Van Allen spoke plainly about the radiation belts beyond earth orbit being *"an obstacle for practical space travel to the moon and beyond"*, just as Kelly Smith of the "Orion" mission did.

Van Allen himself said this, immediately after NASA sent probes with Geiger counters into the radiation belts in 1958:

"Our measurements show that the maximum radiation level as of 1958 is equivalent to between 10 and 100 REM per hour, depending on the still undetermined proportion of protons to electrons. Since a human being exposed for two days to even 10 REM would have only an even chance of survival, the radiation belts obviously present an obstacle to space flight."

Click **HERE** to read: "Van Allen Belts Deadly Radiation".(The above comments are at the very end of the article.)

(Continued on Page 28)

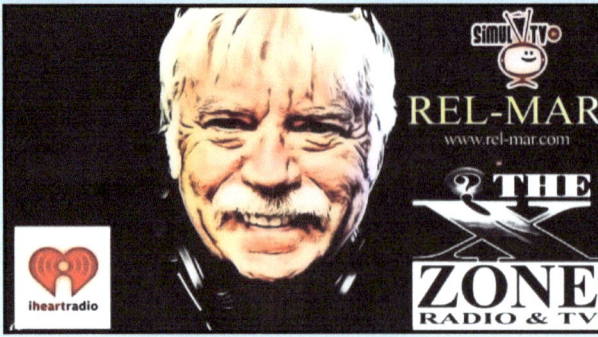

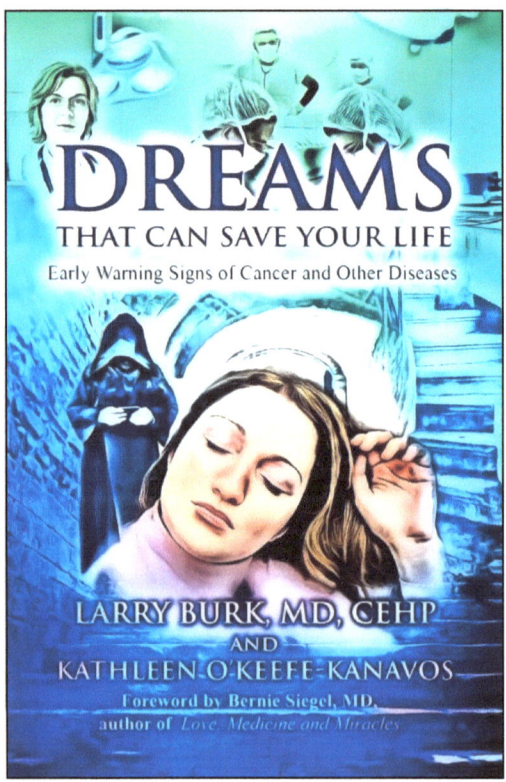

Know the Name
Know the Person

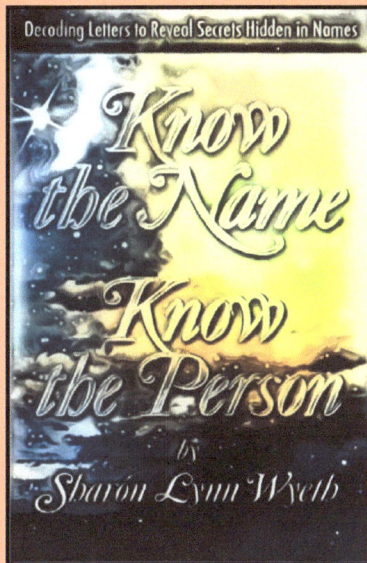

Decoding Letters to Reveal Secrets Hidden in Names

Know the Name Know the Person by *Sharón Lynn Wyeth*

What does your name say about you?

What's in a name?

More than most of us realize. Discover personality secrets hidden in the arrangement of the letters in names. In our busy world, we must make decisions about people quickly, to hire or not; to share personal information, or not; to do a business transaction or not; to trust with money or not. Often there is not enough time to know the person sufficiently before making a decision that could cost both time and money along with one's reputation. Knowing what to look for in a name provides an immediate insight into others, as well as our own, personality traits. This is a must read for everyone who wishes to have insights into others.

After reading this book, you will be able to analyze any name.

By learning Neimology you will:
• Find out how first, middle and last names, as well as nicknames, affect behavior and thinking.
• Realize potential conflicts with others and how to avoid them.
• Discover how to meet and connect with someone immediately.
• Know what types of gifts are appreciated.
• Learn how to sell to people in a style so that they will want to buy.
• Learn how to quickly access strengths and identify what support is required for yourself and others in order to succeed.
• Become an excellent conversationalist depending on the name of the person you are addressing.

We are our names. Recognize what others reveal in their names, and what others immediately know about you, once you know Neimology.

Neimology: The study of the placement of the letters in a name and how they interact with each other to reveal hidden secrets about one's character.

Visit www.KnowtheName.com & Available at Amazon.com

ABOUT THE AUTHOR: As the creator of Neimology® Science, Sharón Lynn Wyeth has supported thousands of people around the world in understanding themselves and others better. In her seventh year of teaching math, having been a math major herself, she noticed that she was getting impressions of how a student would behave when she was making seating charts at the start of the year from the person's name. Her curiosity led her to write down her impressions, as she wanted to get to know her students for who they were. After three months of teaching she read her initial impressions and was amazed at the accuracy. Generally Joshua's were brilliant and a bit obnoxious, Stephanies were stubborn, and Rachels pretty, etc. She followed her fifteen years of research conducted in forty-nine of the States with three years of field work in over seventy countries testing her theories. Everywhere she spoke people asked how to find out more information so she wrote the Amazon bestseller, "KNOW THE NAME, KNOW THE PERSON: Decoding Letters to Reveal Secrets Hidden in Names". Her book has garnered frequent praise and has earned a Literary Excellence Award. Wyeth is an educator and former school administrator, and has appeared on numerous radio and television shows. Sharón also teaches and certifies people to become Neimology® Scientists. **Available on Amazon.com.**

Did Astronauts Go 1000 Times Farther 49 Years Ago Than They Can Today?

Continued from Page 25

Occupational safety limits for radiation is *5 REM over an entire year*, as the danger is calculated by the amount of REM and the period over which it is received, and thereby gradually absorbed, so that the body may have time to incrementally expel the radiation before it reaches a lethal level. Absorbing 5 REM of *radiation in just an hour, rather than a year, is 24 times a lethal dose.* 10 REM of radiation absorbed in an hour is therefore *48 times more lethal a dose* than 10 REM gradually absorbed and expelled over two days (or 48 hours), which Van Allen himself said *was already a lethal dose* (as calculated by it killing 50 percent of those exposed to it). Rounding 48 times a lethal dose per hour in the radiation belts up to 50 (for the slightly longer than an hour trip through them to leave Earth orbit and reach the moon) and then doubling the amount for the return from the moon through the radiation belts again to reenter Earth orbit, this is, according to *Van Allen himself, a minimum of 100 times a lethal dose and a maximum of 1000 times a lethal dose* for the trip to the moon and back.

The "Apollo" spacecraft had inferior shielding (1/8th of an inch of *aluminum*) compared to that of a medical x-ray technician, who wears a much more effective *lead* vest (lead being prohibitive to launch into space because of its exceeding excessive weight), even though the radiation exposure to a chest x-ray is 1/5000th of the radiation exposure to the Van Allen radiation belts, and that only for a split second, rather than *continually for more than two hours* during the alleged trip to the moon and back. Some misinformed and grasping NASA fans have falsely claimed that the Apollo astronauts did not go through the radiation belts while others claim that they only went through weak fringe parts thereof (though NASA never made any such claims), yet this is a scientific impossibility unless the launches took place at the North or South Poles where there are small openings in the belts (as Van Allen clearly stated at the end of the above article), as there was no additional fuel available to zigzag around them and launching closest to the equator as possible, where the radiation belts are strongest, permitted the necessary fuel savings.

Launching at the poles would be virtually impossibility due to the cold temperatures, at least 50 degrees Fahrenheit (19 C) or more *below safe launch temperatures* (because the cold dramatically deteriorates sensitive launch equipment), as the Space Shuttle Challenger's cold launch explosion at just 36 degrees Fahrenheit (2 C) already proved was deadly. What these diehard unresearched supporters of the fraud have inadvertently admitted, is that *yes indeed the radiation belts are deadly,* just as Van Allen and NASA's own Kelly Smith acknowledged in the "Orion" mission video press release. By desperately

saying the crews went around the radiation belts in a forlorn attempt to prove the missions were real (even though NASA claims the crews went right through the most intense part of the radiation), in their acknowledgement of the belt's lethality, they have themselves unknowingly conceded that the missions were scientifically impossible.

Even self-proclaimed "moon" astronaut Alan Bean, when I interviewed him unprepared for my challenging questions, accidentally admitted *on camera* that he did not travel through the lethal Van Allen radiation belts (which he would have to in order to reach the moon). When I pointed out this error to him, he corrected himself by saying, "*Maybe* we did (go through the radiation belts)". When I asked him if he experienced any unusual phenomenon from traveling through the radiation belts, he said "No". When I pointed out to him that a crew of the space shuttle, decades after his alleged moon mission, on the highest altitude of any space shuttle flight, more than 600 miles away from just the beginning of the intense radiation belts, experienced radiation that was so severe, even from that great distance away, that they could see the radiation as sparks of lights through their closed eyelids, Bean then *suddenly remembered* seeing the same phenomenon! When I pointed out to him that I believed that this space shuttle crew was the first of any astronauts in history to report this strange optical radiation phenomenon, he changed his story a third time to keep up with the revelatory information, and immediately recanted what he had just said about seeing the radioactive "sparks of light" in the first place! . . . Absolutely amazing! (Did I mention the fact that each astronaut who was interviewed by me at length asked for Two Thousand Dollars an Hour in cash for the honor of being lied to?)

(See Alan Bean's accidental Truth telling, and failed attempt to cover it up, at 13:41 – 18:53 in **"Astronauts Gone Wild"** by clicking **HERE**.)

(You can also see at time 27:31 – 27:45

in **"Astronauts Gone Wild"** by clicking **HERE**, that Eugene Cernan said that the descent engine to the lunar surface was *"very loud"*, while Bean says that *"you couldn't hear it because of the vacuum of space".*)

Which is it guys?! Get your stories straight!

In August of 2009 it was reported, albeit as a news oddity (and it certainly was) that a "moon rock", personally given to the president of the Netherlands by Neil Armstrong in 1969 (who supposedly hand picked it off of the moon's surface himself), was opened forty years later from its hermetically sealed container by a curious museum curator after they had watched *"A Funny Thing Happened on the Way to the Moon".* Following microscopic examination, the rock was verified to actually be a forgery! (A deceptive "another worldly" looking piece of *petrified wood* instead!) Yet again, not a single journalist, except for myself, asked the question, "If the moon rocks are fake . . . What about the moon missions?" (You can read the story about the fake "moon rock" by clicking **HERE**.)

After Neil Armstrong's departure from this mortal coil, in 2012, his widow found a "bag of moon souvenirs" in the back of his closet. The problem is, for Armstrong's *entire life*, he said that these specific items were *left on the moon!* (Talk about "coming out of the closet"!) Again, *more proof* that the "moon missions" took place *on earth was completely ignored by the media.* (You can read the story by clicking **HERE**.)

(Continued on Page 31)

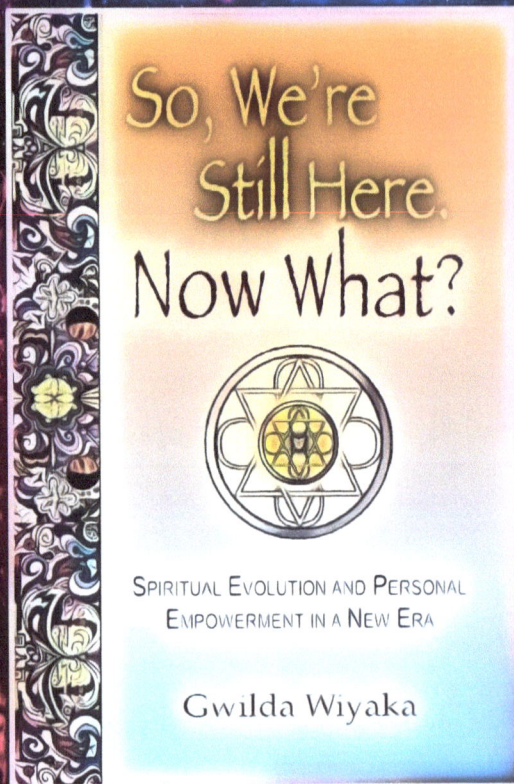

Did Astronauts Go 1000 Times Farther 49 Years Ago Than They Can Today?

Continued from Page 28

When I discovered absolute proof (actual, on camera evidence) that the Apollo astronauts never left earth orbit (contained in a newly discovered unedited NASA reel which was never broadcast to the public; debuted in *"A Funny Thing Happened on the Way to the Moon"* and showcased below) and presented this controversial videotape to a news director at NBC, he turned pale white, practically fainted, and collapsed in his chair exclaiming, *"Oh, my God! It looks like we didn't go to the moon!"*

"I know", I said, "What do we do?"

This man, who held the betterment of America in his hand, thought for a long time . . . and then eventually . . . "chickened out". He said, *"I cannot broadcast this with a clear conscious. It will cause a civil war. I will not be the one responsible for that."*

While I disagree that the public knowing the Truth about the "moon missions" would cause a civil war, Americans would probably demand immense government reform, or possibly a new institution thereof, as well as start investigating other matters of their yet uncovered dark corruption and deception. Naturally, government criminals would rather not get caught and preserve their underhanded way of life, *which the release of this Truth would inevitably bring*. This is precisely why my film has never been broadcast, only to be seen on DVD and Youtube. Instead, numerous networks (owned by bedfellows of the government) have broadcast a dozen full-length documentaries as to why my well-known film's accusations are *"unfounded"*.

If more people would only view with an open, deprogrammed mind, *"A Funny Thing Happened on the Way to the Moon"*, which contains newly discovered video evidence of the moon landing fraud, then they would see, with their own eyes, these recently uncovered unedited behind-the-scenes outtakes of false photography from the first "moon mission", which prove the deception beyond any doubt. In fact, four out of five people who actually view this footage, who previously thought the alleged "moon landings" were real, recant their faith in the supposed mission's authenticity. Thusly you can see why broadcasters are terrified to present this extremely condemning evidence to the public. If they did so, plainly acknowledging as the news director did that this proves the "moon missions" were a government deception, then not only would they be admitting the mainstream media's own complicity in the fraud by being the means through which this lie was disseminated, the public would also call into question the very foundational integrity of the government, possibly leading to its immediate restructuring, as well as the media's, for their own participation in this deplorable dishonesty.

The unedited outtakes of which I speak, were never broadcast to the public. In them, Neil Armstrong is using a one-foot diameter model of the Earth, inside of the spacecraft from low Earth orbit, to create the illusion for the television audience, that he and his crew are halfway to the moon, when they are, in reality, still in Earth orbit, from which they never left. (After all, this is as far as an astronaut can travel today, fifty years later.) This is absolute proof that, though they were on the rocket at launch and achieved Earth orbit, the crew never went any farther, again, just as far as they can go today, with *half a century* improvements in rockets and computers.

This revealing footage is even dated by NASA's own computer clock as having taken place two days into Armstrong's flight, when he is supposed to be halfway to the moon, or some "135,000 miles away from the Earth", yet he and his crew are clearly shown in these revealing outtakes to still be in Earth orbit two days after the launch, and are instead, falsifying the television photography to deceive the viewing public as to their real location. The CIA is even heard on a private, *third audio channel*, prompting Armstrong to respond to Mission Control's questions only *after four seconds have elapsed*, in order to create the false impression of *an increased radio delay*, so as to *appear* to be much farther from the Earth than he and his crew actually were. To best understand this important evidence, a second viewing may be advised, as I too had to look at the newly discovered footage again to realize its incredible significance.

Jump ahead to time 32:03 – 40:50 in *"A Funny Thing Happened on the Way to the Moon"* by clicking **HERE** if you do not wish to repeat the viewing of the entire forty-seven minute documentary and only see again these newly discovered unedited outtakes of Neil Armstrong falsifying mission photography during the historic and now infamously falsified flight, as well as hear the CIA themselves secretly prompting the crew, instructing them to wait four seconds before answering NASA, in order to give the false impression of the great distance of claiming to be half way to the moon at that time, which would cause an increased radio delay in their response.

Due to the obvious genuineness of the footage I uncovered (as it precisely matches NASA's other broadcasts in which they claim the very same footage to be "authentic"), NASA had to acknowledge that this newly discovered unedited behind-the-scenes video from the first "moon mission" (which debuted in *"A Funny Thing Happened on the Way to the Moon"*) is indeed authentic, they simply said that I was *"misinterpreting"* it. Misguided die-hard fans of NASA and detractors of my documentary on the internet elaborated a bit more, to their very own demise. They plainly acknowledged the simple fact that the crew *was indeed falsifying the photography of being "halfway to the moon"* in these newly discovered outtakes of mission photography (*as nearly everyone has the mind to see and admit after examining it*), claiming instead though that the crew was doing so to merely "rehearse" an upcoming scene for the television viewers.

The fact is, this "moon mission" cost about Thirteen Million Dollars Per Minute in today's value. As such, the last thing the crew would do, would be wasting their precious time, and limited weight, carrying and creating a model of the Earth in space at an alleged distance of halfway to the moon, when the real Earth from a distance halfway to the moon was supposed to be right outside their window! If the crew was "rehearsing", then they would have just "rehearsed" with the real Earth out the window rather than wasting valuable time creating an unnecessary model of what supposedly really existed a few feet away! Furthermore, the edited and approved segments of this exact footage, those without the errors I uncovered which give the illusion away, appear in numerous NASA documentaries where their narrator refers to the very same material as "genuinely" being half way to the moon! Additionally, with their already being talk at the time by 10% of Americans that the mission was disingenuous government propaganda, the last thing NASA would ever do, if the mission was real, would be to risk falsifying any of it, for the fear that they would be accused of such dishonesty, if indeed the mission was real.

(Continued on Page 32)

Did Astronauts Go 1000 Times Farther 49 Years Ago Than They Can Today?

Continued from Page 31

What critics have inadvertently done, is *acknowledged* that the first "moon crew" falsified *part* of their photography!

Thank you!

Now you see why broadcasters will not present my film with this clip in it.

The fact is, if they *really* went to the moon, there would be no need to falsify *any* of the photography!

Just as if only *one* ingredient at a salad bar is contaminated with poison it fails the entire health inspection, having discovered only *one* reel of false footage is enough to disqualify the "reality" of all the missions!

All that critics were left with to say in their desperate attempt to extinguish the blazing fire of the Truth contained in this remarkable newly uncovered, unedited behind-the-scenes footage of outtakes of blatant false photography from the first "moon mission", was a feeble effort to diminish its significance by falsely claiming that it was "no big discovery because the video is readily available to the public". These people are *obviously* lying through their teeth. It says in big letters, right at the beginning of the newly discovered reel, *"Not for Public Distribution"*.

When someone has to lie to defend something, this is proof itself that what they are defending is a lie.

Take it from someone who has *personally* and *exhaustively* gone through the entire NASA archives, more than any journalist or die-hard fan of the "moon missions" has ever done. This is the *only* un-edited reel available. Absolutely *everything* else is *pre-edited*. My detractors know this, and shortly after my film debuted, they borrowed some of the footage to hastily put into their new *pro*-NASA releases (as it was never shown previously, proving conclusively that is was not "readily available to the public"), in their dying attempt to minimize the important discovery. In *their* version of my newly discovered footage though, they specifically *deleted* the most incriminating video segments, as well as the *revealing audio of the CIA prompting the astronauts with "Talk"* at the beginning of the deplorable fraudulent footage, done so to remind Armstrong to respond to Mission Control's questions only after four seconds have elapsed, so as to create the false impression of an increased radio delay and thusly *appearing* to be much farther away from the Earth than he and his crew *actually* were. Why would they delete this important *betraying* audio in their films, if this newly discovered hidden track of secret communications revealed nothing of the forgery?

Some despondent critics have even

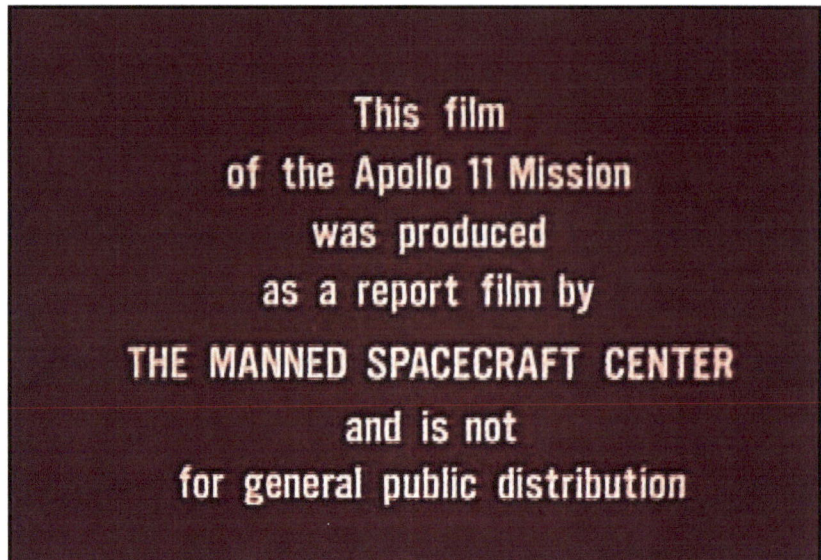

suggested that I am the one doing the deceiving, simply because in my documentary I move from one relevant part of the new footage to another. Come on, really? As my film is only forty-seven minutes in length and the unedited reel is one hour forty-eight minutes long, this is no more "deceptive" than a news sportscaster, with limited time for their program, showing just the *highlights* of a football game. Some, believe it or not, are so desperate to keep the Truth buried, that they have even suggested that I staged the violent attacks which I received from the various angry astronauts in "*Astronauts Gone Wild*" ! (LOL . . . At least they are being creative!)

I am constantly assailed with the *age-old* juvenile, ineffective, and disreputable technique of assaulting the *messenger* of bad news, rather than the message itself, by those who feel they have no other course of action because the reality of my position speaks for itself and cannot be truthfully refuted otherwise. The fact that critics resort to attacking the *messenger* of bad news is proof itself that the *message* is Truthful, otherwise they would have no need to do so in the defense of their position, if their position was not so dramatically faltering to begin with and in such dire need of *misdirection from the condemning evidence.*

In coping with the pressures of such professional and personal ostracization, I once gave prescription antidepressants a try. In doing so while engaged in a prolong fast (sixty days without food), I had an allergic reaction, which resulted in an emotional outburst over a disputed parking place, where I walked across the hood of my adversary's car, denting it in the process. While the "investigative journalist" to whom I personally gave copies of the fraudulent moon landing footage years earlier completely ignored reporting on this *felony* of the United States Government, they found it noteworthy to report on a *misdemeanor* of such a whistle-blower, adding false aggrandizations in the process.

This reminds me of the 2016 leaks of the Democratic Party leadership obtained from hacked computers. Instead of the FBI pursuing the criminals who brazenly rigged a presidential primary, one in which the candidate with the most votes (Bernie Sanders) repeatedly received

the least delegates (a revelation of such corruption that the people involved resigned in humiliation from their lofty positions at the disclosure of this unethical behavior), the federal "policing agency" chose instead to start a prosecutorial investigation into those who merely *released the condemning Truthful information of the illegal acts* (the messenger), rather than pursue those who *actually committed the unlawfulness in the first place!* What a sad, sad joke of our country's government. How on earth my personal error on a random street became so quickly known and disseminated to the press, I have no idea. Someone, somewhere is keeping up with my every move. Why would this be necessary if they *really* went to the moon?

We have to remember that General Motors president, James Roche, admitted during a United States Senate Investigative Hearing, that he had *hired private detectives to follow consumer advocate Ralf Nader* in an effort to "*harass and discredit him*", simply for pointing out errors in the automaker's safety. As one who is spearheading a *much more horrendous* revelation of the much more powerful Federal Government, you can imagine why any misstep I take in private, may mysteriously make its way to a government affiliated public "media" forum in an effort to discredit the messenger.

My tenure of two years as news editor at an NBC affiliate has been falsely identified by my leading critic as two "*months*", in an unscrupulous effort to discredit my professional experience. I worked there through two consecutive "Christmas" holidays and then some, so I and a dozen eyewitnesses know better than he how long I worked there. If my leading critic has to lie to make his point, then his point is not valid to begin with, as valid points don't need lies to support them. If he was simply "mistaken", then his inept powers of research prove that if he cannot uncover the Truth about one simple fact *on earth in his own country*, then how could he possibly discern the numerous intricacies of CIA intrigue as to what may or may not be taking place *on the moon*? The great thing is, either way, his own false statements regarding such a simple thing, prove himself wrong on the more complicated issue.

(Continued on Page 33)

Did Astronauts Go 1000 Times Farther 49 Years Ago Than They Can Today?

Continued from Page 32

The fact that I, during a past occasion used to drive a taxi on weekends to help pay the bills during an economic downturn, is used by some desperate critics to negate the fact that I have been a professional filmmaker for more than thirty years, winning "Best Cinematography", "Best Editing" and "Top Ten Director" from the American Motion Picture Society, and as such, can highly discern fraudulent photography when I see it. (See a list of my films, whose budgets ranged from $2000 to $500,000, by clicking HERE.) If you really think about it, what these lovers of denial are saying is that if you have ever driven a yellow car on weekends, this disqualifies you from being able to perceive the Truth. Anyone who makes such a nonsensical argument to begin with, is likewise proving, by their own ridiculous argumentation or deliberately false or unresearched statements, that it is *they* who lack the ability to perceive reality.

Completely fabricated, and highly outrageous accusations have been made against me, for simply telling the Truth. I even regularly receive vulgar curse filled death threats . . . all for simply saying that I think the Federal Government lied to the public on at least one occasion. The fact that some people react like vicious and insane rabid dogs from a mere statement of opinion, is further proof that the statement is True, as a sword with no point causes no injury.

"The further a society drifts from the Truth, the more it will hate those who speak it."
-George Orwell-

Not too long ago, I interviewed the second man to not walk on the moon, Edwin "Buzz" Aldrin. He sat down with me thinking that I was going to interview him in order to help him make money off of a book he was promoting. Instead, I had a television monitor set up to ask him about the newly discovered unedited outtakes of false photography from his "moon mission", in which he was actually the *camera operator* orchestrating the deception.

You have to understand, at that moment, with two professional television cameras there, a crew of about five people, as well as professional lights and microphones, Aldrin thought, for a brief moment, that the news story of the moon landing fraud had just broken worldwide. It was at this time that he exclaimed in anger (at time 8:58 – 9:11 in the sequel to my film entitled **"Astronauts Gone Wild"**, showcased in the link below), "*And this makes you a real famous person that has discovered this and reveals all this stuff! What an ego you must have to want to propel yourself (your career) like this!*" The question is, if I was wrong with my discovery, how could I become famous from exposing nothing? Therefore, this statement itself is an admission of guilt, as he

didn't say I was *wrong* with my revelation, rather he said that I had *impure motives* for revealing this Truth to the world. (You can see these remarks of his in **"Astronauts Gone Wild"** by clicking **HERE**.)

Aldrin even shouted back (at time 8:30 – 8:38), "*Well you're talking to the wrong guy! Why don't you talk to the administrator of NASA! We're (only) passengers! We're guys going on a flight!*" (See this remark of his by clicking **HERE** in **"Astronauts Gone Wild"**.)

As Aldrin was "*only a passenger*", as he plainly stated, then that certainly means that he never piloted the lunar module to the moon's surface, as he previous claimed, because a *passenger* and a *pilot* are certainly very different from one another. (Merely orbiting the earth for eight days, entirely under the control of NASA, is what made him a *passenger*, not a pilot, as he firmly admitted.)

Aldrin finally remembered that I was not with "ABC" (news) as he previously believed, rather "ABC-Digital", the name of my independent television production company at the time. At this point, when he realized that the discovery of the fraud was isolated, by an independent television producer, not yet broadcast worldwide by a major television network, he started backpedaling on his admission of guilt and started to reassert, though not very convincingly, his mission's alleged authenticity. When Aldrin finally realized that he had made critical errors in judgment by acknowledging *twice*, with the above two statements, that I was right in regard to my discovery of the Truth, he threatened to sue me if I showed his on-camera admissions of guilt to anyone. Certainly if these two statements were *not* admissions of guilt, he would have no problem releasing them to the public. (See Aldrin's threat of a lawsuit at time 10:11 – 10:18 in "*Astronauts Gone Wild*" by clicking **HERE**.)

Seeing how my job as a filmmaker of more than thirty years is to make fake scenes look real, this specific expertise of mine is how I first discerned that the "moon missions" were

filmed inside of a television studio with electrical light, rather than with sunlight on a natural exterior landscape as was falsely claimed. In fact, more than two decades ago, in showing a colleague of mine (with many more years of professional filmmaking experience than I had at the time) a recent dramatic film I had just completed, he complimented me by saying, "*I really liked the way you captured the sunset at the end of your movie.*" I smiled and said, "That was *actually* an *electrical* light, *not* the sun."

In the case of the "moon" scenes that were allegedly lit solely with the bright sunlight on the atmosphereless moon, the shadows from one object (or person) compared to another, should always, without exception, run parallel with one another and never intersect. Yet, in several of the photographs allegedly taken on the moon, shadows from one object or person run at a different angel than the other and eventually intersect. This would absolutely never happen in sunlight, as the sun, the alleged only light source in the "moon" pictures, is one million times bigger in volume than the Earth, and therefore evenly lights in the exact same direction of any given area over the entire Earth.

(Continued on Page 35)

Shamanic Healing is the Key

To Personal Empowerment and Spiritual Evolution!

All four levels of our being: physical, emotional, mental and spiritual, must be addressed in order for us to enjoy balanced, healthy, abundant lives. Shamanism is a spiritual healing modality that has been around 50,000 years and practiced by healers of nearly every indigenous culture.

To find quality shamanic healing you can trust, regardless of where you live, you need look no further than Find Your Path Home Long Distance Shamanic Healing Program.

All Path Home Long Distance Healing practitioners have been trained and certified through the Path Home Shamanic Arts School, a Colorado State Certified Occupational School. They have been handpicked and personally trained by Founder/Director Gwilda Wiyaka to uphold the excellence of Find Your Path Home's Long Distance Program.

Change your life. Live abundantly. Schedule a long distance shamanic healing session with Gwilda Wiyaka or one of her quality practitioners today.

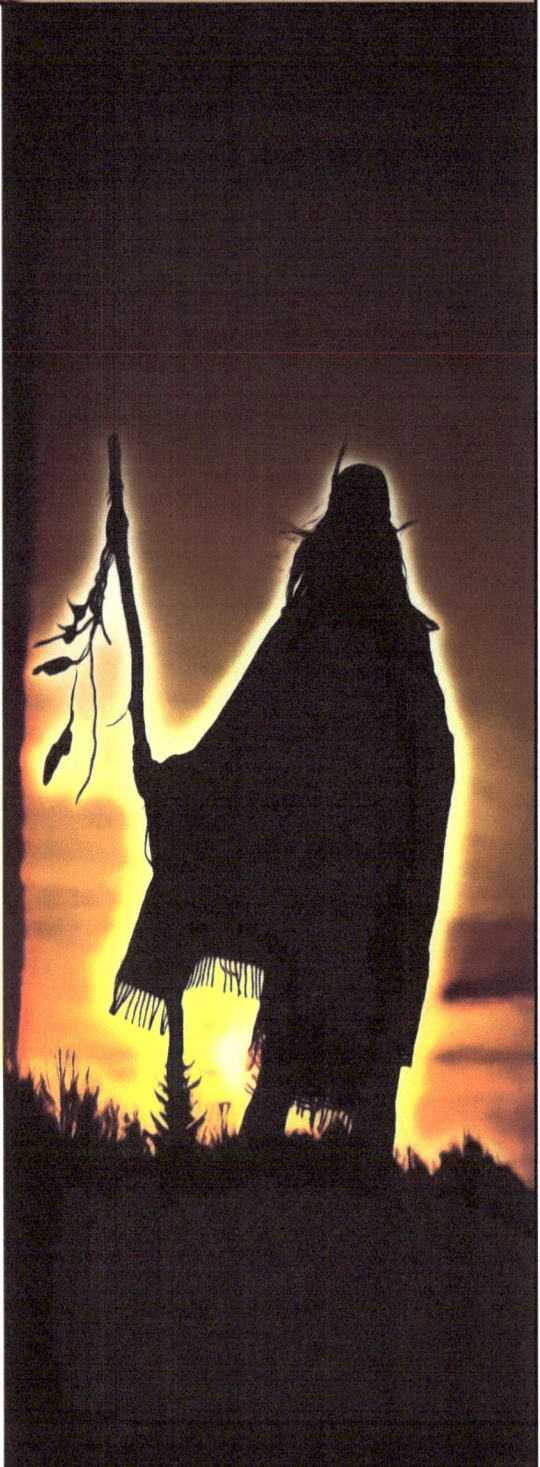

Call 303-775-3431

Visit: http://findyourpathhome.com/shamanic-healing-sessions

Email: touchin@findyourpathhome.com

Did Astronauts Go 1000 Times Farther 49 Years Ago Than They Can Today?

Continued from Page 32

See the direction of the SHADOWS below.

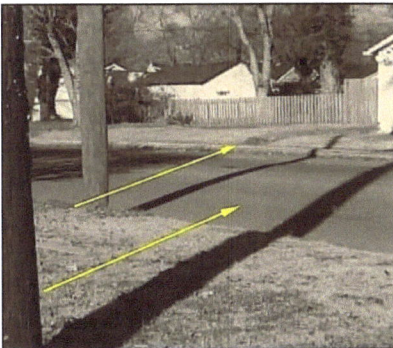

Natural Sunlight, as Claimed (Parallel Shadows)

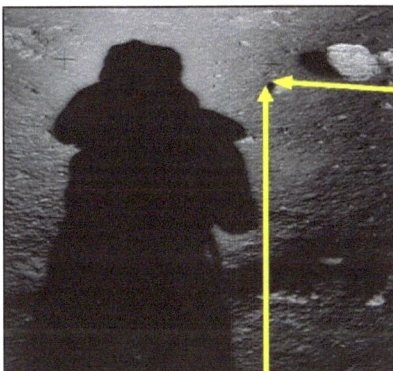

"moon" (Intersecting Shadows: Electrical Light)

According to NASA, no electrical lighting whatsoever was used on any of the "moon missions", simply because of allegedly being on a heavenly body in very bright sunlight, which doesn't have clouds or atmosphere, made supplemental lighting completely unnecessary and a waste of precious electrical power and weight. In fact, according to NASA, because the moon has no atmosphere of any kind, the sunlight there is twenty times brighter than on the Earth, so the last thing any photographer on the moon would need is an electrical light that would cast intersecting shadows, unless of course they were *really* in an enclosed film studio.

In a "National Geographic" television special on how the moon landing hoax was supposed to not be a hoax at all, in a vain attempt to bury the emerging Truth, they went to a California desert *at night* to "simulate" the alleged conditions on the moon. They dressed up an actor in an "astronaut" costume, had them stand a few feet apart from a fellow television crewmember, brought in one electrical light to simulate the sun, and basically said, "See! The shadows of the two people standing near one

another *do* intersect in our 'moon simulation', so filmmaker Bart Sibrel is wrong."

The very simple fact is this: Why didn't they just wait 12 hours and use the very same desert during *the day* with *real sunlight* to accurately depict the very same *sunlit* condition on the moon?! The filmmakers claimed, "*We can't duplicate the sun*", yet they easily *could have* if they only filmed in the very same spot 12 hours earlier, in natural sunlight! They went on national television trying to prove "*A Funny Thing Happened on the Way to the Moon*" wrong with the exact same evidence that *proves me right* . . . all the while telling the viewers *the exact opposite!*

The point is, their shadows in their little demonstration intersected because their "moon simulation" was lit with electrical light! . . . All the while they claimed that this proved that the moon missions were real, when their very demonstration proved that the moon missions were *fake* instead! Think about it! In their "moon simulation", *with electrical light*, the shadows did intersect, just like in some of the NASA "moon" pictures. Yet, they said, "*These results directly contradict the conspiracy claims*" (which are that the pictures from NASA on the "moon" were lit with electrical light, not sunlight). They told this *blatant lie* in a deceptive attempt to confuse the viewer from seeing the Truth, when in fact, these very results of theirs *proved* the conspiracy claims to be *True* rather than false!

Do you see this?!

They went to the desert at night, allegedly, to get a black background like on the moon, *yet this was not the point of the experiment.* The point of the experiment was to see which of the two casts parallel shadows: *sunlight* (as claimed by NASA) or *electrical light* (as claimed by me), because the assertion I made in my film was that the reason the shadows intersect in some of the NASA pictures is *because* they were lit with *electrical light* in a film studio instead of sunlight outside on the moon as they falsely claimed, where the shadows would *never* intersect!

Did you get this?

The "National Geographic" Channel (a propaganda arm of the United States government) simulated the "moon" pictures (matched them) by using *electrical light, not sunlight,* which means that the Apollo pictures were taken with electrical light, not sunlight, meaning they were *taken on earth!* . . . All the while they tried to *mislead* the audience into believing *the exact opposite of the Truth*, that this deceptive "evidence" of theirs proved the moon mission's authenticity, when in fact this *exact evidence* proves the *exact opposite*, that the NASA pictures were also taken with electrical light, and this is *precisely why* the shadows *intersected* in their reenactment, as well as the NASA pictures, because they were *both* taken on Earth with *electrical light*, which caused the intersecting shadows!

The National Geographic program further lied in their "special" when they said "*only a very small group of people believe that the moon missions were fraudulent*". Really? Is

60 million of 300 million Americans a "*very small group*"? (Not to mention approximately *4 billion* others, in other non-brainwashed countries, that perceive the Truth!) If the group of believers of the Truth is so "*very small*", as they falsely claimed, then what is the esteemed "National Geographic" Channel doing wasting an entire expensive hour of television, and tens of thousands of dollars in production costs, trying to convince such a "*small minority*" out of their "*crazy*" and "*insignificant*" error? Obviously these extensive resources are being spent because of the growing *millions* of Americans who are awakening to their senses, that networks like these are trying to keep the multitudes perpetually deceived and asleep to overlook their ongoing crimes.

(Continued on Page 36)

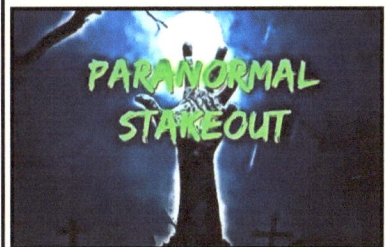

36

Bart Sibrel: "Did Astronauts Go 1000 Times Farther 49 Years Ago Than They Can Go Today?"

SIMULTV

Did Astronauts Go 1000 Times Farther 49 Years Ago Than They Can Today?

Continued from Page 35

Their own "expert" on the program, as to the "moon landing's" alleged authenticity, the one of such astuteness that he proved my film right when he was trying to prove it wrong, admitted that his life's work is to convince people that the "moon landings" were real. Why would this be anyone's life's work if the "moon missions" were so "unquestionably real", the numbers opposed to him were so "very small", and the people opposed to his belief were merely "crazy" as the program insinuated? Would you spend your entire life's energy trying to convince crazy people who thought that the country's first president was Mickey Mouse that it was really George Washington? Of course not. The amount of time, energy, and expensive resources spent on this and a hundred other films and websites to convince accused defective simpletons of the alleged "obviousness" of the claimed moon landings, itself speaks of deliberate propagandizing of a lie.

Even the scene at time 30:38 – 31:06 in *"A Funny Thing Happened on the Way to the Moon"* (Click **HERE** to view), in which the astronauts appear to be "floating" around in 1/6th gravity, is so obviously a simple, yet very convincing, "slow motion" effect, that when they showed the same clip from my film in their deceptive "National Geographic" television special, which was specifically created to disprove my damaging film, they deliberately "zoomed in" on this footage, far beyond the soles of the astronaut's feet and the dirt on which they walked, intentionally so that the viewers could not see the astronauts only getting the same half inch above the ground as they also do here on earth, which my film specifically exemplified as condemning evidence. When you simply double the speed of the footage with professional video equipment, it becomes blatantly obvious that the seemingly convincing "1/6th gravity floating effect" is nothing more than a rudimentary, yet effective, "slow motion" effect. Truly, this alone proves that they were not on the moon, where they should have been able to leap several feet off of the ground, which they accomplished in later "missions" with hidden cables to overcome this initial error on their part. This program's *deliberate* concealment and misrepresentation of the facts *itself* proves that my claims are true, otherwise they would have no need to do this.

"Myth Busters" did the very same thing as the "National Geographic" special, by lighting their simulated "moonscape" with *electrical* light rather than *sunlight*, in an inverted attempt to simulate the lighting conditions on the moon, when in reality what they really did is prove that NASA's "moon" picture were taken with electrical light rather that *sunlight*, meaning they were taken in a film studio, as no electrical lights were brought to the moon. Why they, like the others, did not use sunlight to simulate *sunlight* is beyond me,

unless their *real* intention was to deceptively *mislead* the television viewers into *wrongly believing* this "reenactment" of theirs with electrical light proved the mission's authenticity, when in fact this very *methodology actually* proves the *exact opposite*, as they too duplicated the intersecting shadows of the "moon" pictures with *electrical light* rather than *sunlight*, proving again that NASA's "moon" pictures were lit with *electrical* light rather than *sunlight*, therefore in a film studio, likewise all the while they too *lied* to their television audience by saying that their deceptive technique proved the *exact opposite* of the Truth . . . Amazing.

As before, if this misrepresentation was *intentional*, then *deliberately lying* to make a contested point proves that their position is false to begin with. If such an inversion of the Truth was *accidental*, then it proves their complete *incompetence on the subject*. Either way, it *proves* that the "moon landings" were lit with *electrical* light and thereby *indeed* false, completely contrary to their grossly misleading presentation.

It was when I pointed out these deceptions or errors of theirs that the producers of these two shows (who I believe were NASA surrogates) recanted to have me on their programs, or deleted my previously recorded interviews from their content, because not only did I prove that the "moon landings" were fraudulent beyond any doubt, I also exposed their blatantly deceptive and backwards methodology to make their misleading points to a beguiled public, something they were not about to broadcast.

If a television program about the moon landing "conspiracy theory" refuses to have on their show the *world's leading advocate on this very subject*, or *deliberately deletes conclusive evidence from him of the fraud from their content*, then how can they at all be trusted to be presenting the Truth in the first place? If the "moon landings" are so obviously real and incontestable as they falsely claimed, then they would let me speak uncensored about their fraudulent methodology, and show the newly discovered, and highly condemning, unedited video evidence without any fear whatsoever, which neither of them risked doing. Thusly, the final *lie* of theirs was that their program on this subject was a real open debate of the issue, rather than a production whose sole purpose was to reassure the doubting public that this age old deception which is steadfastly coming to light is still trustworthy despite overwhelming mounting evidence.

Do you see how *upside-down* the Truth is presented on television? The real "myth" is that the "moon landings" took place with 1960's technology, on the very first attempt, allegedly going 1000 times farther than the space station is or any man can travel today, with five decades older technology. *This* is the *myth* they should be busting. Instead, they are a propaganda arm of the corrupt United States government and the CIA, whose native language is lies, saying that the Truth is a myth, and that a myth is the Truth . . . all the while the corrupt government charges their citizens, billions of dollars in taxes, for the honor of being lied to by their deceptive "leaders" . . . Utterly disgusting.

Do you have eyes that Truly perceive . . . or only eyes which see, what the magician wants you to see?

NBC, my old alma mater, for a program on their affiliate the *"Discovery* Channel", paid me thousands of dollars, flew me to New York City, put me up in the very expensive Waldorf Astoria hotel, all because a new, independent-minded producer of theirs wanted to air my side of the story, as well as exclusively showcase the first network broadcast of my newly discovered unedited video evidence of the behind-the-scenes photographic fraud from the first "moon mission". (Remember, another NBC news director previously viewed the very same evidence and promptly concluded that it *conclusively proved* the moon landing fraud, though disappointedly said, "I cannot air this. It will cause a civil war".) This new NBC producer told me, after editing my interview and transferring the condemning footage in preparation for a special broadcast, that NASA somehow found out about her program and threatened NBC, and all of their affiliates, with permanently disconnecting their live camera aboard the International Space Station and never cooperating with them ever again as retaliation if they broadcasted this revealing television program of theirs. Seeing how NBC and the Discovery Channel regularly used and boasted about video feeds from this camera of theirs on-board the International Space Station on numerous ongoing television programs on on numerous channels of theirs, NBC succumbed to the NASA blackmail, canceled their television special showcasing this amazing discovery from the *"Discovery* Channel", and never aired the interview they filmed of me painstakingly explaining the newly discovered condemning NASA footage, which they had already excitedly purchased the exclusive rights to, even though it cost them tens of thousands of dollars of loss in the process.

Do you still believe there is a free press outside of government control?

How the federal government found out about this special broadcast which the producer tried to keep confidential from them is a mystery to me, unless my work is being monitored. The question is, why would my "silly" work about the moon landing fraud be monitored by the government if they really went to the moon?

In an effort to find out, I went the NASA launch headquarters in Florida to see what would happen. When I encountered a retired "Apollo" astronaut and asked him to confirm that he *actually* left Earth orbit (because I had newly discovered evidence to the contrary), I was promptly, and forcibly, removed from the public property, which was opened to the public, by security forces, with the threat of arrest if I persisted with my questions. If you had been there and witnessed this firsthand as I did, you would have sworn that I was in oppressive North Korea or China, rather than the "free" United States of America, with an alleged "free" press.

(Continued on Page 37)

Bart Sibrel: "Did Astronauts Go 1000 Times Farther 49 Years Ago Than They Can Go Today?"

37

Did Astronauts Go 1000 Times Farther 49 Years Ago Than They Can Today?

Continued from Page 36

The only television program to ever broadcast my newly discovered condemning footage of unedited outtakes of false photography from the first "moon mission", with its most revealing secret audio channel of the CIA prompting the astronauts during their deception, was "Tech TV's" enormously popular national cable talk show called "Unscrewed", who mistakenly broadcast the revealing footage without prior executive approval. In fact, the show was so successful, that their viewership doubled every thirty days for the first two years it was on the air! Despite being the highest rated program on the entire network by far, bringing in the owners of the channel untold millions of dollars, the show was abruptly canceled immediately after airing this inflammatory footage of NASA's forgery, especially when someone powerful higher up witnessed the studio audience reacting with horror and indignation when they saw it. This cancellation was a not so subtle warning to other broadcasters who might make the same error in judgment. Since then, knowing this penalty of termination hanging over their heads, no other network has dared to air, on any of their programs, any condemning portions of this monumental evidence, which emphatically proves, to both an NBC news director and producer, as well as many other professionals, that the "moon missions" never left Earth orbit, as is their limit today, with fifty years better rockets and computers.

The simple Truth is, if I really walked on the moon, and someone thought otherwise, I would find that hysterically funny! If someone asked me to swear on the Bible to that "fact", why in the world would I object to taking an oath of such an "obvious" event? Instead, the astronauts in question reacted to the request as if I walked up to them in the company of their wife and asked them how their secret mistress was doing! If they *really* walked on the moon, me saying otherwise would be like throwing a feather at them. Why would anyone be violently mad at someone for throwing a feather at them? If, on the other hand, I were exposing a *real* crime of *infidelity* that they had gotten away with for decades and built lifelong financial reputations on, then you could certainly see *why* they would react with such violent hatred. (If you haven't already, or wish to view again, you can see these revealing reactions at time 00:00 – 2:00 in "*Astronauts Gone Wild*" by clicking **HERE**.)

I even met privately with "investigative journalist" Geraldo Rivera in New York City to personally give him a copy of "*A Funny Thing happened on the Way to the Moon*", which includes the newly discovered condemning video evidence. While I later appeared as a guest on his show to discuss this topic, he made it clear to me that though he may be personally suspicious of the "moon missions" authenticity,

he is not able to say so publicly and keep his job. The only way that I could appear and present my case on his program was *if I did not show the number one key piece of evidence of the fraud*. Why would this matter . . . if they really went to the moon? Instead of showcasing the recently uncovered absolute proof of the fraud, Fox television chose to sensationalize the violence I received in pursuit of the Truth. Subsequently, one has to question Geraldo's (and other's) credentials as a real "investigative journalists", rather than pop-culture propagandists, especially when they privately confide in me that they know the hidden Truth and refuse to share it with the public, whom they claim to look out for, out of fear of personal reprisal.

The same is true of the "New York Times". While "investigate reporter" John Schwartz interviewed me in-depth on the topic of the moon landing fraud, the story which he actually wrote was about "how interesting it is that some people doubt the moon landings", rather than an actual *investigation* into the *real possibility* that indeed the missions were a Cold War deception. When I asked him about the newly discovered condemning video evidence of the astronauts staging their photography of being "halfway to the moon" when they were still in earth orbit, he replied, "*I can't explain that*", and then he went on to say that such an investigation of his along these lines would result in his termination by his superiors.

"USA Today", along with many other newspapers, television and radio stations, "reviewed" my documentary "A Funny Thing Happened on the Way to the Moon", yet repeatedly toted the status quo. In each and every case, with the exception of John Schwartz who was admittedly dumbfounded by the newly discovered condemning video evidence, when I tracked down the actual person who wrote the critical review of my film and asked them, "What did you think about the newly discovered unedited footage of false photography from Apollo 11 showcased in my movie?", they all replied, "*Well . . . I didn't actually watch the movie. I wrote the review on the concept of the film, not the actual content.*"

The fact is, four out of five people who actually watch the forty-seven minute documentary, with the condemning new evidence debuted in it, reverse their opinion as to the "moon missions" authenticity.

90% of *allegedly* professional "journalists", for major magazines, newspapers, and television stations, actually wrote reviews about a film which they didn't even watch! . . . Can you believe this?! Why aren't people like this fired for incompetence or dereliction of duty, instead of being promoted to positions of national media authority?!

Four networks, so far, have paid thousands of dollars for the exclusive license to broadcast this newly discovered amazing NASA footage, only to be told at the eleventh hour not to do *it* by senior network executives (who are likely bedfellows of the CIA, by bribe or by blackmail, whose criminality would be exposed by airing it). The BBC did this very thing only three days before my film's scheduled broadcast, after they had licensed the condemning footage nearly a year in advance at the cost of thousands of dollars. I was privately

informed that a senior US government official personally telephoned the president of the BBC and put pressure on them to not air the program with its condemning new evidence. The BBC even bribed the executive producer of my film with additional thousands of dollars to sign a contract not to publicize their reason for recanting. Again, why would all this be going on, if they *really* went to the moon fifty years ago on the first attempt?

In fact, this executive producer of which I speak, who wishes to remain anonymous, who put up approximately one million dollars to help produce these films of mine exposing the moon landing fraud, has an IQ nearing 200 and is a board member of an aerospace company which is presently building rockets for NASA! Wouldn't such a person know whether the "moon landing" of 1969 was possible or not with 1960's technology? Of course they would. They do know. They *know* that the missions were *staged*. They *know*, from an *engineering* standpoint, that 1960's NASA "low bid" equipment, which killed three astronauts on the ground two years earlier without even igniting an engine, could *never* have successfully landed on the moon on their first attempt with 1960's technology, especially considering the fact that the feat cannot be repeated today with *fifty years* more advanced computers and rockets, with astronauts now only being able to travel 1/1000th as far from the Earth as was claimed a half a century ago!

Although the technology allegedly used to "put a man on the moon" was not classified, because the missions were "supposed" to have been done by a non-military "civilian" government agency (NASA), all of the specific blueprints of the hypothetically miraculous machinery, according to NASA, are nevertheless "unavailable". This is because all of the flight telemetry data, as well as all of the technical specifications of the "Apollo" spacecraft, were *deliberately destroyed by NASA* after the "moon missions". You would think that such important, one of a kind, and supremely valuable and expensive designs, at a cost of *One Hundred Fifty Billion Dollars* in today's value, would be kept for just short of all of eternity, in case such costly to attain information and equipment would be needed again in the future . . . Yet the *exact opposite* is the case. (Click **HERE** or on the below window to see this amazing confession.)

How did the lunar lander power air-conditioning against an outside temperature of 252 degrees Fahrenheit (122 C) down to an amazing 72 degrees Fahrenheit (22 C) inside a boiling spacecraft for three days nonstop with a bank of, essentially, car batteries? No one will ever know. All of the schematics and electrical diagrams of the lunar lander *were deliberately destroyed!* How did the "moon" rocket go 1000 times farther than the space shuttle with decades less advanced technology? No one will ever know. The rocket diagrams and *blueprints were removed from the national archives and are nowhere to be found!*

(Continued on Page 38)

38

Bart Sibrel: "Did Astronauts Go 1000 Times Farther 49 Years Ago Than They Can Go Today?"

Did Astronauts Go 1000 Times Farther 49 Years Ago Than They Can Today?

Continued from Page 37

Imagine Bill Gates spending *One Hundred Fifty Billion Dollars* to build the first computer, and then once successfully completing it, throwing the computer with its blueprints into a furnace . . . Would anyone *ever – ever – ever* do such a crazy thing?! . . . Of course not . . . yet . . . this is what NASA did with the "technology" which they claimed could reach the moon in the 1960's.

This is proof itself that the "moon missions" were fraudulent . . . Here's why . . .

If you *really* went to the moon and spent *One Hundred Fifty Billion Dollars* to do so, you would *never – ever – ever* deliberately throw away such precious hard earned technology . . . *Never!* Has anyone *ever* deliberately thrown away breakthrough technology in the entire history of the world? . . . Of course not. Even the atomic bomb, though this technology *should* have been thrown away, was *cherished with relish,* protected with all security, and then *multiplied and improved upon one hundredfold within just ten years*. Thusly, if the moon landings were real *fifty years* ago, then men would have walked on Mars *decades ago*.

On the other hand, if NASA faked going to the moon, and a detailed analysis of the engineering specifications could *prove mathematically* that the rocket did not have enough fuel to reach its destination and return, or that the onboard computers were not fast enough to process the complicated trajectories in real time as the mission required, or that the power in the lunar module batteries was not sufficient to supply the air conditioning to combat exterior temperatures of 252 degrees Fahrenheit (122 Celsius) for three days without cooking alive the crew inside, *then yes indeed NASA* would *definitely* destroy any and all proof of their deception, which is *exactly what they did*.

Again, if NASA *really* went to the moon, they would *never – ever – ever* destroy that important technology. If, on the other hand, NASA *faked* going to the moon, then they would most *definitely* destroy the evidence which would prove it a technological impossibility. Thusly, the fact that NASA *did* destroy the evidence is *concrete proof itself* that they did not go to the moon. End of story.

All of this intentional file burning was done so that if a curious and astute propulsion or electrical engineering student in the future were to do the actual mathematical calculations, they would not be able to expose the fact that the "lunar lander", in reality, did not have the electrical battery capacity necessary to power the air-conditioning down 180 degrees Fahrenheit (82 C) from the outside temperature nonstop for three days, nor did the onboard rudimentary computers have the processing power or speed to calculate the complicated

trajectories in real time to avoid a fatal catastrophe, nor did the main "Apollo" rocket have the fuel necessary to leave Earth orbit to begin with, as the newly uncovered video evidence clearly proves by the crew's falsification of being halfway to the moon.

Don't believe me? Watch the video clip below in which I read the super intelligent "Apollo" rocket designer's original mathematical calculations to "moon" astronaut Eugene Cernan as to the *only* way possible to reach the moon, a methodology which NASA *never* used. (You can see Cernan squirm and sweat as he realizes that he has just been caught in a lie.) Wernher von Braun, the astute mathematician and rocket scientist, said this regarding the *only* way to reach the moon:

"It is commonly believed that men will fly directly from the Earth to the moon, but to do this we would require a vehicle of such gigantic proportions that it would prove an economic impossibility. Calculations have been carefully worked out on the type of vehicle we would need for the nonstop flight from the Earth to the moon and to return. The figures speak for themselves: Three rockets would be necessary, each rocket ship would be taller than the Empire State Building (1250 feet) and weigh about ten times the tonnage of the Queen Mary (800,000 tons)."

The "moon" rocket the United States Government could afford weighed just 2500 tons (a difference of 32,000 percent) and was just 363 feet tall . . . and there was just one of them, rather than the *three* stated as *required*. Furthermore, Braun went on to say that a Space Station must *first* be constructed *before* a manned mission to the moon, from which to ferry the three rockets and the necessary fuel to the moon and back. (The International Space Station was not completed until 2011.) Braun further insisted that after once landing on the moon, crews would have to find or dig a cave in which to shelter themselves from *thousands* of micrometeorites per hour hitting the moon's surface *traveling at speeds in excess of 20,000 miles per hour*, which would inevitably puncture the spacecraft, as well as the astronaut's spacesuit, causing catastrophic, and fatal, environmental decompression. This, of course, like the other requirements, was *never* done. (See this confrontation with Eugene Cernan at time 31:40 – 32:46 in "***Astronauts Gone Wild***" by clicking **HERE**.)

When the government told the man in charge of the "moon" rocket to adjust his numbers "a little bit" to reflect a fictitious way to reach the moon with the available resources and technology of the time, he immediately, and obediently, dramatically recanted his published and respected findings. Did I mention that this man in charge of the "moon" program's authenticity, Wernher von Braun, was a former World War Two Nazi whom our own government's State Department is on the record for saying that, had he not prematurely died shortly after the "moon missions", he would have been immediately thereafter indicted for War Crimes for overseeing the genocide, *and the cover-up thereof,* of hundreds of innocent people during the war? This threat of blackmail, and likely bribery as well, was likely used to gain his obedient submission to the government deception and his "adjustment" of irrefutable mathematical calculations. (*"The figures speak*

for themselves.")

Not only are all of the specifications, blueprints, and telemetry data of the miraculous NASA 1960's technology that allegedly went to the moon on the very first attempt nowhere to be found because it was all *intentionally destroyed*, all of the original television transmission videotapes, estimated to weigh about two tons, have also been mysteriously "lost" inside the Federally Secured National Archives. Why? Because naïve director Ron Howard, whose own wise grandfather warned him that the "moon missions" were staged, ignoring that advice, requested that all of the original videotapes be transferred to High Definition for an I-Max documentary he was producing to gleefully commemorate the "moon missions", as he *believed*, at that time, that they were real. Prior to Howard's request, the highest quality version of the television footage that anyone had ever seen was *deliberately* a fourth generation copy (a copy, of a copy, of a copy), in order to diminish and disguise the falsification detail and resolution of the fake "moon" landscapes, so that any imperfections that might give away the illusion would be minimized.

When this moon-landing-believing prominent film director asked for the *original* NASA videotapes of all of the "moon walks" so that he could transfer them to High Definition video, in order to be projected *for the first time in history* onto a screen that was nearly 120 feet by 100 feet, *for all the world to see at a resolution that was at least four times greater in detail than had ever before been witnessed*, within days of his request, all of the original "moon landing" videotapes *vanished* from the Federal Archives! But of course, we still went to the moon, right?

Proof of this bewildering predicament, is that when Howard's documentary commemorating the "moon missions" was finally produced without this essential material, he resorted to filling about *95 percent* of his landmark film with "*reenactments*" of the supposed moon walks, which he likewise filmed in a television studio. In fact, there was so little actual original footage available of the alleged greatest event of mankind, that this multimillion dollar director had to resort to renting VHS tapes of other filmmaker's previous work on the subject at Blockbuster Video in order to have at least *some* of the vanishing NASA footage! He was so ashamed of the low quality of the VHS images that he was forced to use, because of the scarcity of them, that he reduced their size within the nearly 120 foot by 100 foot screen to only about 10 percent of the available space to minimize the now *fifth* generation copy quality.

(Continued on Page 39)

Fact*oids

- Pumice is the only rock that floats.
- Cats walk on their claws, not on their paws.
- If a month starts on Sunday, it will include a Friday the 13th.
- Chow dogs have black tongues.
- Sharks are immune to every disease including cancer.

Did Astronauts Go 1000 Times Farther 49 Years Ago Than They Can Today?

Continued from Page 38

In case you were wondering "what if", someday, the mysteriously vanished original videotapes were to one day be found? . . . Oops! . . . Did I forget to tell you? . . . The only machine on the *entire planet* that could *ever* play these one of a kind format videotapes was *deliberately disassembled* and destroyed by NASA, right after the original tapes got "misplaced", making that scenario absolutely impossible. Funny, isn't it? The National Archives has the original "*Declaration of Independence*", more than *two hundred forty years old*, yet "*misplaced*" *every* original document about the "*greatest achievement of all mankind*" *(amounting to several tons in weight)*, which is only *fifty* years old!

As various nations and private enterprises finally, after nearly fifty years, have the capability to send microwave oven sized probes to the moon (*still no men*), NASA has quickly drafted regulations to keep their alleged manned landing sites of the Nixon administration completely *off-limits*. They have said that any flyovers of these locations, or ground incursions thereof, by probes of any nations, *including their own*, to prove or *disprove* the "moon missions" authenticity, are *strictly forbidden*. (Since when does the US government own the moon?) You would think that they would gladly welcome independent proof (of which there has never been) that their outrageous scientific claims of 1960's technology *were* real (even though the feat cannot be repeated today, half a century later), especially in the face of growing universal doubt to the contrary, yet again the *exact opposite* proves to be the case. It is like a murderer who boasts about their innocence, all the while refusing to give a personal DNA sample, which they know full well might incriminate them.

China, a trillion dollar trading partner of the United States, recently sent an *un-manned* probe to the moon. As all of the moon is uniformly desolate and one landing site is just about as good as any other for exploration, I would think that the *perfect* and most logical place to land would be that of the United States' alleged first "moon mission", to prove to the world that their probe was *really* on the moon. Yet if the American government's "moon landing" artifacts are *not there themselves*, this might be biting the trillion dollar trading-partner hand that feeds them. Subsequently, China steered clear of any supposed NASA "moon landing" sites for any of their unmanned lunar probes, even though these were the most logical places to land.

Astrobotic Technology, a private firm, had also planned to land an unmanned probe precisely at the claimed "Apollo 11" landing site, as they too saw this as the most logical choice to prove that their probe was really on the moon, yet *because of pressure from NASA not to do so,* and subsequently embarrass the

organization and government for not having really landed on the moon in 1969, the president of the company, John Thornton, caved in and agreed not to land there as originally planned, even though the moon is not owned by anyone and he was "free" to do so. Is it scientific "freedom" when important exploration is *completely abandoned because of pressure to maintain a falsehood of the CIA?*

If putting a man on the moon is supposed to be "the greatest achievement of mankind", then certainly not doing it as internationally claimed, *lying about it to the entire world*, embezzling *One Hundred Fifty Billion Dollars* in the process, *deceiving* and *misleading* college students, high school students, scientists, academics, *congress, the senate, and future space pioneers who will endanger their lives thinking it was so easy to go to the moon in the 1960's on the very first attempt,* then this event, the *falsification of the moon landings*, out of pride, greed, and arrogance, is *really* one of the most profound events in human history. This is why the *falsification* of the moon landings is more profound historically, than if they had actually gone.

Do you see this?

This Great Truth, as to the True nature of humanity and their governments, *the deceptive, arrogant, and criminal nature thereof,* is being withheld from the majority, by the few people at the top, because they are the ones who committed this crime in the first place and think that they are better than the rest of us.

This Great Truth, which would humble mankind and their governments into changing their character for the *better, before it is too late*, is being withheld from the public, like a cure for cancer, the very *disclosure* of which would bring about its recovery, and *without this disclosure,* our intellectual and moral growth will be forever stunted.

I am sometimes criticized by my fellow citizens as "unpatriotic" for saying that the "glorious" American "moon landings" were a Cold War CIA deception, even though this is the Truth. Our country has hopelessly descended into a realm where liars are heroes, and Truth speakers are villains. If George Washington arose from his grave today and saw all of this unspeakable corruptive government deception, he would grab the first ship back to England. He repeatedly told the painstakingly detailed unflattering Truth of the desperateness of the situation of his Continental Army against the vastly outnumbered and better equipped British troops, to a congress, whom even at that early historic hour, wanted to hear flowery lies of success instead of unpleasant realities. Our leaders have gone from "I can *never* tell a lie", to practically lying *all of the time*. It is not *un-patriotic* to expose corruption, it is *patriotic*. It is *un-patriotic* to have committed this deceitfulness in the first place. If you love Truth and America, then you can see why, "The *Truth* will set you free."

Just as a gangster's children would have a hard time seeing dear old papa as anything but a benevolent patriarch, prideful "intellectuals", as well as deceived "patriots" will seldom admit, without being forcibly shown, that their idolized "science" and aggrandized "government" can be

just as corrupt as pedophile priest.

The fact remains, that if *all* of the scientists from *all* of the nations on earth cannot go to the moon *today* with *fifty years more advanced computer and rocket technology*, and astronauts *now* can only travel 1/1000th the distance from earth as was claimed *half a century ago*, on the *very first attempt*, with *one millionth* the computing power in all of NASA than a modern day cell phone, then it simply means, and it cannot mean anything else, that America did not go to the moon in the 1960's.

Technology does not go backwards . . .
Except in this one case,
and no other instance,
in the entire history of the world.

All of these facts eventually become obvious to anyone with an open mind who does not have a religious attachment to the blasphemous event.[]

About the Author - Bart Sibrel.

Bart Sibrel is an award winning filmmaker, writer and investigative journalist who has been producing movies and television programs for over 30 years. During this time he has owned five production companies, been employed by two of the three major networks and produced films shown on ABC, NBC, CNN, TLC, USA, BET, as well as The Tonight Show with Jay Leno. To discuss his films, he has appeared and been interviewed on The Daily Show, Geraldo, NBC, CNN, FOX, Tech TV, Coast to Coast, and The Abrams Report. Articles featuring Mr. Sibrel's films have been published in Time Magazine, The New York Times, The Washington Post, The L.A. Times, USA Today and many others. His top awards from the American Motion Picture Society include "Best Cinematography", "Best Editing" and "Top Ten Director". As the writer and director of the infamous "A Funny Thing Happened on the Way to the Moon" which exposed the moon landing hoax, Mr. Sibrel has collected over the years innumerous military, government, industrial and private sources for credible firsthand verification of very real conspiratorial crimes against humanity. He will use these contacts and experience in exposing the true and unbelievably horrific intentions of the hidden minority who have diabolical intentions for mankind in his monthly Sleuth Journal column "Conspiracy Corner". Be sure to visit his site at Sibrel.com and subscribe to his Youtube Channel. If you are so inclined, you may Donate to further Bart Sibrel's research with a with a generous one time donation, or a modest $5 per month recurring donation, to help Conspiracy Corner be entirely user supported. Your thoughtfulness is most appreciated. Bart Sibrel is a participant in the Amazon Services LLC Associates Program, an affiliate advertising program designed to provide a means for sites to earn advertising fees by advertising and linking to Amazon.com. When you want to shop on Amazon, please come back to this page and click HERE to visit the Amazon homepage, or copy and paste the following url into your browser's bookmarks as "Amazon.com" for future use (http://amzn.to/2bvcs9I).

Thank you!

Moving From I To We In A Climate Changing World

by Stephanie Mines, Ph.D.

Before I became a neuroscientist, I was a poet and creative writing teacher. This was in the halcyon days of San Francisco, when writers like Allen Ginsburg and Diane DiPrima gave readings spontaneously in Golden Gate Park. I ran a writing workshop in the thriving Noe Valley district where Lawrence Ferlinghetti, Gary Snyder or Michael McClure might show up to inspire young writers, find girlfriends and otherwise be admired. Dressed in flowing garments, I gave poetry readings with jazz musicians at local bookstores and the San Francisco Museum of Art. I met my fellow writers and musicians in cafes to talk about our latest insights and love affairs. We believed we were recreating the ambience of Sartre and Simone de Beauvoir. It was an exciting, rich time.

I remember exactly when it shifted. It happened shortly after the death of Anais Nin. She had been my mentor and I was organizing her memorial at San Francisco State. I was bereft, and felt her loss as if she were my mother. In this mood of eerie abandonment, I returned after a day of planning meetings to my little house amidst wild gardens.

When I woke after a restless night, I felt terribly ill. I cancelled my day and stayed home to vomit for hours, reeling with stomach cramps. It got so bad, I was rolling around on the floor to find relief. It made no sense based on anything I had ingested or drank. I was worried, confused and relentlessly uncomfortable.

Anais Nin had validated my lifelong pursuit of curative writing, so I quite naturally began, in the midst of my disturbance, to write spontaneously in my journal. My whole life came pouring out, like the gunk I was spewing. My bohemian days stopped on a dime as I realized how the violence of my formative years in a home where my father beat my mother, sexually abused me, deserted and abandoned us for other women, and fathered other children whom I would never know, had shaped me to pursue loss after loss. It took a doctorate in neuroscience, however, for me to really grasp the implications of my somatic discoveries and their implications for others as well as myself.

Once I did, though, I was free to become more than trauma repetition. My habits of self-sabotage, repeatedly risking my life and choosing abusive relationships, were neurochemical habituations that I could, with discipline, shift into empowerment and growth. The resources that allowed me to do that also led organically to the development of leadership skills that I continue to cultivate every moment, and that never cease to amaze me.

Fast forward to this era we inhabit, that Joanna Macy calls the Great Turning. This is a time when the fate of all humanity hangs on the thread of our abilities as citizens of the world to create a legacy for the children of the future. What my life reveals is that the movement from I to We is a weaving of personal and collective needs. The leadership that is latent in all of us can only step forward as our personal traumas are sequenced and integrated sufficiently to elevate consciousness.

This is not a clearly defined movement from the economy seating of being enmeshed with trauma to the clarity upgrade. It is a continual back and forth, with each level of expansive consciousness, compassion and empathy inviting new challenges to personal development. Yet at a certain point, the dance across a threshold is sensed somatically and one knows that whenever trauma is reactivated, it will be met not only with self-regulation, but with an embrace of comprehension that leads to enhanced leadership. Climate change demands of us that we become leaders and fulfill as soon as possible our purpose in embodiment.

Western culture has become stuck on the dream of comfort, possession, appearance and seduction. It is time to for everyone to call out that the emperor is naked. For neuroscientists who have invested in resolving personal and collective trauma, this means generating heightened efficiency in resolution protocols that are not faddish because they are quick, but effective because they are thorough. This demands a non-formulaic approach. There is no "one size fits all."

The mastery is not in a three or four step protocol. The mastery is in the depth to which we attune to the truth of another, and meet it with mirrored interventions that uproot the original causative burden. Then the nervous system springs free. I confess to hoping that this outcome produces leadership for humanity in the movement to mediate climate change and find sustainability at every level of existence. The forms of that leadership are multitudinous. Leadership and action will be unique in different cultures, communities and collective. But one thing is clear. This is about all of us.

I am grateful to hear the call from my healed nervous system and to answer it with energy and dedication. This is the product of devotion to my personal unwinding, and knowing with certainty that I am not the trauma and shock that I experienced, and that I went through the arduous journey to manifest myself for something greater than myself. Knowing this at the core of my being is the healed state I have found and what it calls for, without question, is action. I cannot horde the healed state or isolate it.

I believe in the genius of an optimistic, practical and compassionate collective to evolve living action initiatives and dynamic communities of action so that we can thrive in a climate changing world. That is why I have envisioned and convened a momentous gathering April 20-26, 2019 at the Findhorn Foundation in Scotland called CLIMATE CHANGE & CONSCIOUSNESS: Our Legacy for the Earth (www.ccc19.org).

This is also why I have created a healthcare paradigm called Sustainable Health for a Climate Changing World. These are my most expanded acts of trust and therefore the most glowing advertisement for my own healing. I carry in my regenerated cells great faith that each of us will recognize and act on the essence of purpose that brought us here. I know that we will differentiate truth from the deceit of so-called comfort and the greed that it demands. The emperor has no clothes on and is full of fat and falsity. We can all see that.

I have developed my own approach to the reclamation of personal truth and the energy to vitalize it, but I am not alone in having resources. I know that those sincerely invested in stepping onto their path will find what they need. We will all meet there ultimately and recognize each other when we do.

About The Author - Dr Stephanie Mines:

Dr. Stephanie Mines is a neuropsychologist whose unique understanding comes from academic research, extensive work in the field, and blending Western and Eastern modalities. She understands and has investigated shock from multiple perspectives – survivor, professional, healthcare provider, and trainer of staffs of institutions and agencies. She developed the non-profit TARA Approach for the Resolution of Shock and Trauma, a clinically tested comprehensive treatment design taught internationally. As Director, she disseminates information to communities in need, people with illness resulting from shock and trauma, survivors of domestic violence, families and children, and those with neurodiversity including autism and other sensory integration challenges. Her books on grassroots empowerment based sustainable healthcare include: We Are All in Shock; New Frontiers in Sensory Integration, and They Were Families: How War Comes Home.

www.tara-approach.org

A New Earth Rising: Off With the Old, On With the New

by Charmian Redwood

This is a time of great transformation on the Earth. We are at the end of the cycle of darkness and separation that began with The Fall from Oneness into density in the time of Lemuria.

Memories of ancient Lemuria are coming forward now because we have already lived on the Earth in Oneness and harmony and we will do so again. These memories are helping us to remember who we are as Divine Beings in human form.

We have been living a third dimensional existence on this planet for thousands of years where we have focused on the material, physical plane, believing that only things we can actually see with our eyes or experience with our senses are real. There are many planes above the physical one that have been invisible to us as we lived in density.

Now that the frequency of the Earth is rising and the centers within the brain that allow us to perceive the more subtle planes of the fourth and fifth dimensions are being activated, the higher planes of these dimension are becoming accessible to us. The fourth and fifth dimensional planes are above and beyond separation or duality. There is no good and bad; there is only love, light and Oneness where we absolutely know that we are part of God, as is all of Creation. Quantum physics is now beginning to rediscover what mystics and tribal people have known for eons, that all life is made of the same substance, it all has consciousness and is interrelated.

The Earth has been preparing for decades to make an unprecedented energy shift from the third dimension to the fifth dimension where everything and everyone on her surface will be operating from their God Consciousness. This process is called the Ascension, the Resurrection or the Dimensional Shift.

Living in the old way in the third dimension, we have been living from greed, misuse of power, separation, and "the few" controlling the lives of "the many" as well as most of the resources. In the New Way, this will no longer be possible, as only systems that are heart-based will function on the Earth in her new frequency.

Many of the old structures, which have supported the misuse of power, are crumbling. The banking system, big corporations with political influence, and government by the few over the many, are destabilizing and will continue to do so. New systems of equal distribution of wealth and resources will take

their place. Everything that has been happening with the economic, the financial systems and the many changes of government throughout the world, are part of this process, which is absolutely necessary.

We simply cannot continue to live upon the Earth under the present system of corruption, disregard for human rights, deprivation of basic necessities and pollution of our Mother Earth. So the old order is crumbling, being burned in the fires of transformation, and out of the ashes a New Earth is rising, a return to an age of gold where peace shall reign in the hearts of men and women.

Through our many lifetimes of experiencing suffering, martyrdom, enslavement, violence, we have collected many wounds in our emotional body and many programs and beliefs which are stopping us from walking this Earth as our Golden God selves. These old beliefs and wounds are being triggered now so that we can release them and move on. We have been conditioned from our childhood and from past life memories to believe that we are powerless, we don't deserve, we are not good enough. None of this is true of the " Being" that we are. These beliefs are the residue of what we have seen, heard or experienced in the past.

It is time to release these old self-limiting beliefs and to bring in our Divine Essence, so that we can do what we came to do and assist the Earth in this incredible transformation.

We are all carrying guilt, shame, regret, anger, grief and resentment from the past. These emotions are toxic and unnecessary. Everything that we do is a soul choice and contract. When you discover what the contract is, then make amends and do forgiveness, you can move on.

At this time, the deepest, oldest wounds are coming up to be healed – wounds from our original separation from the Source when our DNA strands were reduced from 22 to 2. After this, we were like robots, easy to control; some of us went into anger and some into despair, and this is the root cause of many of our issues today.

In my individual session work, I use hypnosis as a tool, both to access these hidden

beliefs and release them, and to connect with the Soul or the I Am Presence to experience yourself as God, to ask, "Why am I here? What is my soul purpose?"

About the Author - Charmian Redwood

Charmian Redwood had a NDE 35 years ago where she was awakened to the Truth of who she is. She now guides others to experience themselves as Divine Essence, using Hypnotherapy to connect to their own soul and answer any questions they have about their lives. Her books: Coming Home to Lemuria tells us where we came from and how we lived in harmony and peace on the Earth; A New Earth Rising takes us forward through the Ascension into the Healed Earth where all is restored to harmony.

She offers Lightworker Development Training online.

www.cominghometolemuria.com

Symbolic Attachment: A Way Out

by Helena Anton

I have learned throughout the years that if I want to get rid of a negative thought or action (like a bad habit), there is a simple (I didn't say easy) way of doing it. All actions and objects in life are symbolic, for nothing has any meaning save for what we attach to it. Although there are some social objects, such as the concepts of time that we, as a collective whole, agree upon, individual meaning is subjective and differs from person to person.

For example, if I wanted to get rid of a self-defeating behavior that I perform when I feel anxious or upset…this is what I would do: Since all actions are not about the act in and of itself, rather a feeling state that is achieved from the behavior, it is not about the action at all. It is the feeling state we are after. I would have to question myself thoroughly as to what feeling state is created through the behavior, and list it. It's important to include both the positive and the negative.

Let's say, I get rid of my anxiety, a form of self-punishment, a way to "numb out" my feelings and the avoidance of any anxiety producing situation. One way to think about it is self-medicating through an idea that causes physiological changes in the body.

The next step, since everything is symbolic anyway, is to figure out what is the "main feeling" that underlies the first "surface feeling." For all intents and purposes, let's say the "main feeling" comes down to a feeling of security and safety.

Since it is not about the action, and not about the surface emotional states, I center the next steps on the "main feeling." If it is a sense of security and safety that I want to feel, I will allow myself to have it…NOW. I can sit with a visualization (or just conjure up the emotion) and feel it; let it thoroughly soak through and permeate my being. Talk about instant gratification. I didn't even have to do the self-defeating behavior (action) to get the desired result. I allowed myself to have what I wanted at a deeper level, making the action a moot point, for there is no longer any reason to do the action as I already have the desired result.

It is along the same lines as something that was taught to me years ago when I was nervous about giving a public speech – it is okay to allow yourself to FEEL the fear, but do it AFTER the speech. I did not deny myself of the feelings of fear, along with its accompanying physical effects (sweaty palms, rapid heartbeat…fight or flight response), I just reversed the order in which they were experienced. Since I received the desired emotional state beforehand, there was no longer a frantic urgency to act. This also allows space between my initial desire for the action and the act itself. And within that space lies the freedom.

Empty space is not space, but pure potentiality for co-creation. We live in a matrix of energy. All thought is energy. Our bodies are energy vibrating on different frequencies, depending on our physical, spiritual and emotional state.

In fact, our physical bodies are made up of a greater percentage of non-space than solid matter. The idea of "solid matter" is a misnomer, for on a quantum level, everything is just a swirling mass of particles with great space between them. This is true not only for human bodies, but inanimate objects as well.

This empty space, or "non-matter," connects us to each other and the Universe itself. This "non-space" can be thought of as pure potentiality in which everything exists, all at once. We just choose what we pick out and manifest/experience from this chaotic, pure potentiality.

Ancient Chinese culture has a great way of describing chaos itself. It is not deemed scary or threatening; rather, it is defined and seen as a potential for anything to happen…we choose weather it is manifested as good or bad (our labels).

Using this potential, we can create instantaneously. It is not the outer reality that I am talking about (although that changes too), but our own subjective inner reality. When we alter our perceptions and beliefs, we shift our versions of reality and rules by which we live. For example, if I hold a belief that I am a failure, I will act as though that were true; it defines me. We shift our versions of reality, hence our experiences. This is how the power of manifesting/creating works.

Often, when we actively shift our thoughts, hence our experiences of reality, we become dismayed because events are not playing out according to our "plan." When this happens, it is a red flag that we are using our ego-based perception and not that of our True Self. The ego is limited in its knowledge, whereas the True Self is abundant. We often do not see the big picture, for the perception of our ego is short-sighted. From where we (ego) sit, we have a limited view.

For example, if I were to sit on my porch and look at my neighbor's house, I would not know that there is a fire burning in their backyard (I have a "bird's eye view"). But if I were to climb on top of my roof, my view and my story would change. From that view, I would have more of the picture or a "God's eye view" (instead of a "bird's eye view") and I could see the fire spreading in the yard. I incorporate that knowledge into my understanding to explain my neighbor's behavior of running and shouting towards my house. Without the "God's-eye viewpoint," my story of the shouting neighbor would sound a lot different. Most likely, I would take it as an attack on me or my home.

In order to explain my neighbor's behavior, the brain itself needs and functions to acquire explanations, reasons and compartmentalization in order to understand and make sense of incoming data. The ego takes its limited information in order to form its limited perspective and creates a story which I believe, and which fuels my reaction. My "story" would be quite different from the perspective of the rooftop view (spiritualized view).

When something happens in my life that seemingly goes against the path my ego stakes out for itself, my ego immediately responds by holding a belief that my destiny will not be reached; I am discouraged. But by shifting my thoughts/perception, I can know and trust that the all is unfolding for my highest good. I make a shift from ego to Self, fear to trust. This changes my thoughts and reactions and hence can eliminate the suffering that comes from self-perpetuation.

It is my attachment to the associations I give to symbolic objects in my world (all material life is the projection of the Self) that create or subdue suffering. Everything in the world is symbolic for my Spirit, and by changing my attachments and associations with symbols, I alter my "main feelings" and emotional states of how I experience reality.

The key is to be aware of this process (mindfulness) and stop fighting against it. Running to something is the same thing as running away from something; they are two sides of the same coin – it is STILL attachment.

By being aware without fighting or attacking, you give yourself power to alter it. (In other words, you cannot change that which you are not aware of. It is a self-perpetuated and self-created suffering.) In so doing, we push ego and its accompanying perceptions and beliefs aside and take on the worldview of Spirit. It is a surrendering to your Highest Self.

Surrender is not some idealistic moment or ritual; it is a simple giving up of who, what, where and when; the incessant gnawing questions that our egos try to answer from their limited view which keeps us from knowing and experiencing Truth.

As the old adage goes, the solutions cannot be found on the same level as the problem. Surrender is that moment where you no longer ask the questions and hold the preconceived notions about our situation and ourselves. It is allowing the moment to be, just as it is, without alteration. It is a shift of perception from the doer to the silent observer.

When you are focused and present in the moment, the mind cannot, at the same time, fixate itself on any ego or material matter, thrusting us full-force beyond the concepts of linear time progression and moving into the realm of spirituality. It is a gentle letting go. This full acceptance of the present moment ushers us into the realm of spirituality and conscious creation.

About The Author:

Helena Anton's background education is in world religions (concentration on Mysticism). She is an empath, clairsentient, energy healer, light worker and channel. She works with intention, animal healing, crystals, oils made per intention, energy healing of multiple modalities, tarot cards and spirit guides. "I have had many dark times which thankful for, because how else would I know who I am without experiencing that which I am not? I have learned to see that we are not given the darkness to stay and drown in it, rather, we are given the darkness to rise above like a Phoenix!"

Website: www.abundanthealingwisdom.com
Email: Lilspark7@yahoo.com
Phone: 1-847-721-8961

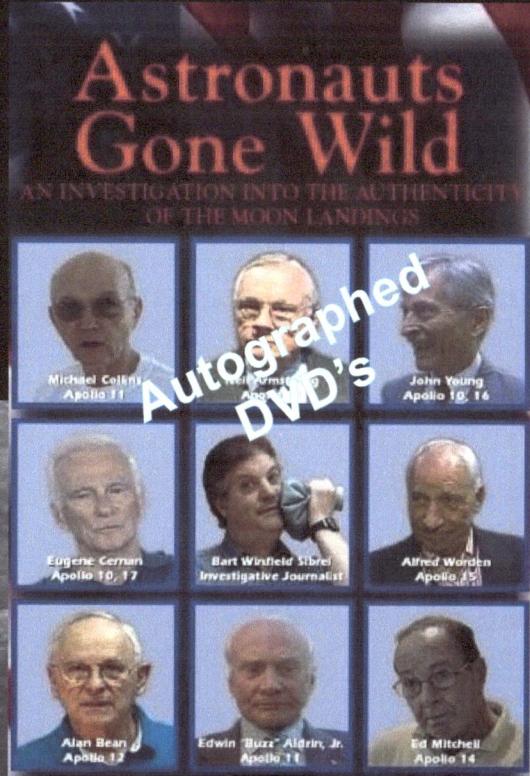

A Breath of New Life After Divorce

by Marilyn Decalo

Faced with Deep Loss

When the decision to divorce happens and the life you once knew – and at one time loved – comes to an end, the healing journey becomes the pathway to regain your power and bring forward new beginnings. In Jungian therapy, a key focus in divorce counseling is to look at what is trying to emerge in the life of the individual as relationship ends. But before the new life emerges, there is usually important and difficult work to be done in the embers and ashes of the dying relationship. Anger, grief, sorrow, and the shadow of those parts of ourselves we will not acknowledge, are most common. As the healing journey weaves through the emotional realm, crossing thresholds of loss and renewal, there is soul and valuable meaning that arises. To confront our own role in the failure of a relationship can be a very difficult thing; but, as with facing difficult emotions, exploring those depths can contribute immensely to greater self-awareness and growth beyond the physical dimension.

Divorce is a life transition commonly experienced as crisis, loneliness and isolation, rife with misunderstanding and doubt. While the experience of loss is very individual, struggle and difficult choices are usually hallmark issues when relationships once characterized by a significant investment of identity, time or love, fall apart. Additionally, the stress of confronting challenging issues while in transition has physical as well as psycho-spiritual ramifications. Divorce might even spark a powerful existential crisis, a "dark night of the soul," or spiritual dilemma for the individual. Multiple layers of shifts, changes and questioning, moving back and forth through different stages of grief, learning to reside in a new consciousness and identity; the healing journey from loss in divorce can be both traumatic and powerfully expansive. In any event, divorce is complicated, and healing requires a supportive orientation that reminds you to breathe into the "new you" you are becoming.

Connecting with someone skilled in psychotherapy can be of great assistance, and it is important to remember that the initial acute pain and subsequent plumbing the depths of loss does not mean divorced individuals will be stuck in emotional distress forever. In his or her own time, in his or her own way, the individual will transform their thinking, feeling, and perspective of themselves and their world. There is a great opportunity in the healing journey to not only feel better, but to transform one's consciousness and awaken to an expanded version of oneself, beyond the limitations of prior beliefs and perceptions.

Ultimately, hope for getting into balance and living a full life emerges. For the individual's journey through divorce to be responsive to the potential for this greater purpose in healing, a transformative, enriching approach to therapy, one that explores the spiritual side and finding meaning in life, will create the more balanced life going forward. An energizing, heart-centered perspective that integrates the spiritual, social, emotional, intellectual, physical and creative elements of human life, views loss as an opportunity to lift the shroud covering the true inner essence, get a better handle on who you really are, elevate your life and gain a deeper understanding of connection with spirit.

The Imperative to Become the One We Carry Within

Many life transitions stem from situations where an individual realizes that "I can't go on living like this anymore." Coming to that conscious realization in a relationship signals acknowledgement of an inner desire for something better, something that feels freer, easier, happier. In situations where the relationship's demise is more cloudy, powerful, conflicting emotions, like feeling simultaneous relief and grief over the ending, lead to confusing paradoxes. In either circumstance, getting through the grips of divorce requires taking stock of where one is in the present moment, mentally, emotionally and spiritually, and accepting responsibility for consciously breathing into one's path forward.

As with most personal growth journeys, establishing an intention, which can be as simple as "feeling stronger day by day" or "prioritizing care of my personal needs," is important for respecting and honoring your experience through the challenge. Remember, even though circumstances can feel out of control in many different ways, you have a part to play in determining your way forward. You will create what you focus on, so intention becomes a practical as well as creative tool for responding to divorce, and you are worth the energy it takes to focus on what you need to heal.

As you embark on the healing path through divorce, it is essential to be willing to engage in an ongoing process daily, which supports you in building self-confidence, releasing perceptions you have taken on from others about your situation and what you "should do," accepting change as catalyst to something better, and being open to a new lifestyle. You start shifting that initial sensation of having lost yourself and the identity you developed in your past relationship by raising your consciousness, and honoring, knowing and loving who you are in the present, no matter what the conditions. Awakening trust and belief in yourself can be the ultimate silver lining of self-discovery one attains through the divorce experience and the unfolding of a more empowered, authentic version of yourself.

The steps you are to take on your healing journey will be lit up much more brightly with awareness of, and access to, your inner strength and core wisdom.

Navigating the ensuing journey of heartache and pain from divorce can leave you feeling disempowered, unsupported and uncertain of yourself at times. Emotions may be overwhelming. Through my own experience of loss and heartache, I found that the surest way out of turmoil is to reconnect with the truth, love and support of my inner-self, listen to the wisdom of my authentic self, and mindfully breathe into the path I was walking, hand in hand with my spiritual nature.

(Continued on Page 48)

A Breath of New Life After Divorce

Continued from Page 45

Taking Steps Forward

There are many different ways to forge a path forward after divorce. Meditation, retreats, support groups, rituals, healing therapies like Reiki and EFT, are all effective tools. From a holistic mind-body-soul integration perspective, the approach of looking at what is trying to emerge in your life when a relationship ends and creating a new identity, is a compassionate and loving method for stepping forward with integrity and ownership of your unique, true power.

Remember, you are meant to live a joyful life, and divorce does not have to be a circumstance that defines limitations to living as you are meant to. Are you ready to claim life on your terms? To let the love that is you – your essence – show you the way forward?

Here are 3 simple ways to identify what is emerging in you and how to integrate it with your divorce plan. Think about these areas of your life:

1. What is still transforming (old paradigm) and what has been clarified?

a. Children - Custody, Therapy, Adult Children Relationships

b. Finances - Alimony, Possessions, Business Interests

c. Relationship with Former Spouse - Communication, In-Laws, Holidays

2. How do you want to live after divorce (new paradigm)?

a. Dreams - What would you like to create?

b. Taking care of yourself – How will you nurture yourself?

c. Stress management - Develop self-care skills

d. Support network - Friends, family, therapy

e. Hope - What are you looking forward to?

f. Work - How will you support yourself economically?

3. What unknowns are you facing?

a. Anniversaries - Be prepared for memories and aware of emotional reactions.

b. Co-parenting - Define how you will do this up front.

c. Coaching - Get the help you need to address crises, goal setting and planning.

d. Finances - If you are not adept at finance find someone who is to help you.

To regain my center and self-confidence, I had to be being willing to be with my emotions, be honest about how I feel.

Accept the negative and positives of the situation, learn to manage your stress, and shift your thinking from what makes you angry and fearful to self-compassion. You might also find that having a support network of those who understand what you are going through, and who are willing to listen without judgment as you experience the ups and downs, is helpful as you move forward. A friend, family member, support group or therapist can make the difference in a day when you are vacillating between hope and hopelessness.

Especially in the early stages, the constant flux of difficult emotions makes it challenging to focus on anything, let alone finding the courage to take next step forward. With life turned upside down, you may not be able to make positive, constructive choices. All too often, people make important decisions about finances, possessions and children in states of confusion and emotional imbalance. This is where being in tune with the truth of your essential self, inviting answers that speak your truth, will inspire perspective, insight and guidance that you confidently act upon.

In my work as a therapist, I find that many people who are looking to heal from divorce are focused on "fighting back" as opposed to clearly thinking about their own future. They are unclear about their priorities or how to start over; afraid of financial repercussions or how they will find meaning again.

Willingness is key. Be willing to fall back in love with yourself and your life. Allow time each day to connect within, intentionally open to the potential for new creative expression that feeds your soul on deep level. Rather than seeking approval or validation from others, find compassion for yourself and everything in your life that led to this point in time.

Humans are beautifully complicated creatures. We want to feel love, yet lack of self-love is the biggest issue holding us back from everything we want. What can you say "Yes" to in your life that evokes the feeling of love? What sparks the breath of new life in you? A favorite park, a beach or a place in the world? Movies, books, or museums? Love may have disappeared in your relationship or marriage, but love remains eternal as the foundational energy of the universe, and all we are. How would love create the future you desire after divorce?

About the Author
Marilyn Decalo

Marilyn Decalo, MA is a transpersonal therapist, intuitive coach, and author of Seeing With The Heart: An Illustrated Journal, a guided exploration of inner wisdom. She writes, speaks and counsels humanity about how to awaken to their unique spark of divinity and integrate spiritual consciousness into daily life experience. Those in crisis seek out Marilyn to align actions with inner truth and clarify their paths forward. Marilyn is a depth-of-knowing intuitive and uses her connection to universal wisdom to help spiritually-gifted people get organized and make their journey of service more joyful and fulfilling.

For further information about Marilyn's services and to read her weekly blog, visit:

Website: www.marilyndecalo.com
Instagram: #marilyn.decalo
Facebook: Marilyn Decalo, MA The Surrender Solution

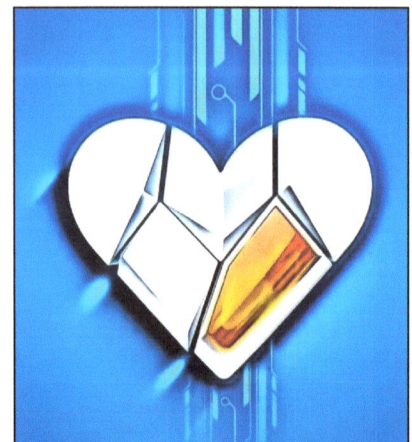

3 Ways to Discover Your Inner-Voice

by Kathleen O'Keefe-Kanavos

"What a wonderful life I've had! I only wish I'd realized it sooner."
~ Collette (1873-1954)

Affirmation: Loving myself heals my life.

Our Outer-voice, the one you use every day with strangers and loved ones, is a reflection of your Inner-voice, also known as Inner Guidance. Do you trust your Inner-voice enough to pay attention to it, or do you consider it a useless woo-woo, nagging neo-science that interferes with logic, despite current research to the contrary?

If you answered "yes" to the woo-woo part of the question, you are not alone.

However, are you missing an important component of your whole being? Your Inner-voice is connected to your Spirit, that part of you that remembers everything you ever experienced in this life and, if you believe in reincarnation, any others you have lived, because the spirit is eternal. So by silencing that Inner-voice, might you be missing out on a fantastic resource for surviving the difficult choices you face on a daily basis for life?

Three ways to connect with your Inner Guidance is through dreams, prayers, and meditations.

Dreams are our Sacred Doorways into the Divine. These dream doorways are used by spirit guides and guardian angels during times of need and crisis. We are all born with guardian angels. We are their job, and they take that job seriously, so it would make sense to take them and your dreams seriously.

How often do we pray for guidance but never listen or watch for the answer that may come from within?

According to research done on a monk in Benedictine monasteries, the chanting of monks is a form of meditation which is outside traditional prayer, yet sanctioned by the church. For some of us, stepping outside our comfort zone of traditional prayer may be frightening. But, try it. You may like it.

Validation is the key to guidance by Inner-voice. Validation is what sets wishful thinking apart from reality, as seen by the dreams that were validated by pathology reports by 41 patients in my book.

Your intuition loves to be tested by you, because it is an opportunity for self-worth and self-belief to shine. Watch for signs, symbols and proof-positive events during the day to verify your innate guidance. It may have been heard as that quiet inner voice. You do not need to search for validation or make it fit into a situation. There is no need to hammer a square peg into the round hole of life.

Validation will find you and fit perfectly into your life. Validation is individual.

An "Ah-ha" moment usually follows the moment-of-truth with the physical response of goosebumps. The next time you wonder if what you are thinking or feeling is correct, check your arms for the telltale goosebumps of validation.

Now that you know how to test your Inner Guidance, how can you use it to create a fulfilled and meaningful life? What has been gnawing at you in terms of truth? Do you have questions about your job or a relationship you find challenging? Should you make a change in some aspect of your life? Perhaps you need a new car but are not sure which one to purchase.

Quiet your body and your mind will follow.

Sit still. Quiet your body and your mind will stop its chatter. Think "Shhhh. Shhhhh." Feel your breath as it glides over your nostrils. Listen for your heartbeat. Now, ask your Higher-power your question. Voice your intention. Then listen for that quiet Inner-voice followed by validation goose-bumps.

About the Author:
Kathleen O'Keefe-Kanavos

Kathleen (Kat) O'Keefe-Kanavos is a TV Producer/Host and Author/Lecturer of Dreams That Can Save Your Life: Early Warning Signs of Cancer and Other Diseases written with Dr. Larry Burk, Foreword by Berne Siegel, which promotes patient advocacy and connecting with Dreams for success in health, wealth, and r e l a t i o n s h i p s . www.KathleenOkeefeKanavos.com

Article Research:

- www.abc.net.au/news/health/2016-06-23/inner-voices-how-internal-dialogue-helps-us-make-sense-of-world/7535538
- Bruno Wang News - www.brunowangnews.com/gregorian-chants-link-to-meditation-and-healing/
- www.amazon.com/Dreams-That-Save-Your-Life/dp/1844097447/ref=tmm_pap_swatch_0?_encoding=UTF8&qid=1517198641&sr=8-1

Fact*oids

- The only animal evidence admissible in American courts is from bloodhounds.
- The only bird that can fly backwards is the hummingbird.
- The cat is the only domestic animal that does not appear in the Bible.
- South America has earthworms up to 8 feet long, 3/4" around, and over one pound.
- Eye gunk that accumulates when you sleep is a combination of sweat, oil and tears.
- Humans suffer from dandruff; in animals, it's called dander.
- The average human loses 80 hairs a day.
- Cockroaches can run up to 3 mph.
- Pessimism raises blood pressure; laughter lowers it.
- Laughing provides an aerobic workout for the body's diaphragm.
- You dream an average of five times a night and each successive dream lasting longer.
- The computer was *Time's* "Man of the Year" in 1982.
- The idling frequency of a diesel engine is 26 cycles per second, the same as a cat's purr.
- A half-ounce of gold can be stretched into a wire 25 miles long.
- Cats walk right foot, right foot, left foot, left foot, instead of right then left.
- The earliest horse was about the size of a fox terrier.
- Galileo made the first thermometer in around 1600.

You asked for more Fact*oids, so we are happy to comply! Keep reading and enjoying The 'X' Chronicles Newspaper.

BOOK OF MYSTERIES

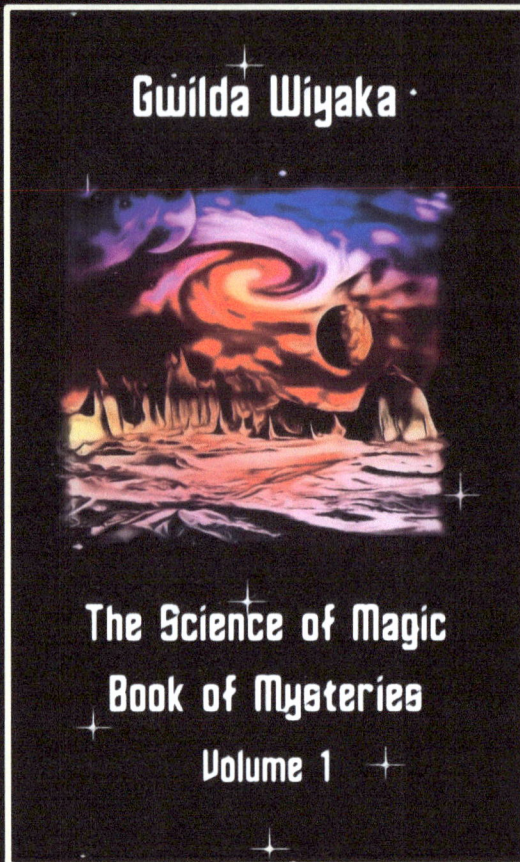

Gwilda Wiyaka

The Science of Magic
Book of Mysteries
Volume 1

AVALABLE AT

http://findyourpathhome.com/store

Gwilda Wiyaka,

Is an author, founder and director of the Path Home Shamanic Arts School, preceptor for the University of Colorado School of Medicine, Consultant for Shamanic Affairs at REL-MAR, and host of the very popular "The Science of Magic Radio Show."

"The Science of Magic Book of Mysteries Volume 1" by Gwilda Wiyaka is the first of a series of books based on Gwilda's writings, opening every episode of "The Science Of Magic Radio Show."

Drawing on the subject matter of each guest and armed with over forty years' experience in shamanism, thirty years in alternative health, and degrees in Psychology and Religious Studies, Gwilda introduces relevant and leading edge information that supports spiritual evolution and personal empowerment.

Rich with wisdom and inspirational quotes, packaged in digestible segments, this is a book that will pull you from cover to cover. It will serve as a daily inspirational reader for years to come.

"The Science Of Magic Radio Show" is produced by REL-MAR McConnell Media Company.

Antilia

by Lee Sumpter

Recently I read a short biography of Christopher Columbus. One of the rumors about what might lie out in the unknown Atlantic was that there was an island or group of islands not far off the shores of Spain and Portugal, called "Antilia." It was often placed on maps of the coasts of southern Europe and Africa.

In the late 1400's, Iceland, the British Isles, the Azores, the islands of Madeira and the Canaries were known. Ships often traded among these islands and Columbus captained such a ship to Iceland.

Antilia was not known. No one had ever been there. Yet, it was supposed to exist and this strongly enough to be included on maps. When Columbus planned his first voyage, he expected to make landfall there and resupply.

Off of the coasts of Portugal and Morocco, there are a number of sea mounts that are less than 200 feet beneath the waves. One such underwater mountain, called Seine Seamount, has a great flat plain on its top that is about 150 feet below the surface. Seine Seamount is part of a bank of ridges that have been responsible for earthquakes and tsunamis along the coast of Portugal.

Frank Joseph, in the latest edition of Ancient American, describes another one called Ampere Seamount, which has been reported by Russian researchers to be covered in beach sand and to even have columns and stairways. He adds that this seamount, which is only 60 feet under water, may even have been connected to the African coast some 260 miles away by a land bridge. Elephant bones have been recovered from the bottom of the ocean in this area.

An internet search will show that there are many high places on the bottom of the Atlantic off the Strait of Gibraltar that could easily have been above water in past times, just like the Canaries, Madeira and the Azores are now. In short, we really have no idea what the eastern Atlantic may have looked like, hundreds or several thousand years ago. For sure, a large island or peninsula off the coast of Africa near the prevailing eastern trade winds would have considerably shortened the trip across the Atlantic to our continent.

Evidently, just such a land mass existed out in the Atlantic off the Strait of Gibraltar, long enough that it was recorded on charts and spoken of by sailors and navigators as the island of Antilia. Today, it is called the "mythical island of Antilia," and it is the origin of our word

Antilles, which is the name that post-Columbus navigators gave to our Caribbean chain of islands.

Now, an extensive channeled history of Atlantis is found on the Earthkeepers website. It gives the names of the five islands that resulted from the initial breakup of the Atlantean continent, which spanned the entire Atlantic basin from the eastern edge of the Americas to the coasts of Europe and Africa. They were named Aryan, Poseida, Eyre, Og and Atalya.

Of course, the latter is possibly a variant spelling of Antalia. We recognize Eyre as the Gaelic name of Ireland. Og is part of the name of a petroglyph script found worldwide, called Ogham. It is considered to be some form of early Gaelic. Aryan is a name for western, Celtic people. Poseida is another mythical name for Atlantis, which was ruled by a king or god of the sea by that name.

The presence of undersea mountains and ridges that reach almost to the surface and that are today very active seismically, the paleontological evidence of land animals and plants in the sea bottom around them, and the name Antalia on navigational charts, is beyond coincidence. That there is spiritual narrative that speaks of just such an ancient land is amazing. We have our geological and archeological sciences, but we have only been paying attention to these things for two or three hundred years. 2,400 years ago, the Greek philosopher, Plato, described the ocean beyond the Strait of Gibraltar as full of islands and treacherous muddy shoals. This is all that was left of a mighty island kingdom where, in fact, elephants were common.

We are reluctant to accept that islands large or small, even continents, may change their geography or disappear. It is an uncomfortable fact of nature. All that may be left is legends or marks on ancient maps. Such myths and legends are to be found all over the world. No doubt, the more we accept the possibility that these legends have some basis in fact, the more we will have a better understanding of history and geology.

About the Author
Lee Sumpter

Lee Sumpter is a retired teacher of languages and has lived all over the world. He currently reside in Florida. Sumpter has studied unorthodox religion, anthropology, maverick history, geology and UFO's, metaphysics, and phenomenology since a very early age. "Fortunately I have gotten to point where I can write about them."

An Introduction To Conscious Evolution: A Theory We Can Thrive With

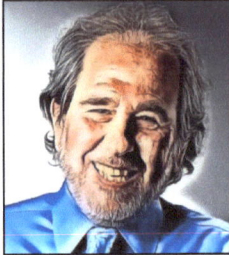

By Bruce H. Lipton, Ph.D.

Today's global crises are symptoms of planetary upheaval propelled by the unsustainable desires of human civilization, which have precipitated the planet's 6th mass extinction event. The mechanisms driving evolution encode the characteristics that determine whether a species survives or becomes extinct.

Since the 1900s, neo-Darwinian theory, with its emphasis on the "survival of the fittest in the struggle for life" and on genetic mechanisms as the metric determining species survival, has shaped the behavioral character of civilization by giving scientific legitimacy to the use of power, greed and violence to "advance" civilization. However, new insights from epigenetic science and the results of the Human Genome Project have completely undermined basic tenets of Darwinian theory.

Epigenetics recognizes that the environment, and more importantly, our perception of the environment, controls genetic activity and behavior and thus shifts the focus of evolutionary theory to the role of the nervous system and consciousness. Because the structural and functional organization of the nervous system in multicellular organisms is so complex, single-celled organisms offer a more productive means for deciphering the mechanisms of consciousness.

Conventional science considered the gene-containing nucleus as the cell's "brain," but new research points to the membrane as the information processor that controls the fate of the cell. Molecular switches built into the membrane translate environmental information into cell behavior and represent the basic physical units of perception, the building blocks of consciousness.

Modeling membrane evolution using fractal geometry offers profound insights into the origin and influence of consciousness and the role of cooperation within and among species. Because conscious evolution theory elucidates the fact that cooperation rather than competition and struggle is the driving force of evolution, it can support the survival of human civilization.

Human civilization is at an evolutionary crossroads where unsustainable human behavior is precipitating the planet's 6th Mass Extinction Event. Five times in Earth's history, life was thriving when some event precipitated

a wave of extinction, eliminating 70 to 90 percent of all plant and animal species. The last mass extinction event, 66 million years ago, noted for wiping out the dinosaurs, was apparently due to a massive asteroid impact in Mexico that upended the global web of life.

Today's severe environmental imbalance is, in large part, attributable to the cultural consequences of Darwinian evolution theory, which holds that struggle and competition are the driving forces behind evolution. But the Darwinian notion that evolution is driven by the survival of the fittest in a continual competition among individuals is giving way to a more scientifically accurate, as well as, more positive theory of evolution that emphasizes the role of cooperation, interaction, and mutual dependence among all life forms. In the words of Lynn Margulis, "Life did not take over the globe by combat, but by networking".

The once universally accepted Darwinian theory about the origin and evolution of life emphasized a two-step process to account for evolution. First, random variations in hereditary traits, introduced during reproduction, provide offspring with physical and/or behavioral characteristics that differ from those of their parents. Second, the fate of "altered" individuals, specifically their ability to survive and pass on their "new" traits to the next generation, is determined by natural selection, a process often abbreviated as the "survival of the fittest in the struggle for life." From this perspective, violence and war are considered to be natural behaviors in determining the "fitness" of our species. Evolution results from a continuous lineage of species expressing ever-increasing structural and behavioral complexity.

Ernst Haeckel famously illustrated the Darwinian progressive lineage of species evolution in his 1879 image of the Tree of Life. Primitive bacteria were positioned at the Tree's base, while human beings, perceived as the most advanced species, were placed at the Tree's top branches.

At the time Haeckel conceived of the Tree, there was no scientific insight about the nature of the hereditary mechanisms responsible for the evolution of the depicted species lineage. More than a decade earlier,

Catholic monk Gregor Mendel's experiments with crossbreeding pea plants between1856 and 1863 had introduced the concept of "genes," though it was Danish botanist Wilhelm Johannsen who first introduced the term gene in 1909. Mendel's seminal research, which founded the modern science of Genetics, languished in obscurity for over three decades before it was resurrected in 1900 by botanist Hugo de Vries, whose own breeding experiments verified Mendel's conclusions.

(Continued on Page 53)

An Introduction To Conscious Evolution: A Theory We Can Thrive With

Continued From Page 52

The question as to which of these macromolecules provided the trait-controlling genes was resolved in 1944 with Avery, MacLeod, and McCarty's research that included two morphologically distinct species of pneumococcal bacteria4. When incubating bacterial species R in a DNA extract from the chromosomes of species S, the R bacteria acquired species S traits. In contrast, extracts of species S chromosomal proteins were unable to transfer S traits to species R bacteria. The results firmly established that DNA molecules are the carriers of genetic information.

The next step toward understanding evolution was to assess the nature of DNA's molecular structure in order to gain insight into the mechanics of heredity. X-ray crystallography studies of DNA molecules by Rosalind Franklin in 1952 led to the discovery of DNA's double helix structure.

Without her knowledge, Maurice Wilkins, a disgruntled colleague of Franklin, gave her unpublished crystallography data to James Watson and Francis Crick. Using Franklin's data, Watson and Crick changed the course of human history when their article, "Molecular Structure of Nucleic Acids" was published in the prestigious British scientific journal Nature in April of 1953. In their paper, Watson and Crick revealed how the sequence of nucleic acid bases (adenine, thymine, cytosine and guanine) along the DNA molecule programs the structure of proteins, the macromolecules that provide for an organism's anatomy and physiology.

The next challenge was to discover the mechanism that controlled the synthesis of DNA. Matthew Meselson and Franklin Stahl revealed the surprising answer to that quest in 1958 when they separated the two strands comprising a DNA double helix molecule and incubated each single DNA strand in a solution containing the four nucleic acid bases that comprise the molecular building blocks of DNA. Each DNA strand served as template for the synthesis of its complementary new strand. During cell reproduction, the DNA double helices split apart with each separated DNA strand serving as a pattern for recreating the double helix. The "obvious" conclusion was that DNA controls its own reproduction.

In the wake of the Meselson-Stahl experiment, Crick published a hypothesis defining the flow of information in biology along a unidirectional path from DNA$\Rightarrow$RNA$\Rightarrow$protein, a chain of command predicated on DNA's autonomous, self-controlling mechanism. Crick's hypothesis led to the belief that genes are self-actualizing, i.e. they turn themselves on and off and thereby represent the sole control of the hereditary characters that shape an organism. This notion of genetic control implied that people had no influence over their genetic fates but instead are "victims" of their heredity. For example, a history of a recurrent pathology in the family lineage, such as cancer, heart disease, or Alzheimer's, implied that children in that family would possess the disease-causing genes and should expect to experience the same fate as their parents.

Crick's theory also emphasized that an accidental alteration in the genetic code, introduced through copying errors in the process of DNA replication, is the initiating factor for evolution. Crick's hypothesis, which he referred to as The Central Dogma, became the foundational principle that shaped the next 50 years of biomedical research. It's a disturbing principle because the Dogma emphasized that evolution is independent of environmental circumstances. The emphasis on DNA's primacy in controlling life led to the Human Genome Project, an effort to identify all the trait-controlling genes found in the human genome. Armed with such knowledge, it was thought that genetic engineering would enable humans to control their fate, as well as offer science the ability to create "new" organisms, in what would amount to human-designed evolution.

But by the time the Human Genome Project got off the ground in 1990, research was undermining the conclusions of Crick's Central Dogma, which, after all, was only a theory he introduced to the public around 1960, though the premise was repeated so frequently over decades that people forgot it was only a hypothesis and assumed it was scientific "truth."

1) The Dogma's unidirectional flow of information was upended by Harold Temin's Nobel Prize-winning research on reverse transcriptase, the enzyme infamous for its role in the propagation of the AIDS virus. Temin's research changed the Dogma's information flow by showing that RNA can alter the information coded in DNA: DNA$\Leftrightarrow$RNA$\Rightarrow$protein. Temin's research was included in Crick's formal journal article in 1970.

2) Cell replication research that factored in the role of the formerly discarded chromosomal proteins also changed the understanding of information flow in biology. This research found that DNA does not control its own activity, but is dependent upon the activity of chromosomal proteins that are controlled by environmental signals. As succinctly stated by Nijhout in 1990, "When a gene product (i.e., protein) is needed, a signal from its environment, not an emergent property of the gene itself, activates 6expression of that gene".

The Dogma's latest information flow chart reads as: DNA$\Leftrightarrow$RNA$\Leftrightarrow$protein.

Then came the 2003 results of the Human Genome Project, which further eroded belief in Crick's Dogma. Science had held that the evolutionary lineage illustrated in the Tree of Life represented a hierarchy of species with ever increasing genetic complexity. Simple organisms near the base of the Tree would possess a small number of genes, and as one ascended the Tree, more advanced organisms would have greater numbers of genes to accommodate their more complex structural and behavioral traits.

Based on the belief that every protein required a gene blueprint for its synthesis, scientists estimated that the human genome would have a minimum of over a 100,000 genes. But the project found instead that despite humans' lofty position on the Tree, the human genome contains only ~20,000 genes9. That result upended the fundamental tenet of modern genetics that one gene codes for one protein. But there was more. It turned out that the miniature roundworm, Caenorhabditis elegans, an organism at the bottom of the Tree comprised of only 1,031 cells, has the same number of genes as humans at the top of the Tree comprised of 50 trillion cells, which led to the project's most profound insight: evolutionary lineage does not reflect increased genetic complexity.

These new insights profoundly revised the foundation of genetics and led to the formalization of a new field of heredity research, Epigenetics. In contrast to the conventional belief of genetic control (i.e., "control by genes"), the prefix "epi" in the term epigenetic control, simply translates as, "control above the genes." It is now recognized that the environment, and especially our perception of the environment, provides the source of "control" above the genes and represents the primary factor that shapes genetic activity. Epigenetic mechanisms can create thousands of different variations of proteins from a single gene blueprint.

The new emphasis on the role of the environment in controlling heredity resurrected Jean Baptiste Lamarck's once ridiculed theory of evolution. Published fifty years before Darwin's Origin of Species in 1809, Lamarck's theory of evolution scored the hierarchy of species in the lineage on the basis of their level of consciousness rather than their level of genetic complexity. Unfortunately, the definition of the term "consciousness," has itself been a source of problems — some definitions of consciousness are philosophically based and take pages to define. At the simplest level of understanding, consciousness can be described as the state of "being awake and aware of one's surroundings." Using this definition, more than two centuries after Lamarck, Margulis successfully argued that primitive single-celled organisms, from bacteria (prokaryotes) to amoebas (eukaryotes), clearly possess a primitive level of consciousness.

Still, efforts to assess the nature of consciousness and the nervous system's role in evolution have been thwarted by the unimaginable complexity of the connectivity and information flow in the brains of higher organisms, which can contain a trillion or more cells. Recent research has focused on a lower organism, the microscopic brain of Caenorhabditis. Histological studies of this worm's brain have provided a complete "connectome," a map revealing all the connections among the brain's 302 cells. Despite this mapping information, the complexity of the information flow has made it impossible to decipher how the brain creates the character of "consciousness," and specifically, how that consciousness would influence evolution.

(Continued on Page 55)

An Introduction To Conscious Evolution: A Theory We Can Thrive With

Continued From Page 53

A different approach to understanding the role of the nervous system is to study single-celled organisms, such as amoeba. Protozoan eukaryotic (nucleus-containing) cells have the same physiologic systems found in human beings that control respiration, digestion, excretion, musculoskeleton, endocrine and immune functions, and most important for this story, a nervous system13. In the single-celled species, cytoplasmic miniature organs ("organelles") provide the same physiologic functions that in humans are provided by the complex organs. As to the question of which of these organelles serves as the "brain" of single-celled species, current biological curricula still point to the nucleus.

But that "fact" has been challenged by enucleation research, in which micropipettes are used to remove the cell's gene-containing nucleus. Though these cells have virtually no DNA, they can survive for weeks and still exhibit complex behaviors. The only function lost in enucleated cells is the ability to reproduce their proteins and even the cells themselves. This research suggests that the nucleus is not the "brain" of the cell, but in reality, represents the cell's "gonad."

My research on cloned stem cells during the late 1960s and early 70s also provided insight into the nature of the cell's brain. This research involved inoculating a culture dish with a single multi-potential stem cell. Cultured stem cells divide every 10 to 12 hours; one week after plating a single stem cell, the culture contains approximately 24,000 cells. All the cells in the culture dish are genetically identical because they are progeny of a single parent cell. I split up the cell population into three dishes, each with different culture mediums, i.e. each with a different environment. In environment A, the cells formed muscle. In environment B, the cells formed bone and in the third environment C, the cells formed fat cells. Because all the cells were genetically identical, the results revealed that the fate of cells is controlled by their response to the environment and not by their genes. These original observations illuminated the role of epigenetics 20 years before this field of knowledge was officially recognized.

The results of these cell culture experiments as well as enucleation experiments, shifted attention to identifying the cellular equivalent of the human nervous system responsible for translating environmental signals into cell behavior. That search led to the bacterial cell membrane, the cell's only structured organelle. With a thickness of 10 nanometers, the physical dimension of the cell membrane is well below the resolution of the light microscope. In fact, scientists only learned that all cells possess a cell membrane when the electron microscope was invented in the late 1940s. In electron micrographs, the cell membrane appears as a vanishingly thin (<10nm), tri-layered (black-white-black) "skin" enveloping the cell.

A general rule in biology is that structure implies function; simple structures have simple functions and complex structures express complex functions. But cell membranes are the exception to that rule. While simple in structure, the cell membrane, which was the first biological organelle to evolve, is far from simple in function. Membranes provide a physical barrier separating the interior cytoplasmic domain from the external environment, but they are also responsible for respiration, digestion, and excretion functions, and serve as each cell's "nervous system" because of their ability to "read" external environmental conditions and then relay regulatory signals internally to control cytoplasmic behavior.

As for the structure of the membrane, its layered appearance in the electron microscope directly reflects the molecular organization of its phospholipid building blocks. Lollipop-shaped phospholipid molecules are amphipathic, possessing both a globular polar phosphate head and two stick-like non-polar legs. When shaken in solution, phospholipid molecules self-assemble into a stabilizing crystalline bilayer.

The molecule's lipid legs, forming the membrane's central core, provide a hydrophobic barrier that physically partitions the cytoplasm from the external environment. While cytoplasmic integrity is maintained by the lipid's passive barrier function, life processes necessitate the active exchange of metabolites and information between the cell's cytoplasm and surrounding environment. A membrane comprised of only phospholipids would not support the transport activities required to sustain life.

Enter the crucial cell membrane's large population of proteins (100,000+) that are unseen in electron microscope images. Because these proteins are physically integrated within the membrane's structure, they are referred to as integral membrane proteins (IMPs). There are two fundamental roles attributed to all cellular proteins.

1) They provide for the cell's physical structure (anatomy).

2) They are responsible for generating the cell's vital physiologic functions.

To understand how membrane proteins perform those roles, it is necessary to consider their shape-shifting structure. Each protein's unique 3-dimensional structure is defined by its "backbone," a linear molecule comprised of a specific sequence of amino acid molecules strung together like beads on a string. After the amino acid backbone is assembled during protein synthesis, it spontaneously folds into a specific three-dimensional conformation (shape) by balancing the electrical charges within its amino acid backbone. A protein molecule responds to an environmental signal, such as an ion, a molecule, or resonant vibrational field by shifting into a complementary physical shape. The binding of an environmental signal to a protein, alters the distribution of electric charges along the protein's backbone. In response, the protein's shape is reconfigured as its backbone adjusts by folding to accommodate the altered electrical charges. Simply, when a protein binds with a complementary environmental signal, it causes the protein to shift from conformation A to conformation B. The movement generated by protein conformational changes is harnessed by the cell to power its physiologic behaviors.

This article will continue in the next edition of The New Age Chronicles November 2018 Edition []

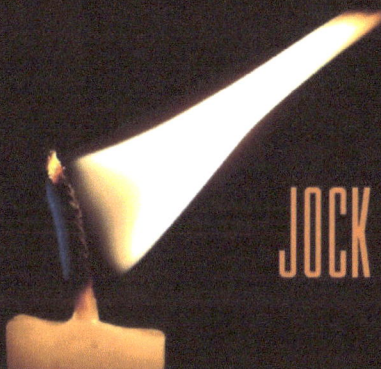

A Modernistic Look at Neptune

by Stephen Judd

Neptune is the furthest most of the gas giant planets of our solar system, with an orbit of 165.7 years and spending just under 14 years in each sign of the zodiac. As with everything Neptunian, there was controversy about who actually discovered it and when it was discovered, although in recent years it has finally been accepted by most astronomers and astrologers that it was discovered in September 1846, and that the French astronomer Urbain Le Verrier should be credited with its discovery. It is noteworthy that Galileo did map the position of Neptune in both 1612 and 1613, but mistakenly classified it as a fixed star.

After initial names of Janus and Oceanus were rejected, the name Neptune became accepted throughout the western world, following in the nomenclature of the other planets, all of which had been named after Greek or Roman deities.

The mythology of Neptune is well defined from the Greek. Born of the mating between Cronos and Rhea, the two must human-like of the Titans, Neptune (or Poseidon, as he was known in ancient Greece), along with his brother Hades (Pluto) and his sisters Hestia, Demeter and Hera (Vesta, Ceres and Juno in Roman mythology), was consumed and absorbed by his father, who was fearful of his children usurping him as he himself did to his father (Ouranus). When the youngest of his siblings, Jupiter (Zeus), freed them from the belly of Cronos, the three brothers split the firmament between them with Jupiter taking the overworld, Pluto taking the underworld and Neptune taking the waterworld. It is for this reason that, in today's astrology, Neptune is seen as ruling the seas and oceans, as well as the astrological sign of Pisces and the twelfth house, the most watery of the twelve astrological signs and houses.

Neptune's atmosphere is primarily hydrogen and helium at the higher levels, on top of a lower atmosphere of ammonia and methane. The combination of these elements create a bright blue appearance, with occasional white clouds and irregular dark blue spots, indicating storm patterns similar to Jupiter's great red spot. It has a faint ring system and a number of satellites, of which Triton is the largest, occupying over 99% of the mass orbiting Neptune. Triton, unlike any other satellite in the solar system, goes retrograde, suggesting that eventually it will impact into Neptune.

Neptune's discovery coincided with a number of different developments in society, all of which can be said to have Neptunian themes.

The first global drug war (the opium war), the invention of the camera, the use of mesmerism and hypnotism for the first time, the first commercial brewing of alcohol, the first common use of anaesthetics and the writing of the Communist Manifesto – are all aspirational developments for a better social order.

If there is one word that would summarize the astrological influence of Neptune, that word would be "nebulous." It could be said that only since July 2011, the time that Neptune completed its first orbit of the Sun since its discovery, has its qualities from an astrological perspective become clearer.

Viewed in a challenging way, Neptune is the planetary energy associated with gullibility, escapism, avoidance, addiction and neurosis. It is where the capacity for fog, cloud, mist, treacle and quicksand in one's life is strong. The gullibility can be seen when planets in the horoscope are squared or opposed to Neptune, and the individual will look at others and only see the good sides of the other person, not the bad ones. The escapism is shown when the individual with difficult Neptune aspects will live in cloud cuckoo land, not wishing or even able to see the reality of their situation. Similarly, this attitude contributes to the avoidance of certain things or issues in one's life to the point of deliberately not wanting to recognize behavior on the part of others, or even of oneself.

The addictive quality of Neptune is not only the capacity for alcohol or drug abuse – it can also be seen in other forms of addiction, such as sugar and chocolate, sex, chemical medicines, junk food or other forms of substance that are not good for one's body or soul. The neurosis can be a combination of any of the above, with the added criteria that the individual will experience the world as being the way that they want it to be, rather than dealing with it the way it really is.

When viewed from a more neutral perspective, Neptune is seen as the planetary energy that deals with all forms of artistic expression, such as art, music, dance, film, photography, theatre – anything that stresses the more artistic and sensual. It is the planet of the dream and the ideal, as well as being the difference between the fantasy and the imagination, in that one stays between the ears or else ends in disappointment, whilst the other can not only be imagined, but also created.

Neptune from a positive perspective is the planet of illumination and enlightenment. It can strongly influence the relationship that one has with the divine, no matter how you view your interaction with divinity. It governs the intuition and to a lesser extent the instinct. Neptune is one's capacity for compassion and empathy, as well as the genuine desire to help others less fortunate than oneself. From a physical health perspective, Neptune is common in the charts of people who have issues with the glandular system, particularly the thyroid, as well as eyesight issues (again, the vague, the nebulous and the uncertain).

By transit, Neptune brings a range of experiences, ranging from dissolution, weariness and fatigue to artistry, a greater sensitivity to the environment and an empathy for those unable (or unwilling) to help themselves. These transitory experiences can last for up to two years, so should not be taken lightly – under a difficult Neptune transit, long term commitments (marriage, contracts, mortgage, etc.) should be avoided, whilst on a positive Neptune transit the opportunity for a more refined, sophisticated and elegant way of life will present itself, whilst the influence of those who attempt to drag you down or keep you the way you've always been will dissipate.

Neptune remains nebulous, even in the 21st century. It can drag you down, make you tired and dissolve things and situations around you. It can also inspire, intuit and refine your life in a way never previously imagined. As with everything in Astrology, one's intent and intentions are the guiding light here, and if used for the right reasons, Neptune will illuminate your path forward and inspire you to a greater spiritual way of living your life.

About the Author
Steve Judd

Steve Judd is a practicing astrologer with 40+ year's astrological experience. Check him out on YouTube or at www.stevejudd.com.

The Magic of Where Our Consciousness is Headed

by Diane Brandon

If you've opened up spiritually and had a spiritual awakening, you've likely experienced the joy that can bring. If so, have you noticed how your beliefs have changed, along with your mindset, outlook, and view of the world? In all likelihood, that new view feels much better. If you're like most who are spiritual, you wouldn't want to go back to a more restricted type of mindset or consciousness.

Because we have seen increasing numbers of people opening up spiritually, we know something is going on, that from a higher vantage point there's a bigger picture of where we're headed -- one that we're all a part of. The question, of course, is what exactly that bigger picture is, and where we as a species are headed in this greater scheme. Sometimes, we can gain a greater understanding of where we're headed by looking back at where we've been.

Humans evolved from small bands of people. We lived in small groups and had to focus on survival. Indeed, we struggled to survive. We had to be wary of threats that could endanger us. We had to be leery of the unknown.

As a result, we tended to trust the familiar.

In all likelihood, all those many years ago, we had a tribal mentality. We identified with our "tribe," the people we knew. We knew and counted upon our tribe's customs and mores. Strangers were thus somewhat suspect and we may have been wary of them.

Does this type of consciousness or orientation sound familiar? As ancient as a tribal mentality may seem, we continue to see it in our modern world: distrusting strangers, judging those who are different from us (other races, nationalities, religions and creeds, even other genders) as "less than," suspicious, or likely to have ill intent. If you think about it, this type of primitive mentality still exists and, in some places, prevails.

So are we stuck in a tribal mentality forever? I seriously doubt it.

Another type of consciousness has been developing. It's actually been both triggered and fostered by advances in technology: a global consciousness.

We know that the world has become figuratively smaller due to technology. The invention of the telephone enabled people to communicate with each other at a distance. Airplanes brought about greater contact with others at a geographical distance. Computers and the internet have further facilitated such communication and sped it up. Advances in video and media have brought news from around the world to us, seemingly instantaneously.

And then the internet came along. And Facebook. And Twitter. We gradually started connecting with others all over the world – not with famous people, but with everyday individuals. We found others throughout the world with similar interests and like minds. I know that I'm connected on Facebook with people in many different countries and from vastly different cultures.

Connecting one-to-one with others coming from such vastly different cultures allows us to transcend differences. We connect with who others are, as fellow humans on this planet who share one extremely significant trait – our common humanity.

Thus, technology has been leading us as humans to move from a somewhat tribal mentality to a more global consciousness.

At the same time, growing numbers of people are becoming more open to animals and wildlife, increasingly seeing them as confreres, fellow beings to whom we can open our hearts and with whom we may be able to communicate in some fashion. The same openness has been transpiring with nature, as we open our hearts to it and as science has been showing us its benefits for our health, how aspects of it (trees and plants, for example) have their own modes of communication and intelligence. This shift likewise leads us to, and amplifies, our global consciousness.

Is this the end position of our human consciousness – or will it continue to evolve? If so, where will it next be headed?

I feel that our human consciousness will continue to unfold and evolve – that its next stop will be a more universal consciousness, and this universal consciousness is even more spiritual in nature.

A universal consciousness will take us past our identification as humans, or even residents of this planet ("earthlings"). It will open us more to connecting with what may lie outside of our self-definition as humans, our human-based limitations and limited perspective.

There are triggers for this type of shift, triggers we've been seeing for several decades. Some of these triggers exist thanks to technology and technological advances, especially in the field of medicine. Because of medical advances, we have been seeing increasing numbers of people surviving lethal situations, being revived and brought back to life. Many of these people have had what we term "near-death experiences."

While there can be great variety in what near-death experiencers go through, many have intensely spiritual experiences – they come back changed as a result. They may encounter God or other loving spiritual beings. They tend to lose their fear of death. And they frequently see their lives transformed as a result of their NDEs.

Because of the increase in near-death experiences over the past several decades, we have seen more people opening up spiritually, along with a greater infusion of spiritual awareness in both our culture and the world. This spiritual opening has also served to loosen the tight existing energy of humans being open only to this planet and their culture of birth, serving as somewhat of a preparation to being open to even more shifts in awareness.

At the same time, I feel that we have been seeded for a more universal consciousness by yet another phenomenon: the ET experience, or encounters with extra terrestrials. It may have started in a more sensationalized manner with UFOs and Hollywood depictions of same. However, it's increasingly appearing to be more spiritual in nature.

When astronauts went to the moon and looked back at earth, several of them had a spiritual awakening. They were able to see earth from a different perspective. It looked not only beautiful, but also less significant compared to the hugeness of the cosmos. Edgar Mitchell was so moved by his experience that he founded IONS, the Institute of Noetic Sciences. The spiritual shift in these astronauts happened in the same general time frame as reports of UFOs and then abduction experiences.

(Continued on Page 58)

The Magic of Where Our Consciousness is Headed

Continued from Page 57

Many people, including those spiritually aware, may have felt that ET experiences were bizarre and otherworldly – further, that they had no connection to spirituality. However, we're learning this is far from true. To the contrary, a significant percentage of those who have undergone ET experiences have either opened up spiritually or found their spirituality enhanced. Some view their ET experiences as spiritual in nature. (F.R.E.E – The Edgar Mitchell Foundation for Research into Extraterrestrial Encounters – has noted this effect in their research, some of which may be found at www.experiencer.org.)

How can we view ETs, those non-humans from other places in the cosmos? Are they weird aliens we should fear or mistrust? Could they be spiritual beings? (Some feel that they are indeed spiritual beings or even beings from another dimension.) Or are all possibilities valid?

Could ETs have any connection to us as humans? Yes, there are theories that humans on this planet were seeded by ETs, but, aside from those postulations, could we have any other connection?

So the ET experience is yet another trigger leading us to open up our consciousness beyond the limits of our humanness. It is to see and to perceive the connection and inter-connection we have as souls to others, irrespective of the physical form or body the soul is temporarily in. Just as we can commune with animals and connect with the embodied awareness or soul they have, so too can this happen with all life forms. This leads us to that beautiful universal consciousness.

There is another phenomenon helping to trigger this consciousness: the Born Aware phenomenon. This refers to those of us who have always remembered what we thought when we were born, whose thoughts and perceptions at birth were spiritual in nature, including memories of the other side before we came here. Those of us (myself included) with these memories intrinsically know that we're souls first and foremost, and that the human experience and perspective is limited and quite temporary.

Those of us born aware were not only in our Higher Soul Awareness at birth, but also have that as our default mode of consciousness. This is the awareness that we have as souls when we're not in a body. Being able to transcend the limits of our human minds and psyches is key to shifting to a universal consciousness.

Born awares also remember the inter-connectedness we had as souls before coming here, meaning that we remember that everyone and everything is connected, irrespective of physical form or place of residence. This in itself is more of a universal consciousness. It is no accident that the Born Aware information is coming out now and dovetails time-wise with increased near-death experiences and ET experiences.

The universal consciousness that we are moving towards is a beautiful one and quite magical. It allows us to view others – irrespective of who or what they are, where they come from or may believe, or the type of body they're in – as fellow beings to whom we are connected and with whom we share a spiritual basis as souls. It allows us to see and feel the beautiful and positive Divine and spiritual energy pervading and inhabiting the cosmos, of which this planet is one tiny part. It allows us to broaden our sense of community. At the same time, it can allow us to perceive things, both our lives and mass events, from a higher spiritual perspective and perceive the higher spiritual purpose of that which transpires. In effect, a universal consciousness can take us closer to the ultimate spiritual perspective, that of a higher level.

This can bring real magic to our lives.

About the Author
Diane Brandon

Diane Brandon is an Integrative Intuitive Counselor, teacher, former radio host, and coach, as well as the author of Born Aware: Stories & Insights from Those Spiritually Aware Since Birth, Intuition for Beginners: Easy Ways to Awaken Your Natural Abilities, Dream Interpretation for Beginners: Understand the Wisdom of Your Sleeping Mind, and Invisible Blueprints. Born and raised in New Orleans, she has an A.B. from Duke University and did Master's work at University of North Carolina. Her website is www.dianebrandon.com.

Is this a UFO flying over North Carolina? No, Goodyear blimp says: 'That's definitely us'

The minute-long video purports to show a space craft eerily hovering in the distance over Lake Norman near Charlotte, North Carolina. And while buzz on the video swings from claims of hoaxing to apparent belief, one iconic airship has claimed responsibility: the Goodyear Blimp

"We don't want to get in the way of a good story, but that's definitely us," the Goodyear blimp's team stated from its verified Twitter account. "We left the Charlotte area 5/29 after covering the Coke 600."

Indeed, Monster Energy NASCAR Cup Series Coca Cola 600™ race took place that week at Charlotte Motor Speedway — kudos to winner Kyle Busch — and the apparent UFO video, from YouTuber Jason Swing, was published on May 29, the date the blimp departed.

In the video, a man states that "this is a space craft" before shakily panning over to the lake, showing a grey, oblong ship in the sky ahead. After more shaking, the narrator exclaims he must leave. The video ends.

Commenters on the footage criticized the shaky camerawork, which some called cover for a hoax. Others, perhaps more inclined to belief, groaned that the cameraman squandered "a once-in-a-lifetime opportunity," as commenter Tom Brown said.

The video went largely unnoticed for weeks before a UFO-focused site, called The Hidden Underbelly 2.0, picked it up, according to The Charlotte Observer. But Goodyear remained confident the ship isn't from Mars or some CGI software.

"Based on the timing, location, and what little visibility is in the video, we have every reason to believe this is WF1," the blimp's team stated, referring to the Wingfoot One member of the tire company's fleet. "We're not aliens, but we do come in peace." []

Optimizing Spinal Surgery

by Dr. David Hanscom

There are well-documented treatable variables that have a negative effect on the outcomes of spinal surgery. Currently the medical profession is ignoring them frequently resulting in catastrophic results:

• It is reported in over one thousand peer-reviewed research articles that anxiety, depression, catastrophizing, and fear avoidance adversely affect the results of surgery.

    o They are better predictors of outcome than the actual pathology.

• Shared decision-making regarding procedures with permanent sequelae is critical.

    o A fusion for LBP is successful only about 25% of the time at two-year follow up.

• Surgeons cannot accurately assess patient stress in the office setting

• Sleep is well-documented factor that affects the perception of pain

• Degenerative disc disease is a part of the normal aging process and has been shown to have little if any correlation with back pain.

• Any surgery performed in any part of the body can create chronic pain as an outcome of the procedure. It occurs 10-40% of the time and it can be permanent. Around 5-10% of time it is permanent.

• High dose narcotics not only create a tolerance but also increase the actual level of pain.

• Physical conditioning and activity are important in decreasing pain.

• Focused structured care can markedly improve both surgical and non-surgical outcomes.

Here is what is currently being done:

• Surgeons are monitored on productivity and discouraged from spending time with patients.

• Less than 10% of surgeons assess stress before making the decision to perform surgery. Therefore, there is little shared decision-making.

    o Frequently major life-altering decisions are made on the first visit with inadequate data and patient education.

• Surgeons feel they can assess mental stress in the clinic. Yet it's documented that they can do so less than 45% of the time.

• Sleep is rarely addressed by anyone.

• In spite of the overwhelming evidence that the outcomes of surgery for degenerative disc are poor and unpredictable there are hundreds of thousands of them performed annually in the United States.

• Narcotic usage is seldom defined and stabilized before surgery.

• Although physical therapy is often prescribed there is often no long-term conditioning plan implemented.

• A multi-faceted approach to resolving chronic pain is often not available. Most physicians are not well-trained to deal with chronic pain and dislike dealing with it.

• Surgery is simplistically viewed as the definitive solution. It is just one tool and is actually dangerous. Chronic pain is seldom mentioned as a complication of surgery.

About three years ago I, along with my team, decided to become more systematic with our pre-surgical process. We coined the term, "prehab." We will not perform elective spine surgery unless the patient is willing to work through his or her part of the protocol for at least six weeks. I also do not perform surgery for back pain.

• Surgical decisions are not made on the first visit

    o Specific educational material is available for a shared decision-making process on follow up visits

• Psychosocial variables are obtained and acknowledged on the first visit

    o Anxiety/ anger/ depression assessed and treated

    o Must have some degree of improvement prior to proceeding with surgery.

• Sleep

    o Should be sleeping at least six hours per night for more than six weeks.

• Medications defined and stabilized

    o Pain consultation if daily opiate intake > 100 mg of Morphine equivalent.

I have observed that patients' post-operative pain is less, rehab is easier, the outcomes are more consistently excellent, and there is a quicker return to full function. What has been surprising is that I have now seen dozens of patients who have had their pain resolve without surgery in spite of having significant anatomical problems that I had planned on solving with surgery.

Janet's Story

The following letter is from a woman who I saw last summer with a large synovial cyst. This is a problem where a sac of fluid is formed off a facet joint off of the back of the spine. It was not only pinching her sciatic nerve it was calcified, which means it couldn't shrink. I immediately offered her a small operation to remove it. The outcome of removing the cyst is predictably positive with few complications. It is one of my favorite procedures. It took every ounce of restraint I had to offer her the prehab process through our pain center. She never returned to see me and I received this letter from her last week.

(Continued on Page 60)

Optimizing Spinal Surgery

Continued from page 59

Dear Doctors,

Last summer an MRI scan revealed a synovial cyst in my back. I had severe pain from cramps in my butt and calf muscles. My family doctor referred me to your office.

I am writing to update you on my status, which is greatly improved. On my initial visit at the Pain Center, the doctor asked me to keep a journal of what I couldn't do.

What I cannot do because of pain:

I cannot get up in the morning in a flash. I need to exercise and stretch my right leg in bed, roll carefully out of bed to ice my butt and calf, do stair step exercises, and then finally do a 20 to 30 minute "working with pain" meditation.

I can't sit in any chair I want because my butt muscle will spasm.

Car seats are hard to sit in. I have to get out at least every 45 minutes to stretch.

I was on Gabapentin, Cyclobenzaprine, and Ibuprofen.

I followed the Back-in-Control program, writing down my thoughts and beginning to focus on what I wanted to do, including returning to dance class. In early October I began sleeping in a semi-upright position, with a pillow under my legs and the cramping began to subside. I also had biofeedback training. By mid-November I was able to get off all pain medications and start lifting weights again.

I have very occasional twinges in my right butt when sitting or walking but I am basically pain free. I am so grateful for the chronic pain management program and extremely grateful that you offered the program rather than immediate surgery on the synovial cyst.

Many many thanks.

Sincerely,

Janet

I had forgotten about her case so I reviewed her MRI scans and was shocked to see the size of the cyst. However I have been surprised at the severity of the pathology with every surgical patient I have witnessed becoming pain free without an operation. In fact, in the first edition of my book, I comment that if a patient has a significant structural problem with matching symptoms that surgery should be performed quickly so as to move forward with the comprehensive rehab program. I thought the pain would be too distracting to be able to participate. The opposite scenario occurred in that when I performed surgery in the face of a fired up nervous system, the pain would frequently be worse. I eventually discovered this problem has been well documented in the medical literature.

Chronic pain can actually be induced as a complication of any surgical procedure, including painless ones such as a hernia repair. One of the risk factors is pre-existing chronic pain in another part of the body.

Ask for This Approach!

I'm excited about this turn of events, although it is becoming a little challenging maintaining a surgical practice. The medical literature has clearly documented that this process is effective. Ask your doctor to help you out with setting up your own program. You don't need a major pain center, as the necessary resources are readily available.

Every surgery has risks and no one thinks a complication will happen to him or her. I have seen them all. They are unpredictable and the outcomes can be catastrophic. Do you really need surgery? Be careful!!

Avoids a Five-level Neck Fusion

I received this email from a physical therapist on the East Coast, who I've never met. Before you read this letter, I'd like to emphasize that research has documented for decades that arthritis, bone spurs, disc degeneration, disc bulges and herniations are not considered a cause of neck, thoracic or low back pain. There is never an indication to perform even a one-level fusion for isolated neck pain. Whenever I perform a neck fusion for spinal cord damage or arm pain, I am clear that the surgery won't alleviate the neck pain. In fact, it can make it worse a significant percent of the time.

The letter

Dr. Hanscom,

I have been meaning to reach out to you for some time. First, congratulations on your new endeavor and I'm excited to see and hear what you achieve. Second, I want to extend my gratitude for providing new, refreshing and empowering information.

I first heard you on the Pain Reframed Podcast with Jeff Moore and Tim Flynn. Your story, and the information you provided helped change my practice as a physical therapist.

At the time, I was working with a patient who was very focused on the pain she was having in her neck and some intermittent tingling in the left forearm. Midway through our time together, she had an MRI which showed degeneration, and disc bulging. Of course, her symptoms increased after reading the imaging report. I relayed that this was normal for her age (75 years old) and we went through a lot of effort to de-educate her and give her some hope.

She followed up with an orthopedic spine surgeon who recommended a five-level cervical fusion. At the time, she was convinced that she needed to have the surgery because her doctor said so. Her strength was excellent. Her reflexes were intact and equal bilaterally in the upper and lower extremities. I went through extensive phone conversations, face to face discussions that ultimately ended in frustration. She also has a son and she is his primary caregiver. The surgery would significantly impact his life as she recovered...I was at a loss...

Then, I tuned in for my weekly listen to Jeff and Tim's podcast. When you walked through your 5-step process, I immediately started taking notes. I put together a printout for her and we discussed each step one by one. We went through each step over the course of about one month. She would periodically call me with questions and we would talk through any issues she was having implementing each step. One

day she called, and her tone sounded different. Her surgery was scheduled for the following week, so I wasn't sure what to expect. She said "Steven...I decided to cancel my surgery." I was at a loss for words. She started to notice improvements in her symptoms and her ability to control her body's response to different stimuli. We keep in touch and she still reaches out with questions and to get more information on how to improve her wellness.

I want to thank you for putting your message out there! I want to thank you for helping people that you have never met! I want to thank you for helping me and a patient who were at loss!

Without your willingness to change your practice and seek ways to serve your patients better, she would've had the surgery and who knows where she would be now. I'm sure you've done the same for many people, but I truly hope hearing these stories never gets old for you.

Thank you and keep spreading your message!

My thoughts

I am always inspired to keep moving forward when I hear stories like hers. I'm grateful that I have been able to give back in a way that's consistently effective. We hear stories like this every week in and out of our clinic. At the same time, I am disturbed that my profession would remotely consider a five-level fusion as a reasonable option. It's a big operation with a significant chance of complications, such as trouble swallowing, having food go into her lungs, and vocal cord problems. I can quickly think of eight cases of one and two-level neck fusions that died after the operation. Additionally, not only is there a low chance of improving her pain, there is at least a 40% chance of making her worse.

This story could have been written under the "Are You Kidding Me?" post. None of it is rational. I'm happy that somehow, she was able to not only halt the procedure, but she has largely recovered with minimal interventions and no risk or cost.

About the Author
Dr. David Hanscom

Dr. David Hanscom is an orthopedic complex spinal deformity surgeon who now understands that most chronic pain from any source is solvable – usually without surgery. He is the creator of the DOC (Direct your Own Care) program, which is the subject of his book, Back in Control: A Surgeon's Roadmap out of Chronic Pain. He also publishes a weekly blog and maintains a website, www.backincontrol.com, to provide resources for chronic pain patients and their families. Dr. Hanscom distinguishes himself from many spine surgeons in that he strongly encourages non-surgical solutions for his patients.

Part Two of Optimizing Spinal Surgery will be continued in the November 2018 Edition of The New Age Chronicles Newspaper.

An Interview with Jock Brocas

Interviewer: Tell us about yourself.

Jock Brocas: There is very little to tell. I am a normal guy that has experienced a varied life. I spent my youth striving for spiritual knowledge and wisdom and when others were heading on big holidays an exciting outdoor adventures, I would prefer to spend my time with monks and nuns of a religious community. My Uncle was a monk and I had a fascination and desire to serve god. The easiest way that I could think to do that was to become a priest and serve within that same religious community. However, that was not meant to be. I was refused entry to further studies at a senior seminary and so that aspect of my life threw me into a kind of shock. Later, I joined the military and spent time serving queen and country. The desire for spiritual growth still never left me and I would often continue my spiritual studies in private, seeking enlightenment where I could. I am a deeply driven individual and very compassionate as many will attest and I try to live life by my 3 rules of love, forgiveness and compassion.

Interviewer: Describe your psychic abilities and how they work.

Jock Brocas: I laugh when I am asked this, because it reminds me of when people find out I am a medium or psychic and look at me either in shock or ask what I can see around them, and if i had a dollar for everytime, I would be an incredibly wealthy person. I guess before anyone really knows who they are, or what they are, they have these unusual experiences and abilities but can't label them and I had my fair share of dreams, visions and knowing. It was not until later years when I finally found out and then I could label them. So, as we all have psychic and spiritual abilities within us, I guess, I had more of one than another and my natural abilities were forefront in my experience. If I have to put a label on what spiritual ability I have more predominance in, I would say that I am profoundly clairaudient. Even though I have the ability to tap into all my spirit faculties, my clairaudience is what serves me better. It means that I am able to hear spirit speak to me or to impress me in a subjective and objective method of hearing the message. It allows me to deliver messages with a high degree of evidence. However, one is always in development. Nevertheless, a predominant ability that i have and continually work on is my discernment. It is not something I can teach and is not something that is comprehended easily. I believe it is bestowed upon everyone, but like mediumship, some are used more with this spirit faculty.

Interviewer: What is an evidential medium? Is it a same thing as a spiritual medium or psychic?

Jock Brocas: An evidential medium is like any medium, however, the difference lies in the ability to provide highly evidential information to prove the continuation of consciousness after the death of the physical body. I wrote an article on evidential mediumship and if i may, I will quote it here as it will give you a full deeper understanding of what evidential mediumship is.

This is taken from an article I wrote in "The Otherside Press"

Think of these two particular points and identify what you perceive to be the best type of validation.

Medium:"I have a father figure here, and he is coming around you with a great deal of love, he passed with a heart or chest condition. He is saying that you were very special to him and that you found it difficult when he passed. He is about 5 ft10 and a bit rotund, wears glasses and smokes and has a great personality. He says sorry for what you went through and identifies that you stepped up to help the family. You could always wrap him round your finger and that he would give you anything he could. He is strong in stature and looks like a powerful man. Do you understand?"

This message to many is perceived as good and the sitter feels validated because certain pieces of information have been covered - especially if they are grieving badly and reaching for anything. Due to the sitters' need to hear the information, she or he accepts it and begins to open up more - offering leading answers that feed the medium such as, "yes he had a heart attack and I was the one dealing with everything". The medium confirms that is what he or she was getting and feels good because he or she thinks she has a hit. The reality is that it offers no real evidence and is not in the slightest any type of evidential message for the individual who is grieving

Now the second medium: *I have a male figure coming through with the name Micheal and what sounds like Thompson or Johnson. He says thank you for talking with him when you were walking through the park yesterday and you thought about him when you stood by the bed of flowers with the statue in the middle. He also says that you were in a store like Macy's and you nearly bought a new pair of shoes but* changed your mind, placing them back. He often comes around you and notes that he was with you when you were mending the chair that you recently broke in the kitchen. He was trying to tell you how to do it and laughs at your attempt. He mentions the name Mateo or sounds like this and also I have to give you Anaheim road or place. Can you understand this? He also tells me that you have an anniversary in July and another on the 5th May. He want's to send love to his wife and the name I am given is mary. He also shows me that you have his watch with you now. Can you accept that?

Now if this information is validated by the sitter in entirety or at least 80%, this would be considered as stronger evidence and even better if more evidence is given the sitter can't validate until much later by another party. This would suggest the sitter had no knowledge and the information would have to be validated by a third party at another time, thus suggesting the information could only have been derived from a communicating entity whom knew the information previously. Obviously how one delivers this type of message has some bearing on how the evidence is offered, but generally there should be no questions or assumptions. The medium should be able to give the name or sounds like as close as possible, it is not good practice to throw out a random letter unless the evidence that supports that is overwhelming.

From this, I believe you will be able to deduce what constitutes mediumship evidence. However, one must also remember that one persons evidence is another's failure.

(Continued on Page 64)

THE SUN IS GONE

A Sister Lost in Secrets, Shame, and Addiction, and How I Broke Free

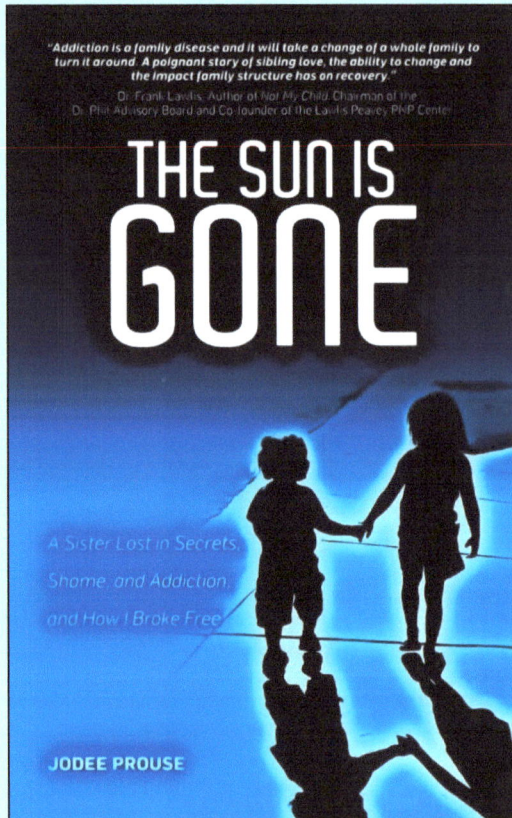

"Addiction is a family disease and it will take a change of a whole family to turn it around. A poignant story of sibling love, the ability to change and the impact family structure has on recovery."
Dr. Frank Lawlis, Author of Not My Child, Chairman of the Dr. Phil Advisory Board and Co-founder of the Lawlis Peavey PNP Center.

THE SUN IS GONE

A Sister Lost in Secrets, Shame, and Addiction, and How I Broke Free

JODEE PROUSE

What they are saying about The Sun Is Gone

"A deeply intimate and moving story of trauma, loss, addiction, tragedy and the possibility of redemption." – **Gabor Maté M.D., author of In the Realm of Hungry Ghosts: Close Encounters With Addiction.**

"Addiction is a family disease and it will take a change of a whole family to turn it around. A poignant story of sibling love, the ability to change and the impact family structure has on recovery." - **Dr. Frank Lawlis, Author Not My Child, Chairman of the Dr. Phil Advisory Board and Co-founder of the Lawlis Peavey PNP Center.**

"A courageous and unflinching portrait of a sister's journey to help her brother and ultimately herself. The Sun is Gone highlights the need to take personal responsibility for our choices, mistakes, and the learning process that is inherent in making real changes in your life." -- **Carrie Wilkens Ph.D., Co-author Beyond Addiction: How Science and Kindness Help People Change**

www.JodeeProuse.com

How many times have you lost yourself in some chronic family crisis, giving and giving until there is no more left to give—and yet you give more. Out of love, out of duty, out of knowing that everyone looks to you?

Whether that awful situation is a result of a horribly dysfunctional family, chronic drug or alcohol addiction, sexual or verbal abuse, living with the mentally ill, raising a disabled or autistic child, the pain of a disintegrating marriage and divorce, the responsibility that comes with parental healthcare decline, a jailed or arrested partner or some other trauma?

As women, we have often learned from childhood that we are the ones that must be the peacemakers, the problem-solvers, the fixers—the ones to make concessions. And we sometimes do this with dire consequences, losing our selves, sometimes our partners and our children -- and even our souls.

Jodee Prouse knows this from experience. Her painfully honest book The Sun Is Gone about trying to halt the alcoholic decline of her beloved brother, amidst a lifetime of family crisis and dysfunction, is both a cautionary tale and beacon of hope for women to find the strength to make painful, but personally healthy choices.

Her story begins as a child where she becomes her sweet little brother's protector as her alcohol-fueled father rages in the night. The grand-daughter, step-daughter, daughter-in-law, sister-in-law, niece, great-niece, aunt, cousin and ultimately sister to alcoholics, she becomes the one pillar of strength in her immediate household as her neglectful and emotionally-withholding mother moves on to a new partner and divorce again. Eventually starting her own family with a loving husband and two children, and beginning a business, Jodee remains her brother, Brett's best friend and safe harbor.

But as his drinking becomes apparent, grows worse and more self-destructive, Jodee is drawn into a maelstrom of pain, co-dependence, and battle of wills with her other family members. Her deep love for her brother propels her forward to make choices and sacrifices that are disempowering for herself, Brett and others.

Yet, finally, despite excruciating emotional pain, she comes to realize that she must put herself and her husband and children first—and set boundaries—that she cannot fix someone else's life. For anyone dealing with an addictive family member, this experience will especially resonate.

But today, Jodee Prouse asserts that the need for women to take back the control over their own lives –and disengage from the maelstrom within a family crisis -- to no longer be an enabler -- is universal.

Now a full time speaker and advocate living in Alberta CAN and Oroville, WA, after successfully building and selling her highly regarded beauty company, Jodee is also urging families to stop hiding in shame from "family secrets"—to deal with hidden emotions by sharing, speaking out and getting help, to lance wounds that lead to pain, addiction, rage, regrets and family crisis.

Says Jodee: "I know what it is like to feel powerless to something that takes control over your life. It is not easy to break patterns of all we have ever known, even when our choices hurt us or hurt the ones we love. I know that sometimes these behaviors are etched deep inside...But when we lose ourselves in someone else's addiction or issue, we are no good to anyone; not ourselves and certainly not the one's we love. In the end, we are not culpable for someone else's path. Just our own."

And that's the deepest form of love and understanding. Through her book and message, Jodee inspires people to: **LEARN. ACCEPT. FORGIVE. HEAL**.

Available at Amazon.com

ON PLANET EARTH ALL LIVES MATTER

www.XZBN.net

MISSION: EVOLUTION
with GWILDA WIYAKA

Gwilda Wiyaka author of So, We're Still Here. Now What? Spiritual Evolution and Personal Empowerment in a New Era, is considered by many to be today's foremost expert on the modern day application of ancient shamanic principles. She is the founder and director of the Path Home Shamanic Arts School, a Colorado state-certified occupational school of the shamanic arts. Gwilda is also a preceptor for the University of Colorado School of Medicine, where she provides instruction to medical doctors on the modern interface between shamanism and allopathic medicine for the University's School of Medicine's Complementary and Alternative Medicine course. Radio Talk Show Host, author, teacher, singer, musician, visionary and much more. Email - gwildawiyaka@xzbn.net

CONNECTING WITH COINCIDENCE
with DR. BERNARD BEITMAN, MD

Dr. Bernie Beitman, MD, author Connecting with Coincidence: The New Science for Using Synchronicity and Serendipity in Your Life, is the first psychiatrist since Carl Jung to attempt to systematize the study of coincidences. He is a Visiting Professor at the University of Virginia and former Chair of the Department of Psychiatry at the University of Missouri-Columbia. He attended Yale and completed a psychiatric residency at Stanford. Dr. B has received two national awards for his psychotherapy training program and is internationally known for his research into the relationship between chest pain and panic disorder. In addition, he has edited two issues of Psychiatric Annals that focus on coincidences. Dr. B is the founder of Coincidence Studies. To contact Dr B - drberniemd@xzbn.net

www.XZBN.net

www.XZBN.net

An Interview With Jock Brocas

Continued From Page 61

Interviewer: So Jock Tell Me "Are Demons Real"?

Jock Brocas: Well let me ask you, is the air you breathe real? Even though you can't see it, you know it's real because without it you would not exist. If you fall, does that mean that gravity is a false perception? Too much of what we are told is real or is not is based on other's perceptions and whether or not you believe in it, does not mean that it is false. From my experiences, Yes, I believe Demon's to be as real as gravity and perhaps that analogy has some kind of relationship, but we can discuss this another time. However, perhaps the issue here is that we are all ready to label something too quickly that we simply can't understand really and do not want to admit that an intelligence that may seen malevolent is more intelligent and knowing than we are, no matter the label, its reality is unrefuted since the dawn of time.

Interviewer: How Dangerous is the Demonic?

Jock Brocas: Personally I think it is very dangerous - especially to the ignorant and the inquisitive individual who wants to delve into the afterlife and immediately after having a few experiences, becomes an expert. Nevertheless, contrary to some medical professionals and religious individuals. Demons are not wandering ready to jump on everyone and the probability of spirit obsession is higher than demonic possession. There's a bandwagon with the title called demon and unfortunately it's got so many people on it that it gets bigger and bigger.

Interviewer: Do You Think Paranormal Problems Are Growing!

Jock Brocas: Absolutely and I will reiterate what I said before, but perhaps one of the biggest issues is the necessity for people to think they can take on a force that is far more intelligent and unseen. The more we have misguided people and even professionals delving into the unseen realms with no real knowledge or rose tinted glasses, then opportunities will increase for the malevolent on the other side of life to manifest within someone's life or domicile. I recently read of a medical professional who immediately labeled one as possessed because of the behavior they displayed. This of course becomes an inherent issue and one needs the very real discernment of a medium that can discern. The more one dabbles the more one spins the chamber of a pistol, at some point someone will win the Russian roulette.

Interviewer: What is your mission in your work as a spiritual medium?

Jock Brocas: My only mission is to help those who suffer grief or who are grieving in both education and demonstration of evidence of the continuation of life after the process we understand as death. However, another part of my mission is to educate those about the negative aspects of the afterlife and to come to the aid of those who need help that may be suffering from some paranormal occurrence.

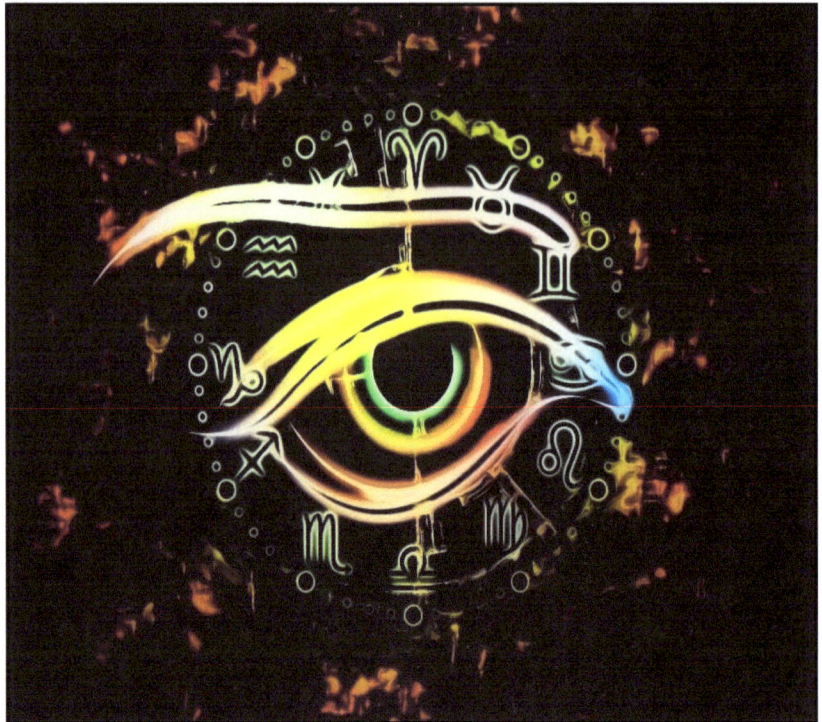

Interviewer: You have real experience dealing with demon oppression and possession. Tell us about this part of your work.

Jock Brocas: This is not something I asked for, I never set out to deal with these cases or issues that people suffer from. It seemed to me that I was chosen by spirit to serve and the more I fought against it, the more I was pushed toward it. It is a very serious aspect of the work I do, yet i very rarely deal with devices and modern tech to do it. I use what spirit gave me including discernment that I continually work on and the ability to harness divine power. I am always looking for others to help me and that I can turn to, but this is hard to find. Many paranormal teams over exaggerate, they create more problems and love to advertise the service for further gain or to gain notoriety. This is a form of suffering and the main concern is those who suffer. First and foremost it is about them and alieving that suffering they have found themselves in and their loved ones. For every thousand people, or investigators claiming Demon, you will be lucky if even 1.5% of that is really diabolical. I prefer to work with science and spirit, blending both together to ensure a safe outcome and I will say, I am not an exorcist, I know boundaries and if I need to bring in other's I will. My work is private, totally confidential and will not be used to sensationalize what I believe is out of control in our world.

Interviewer: How do you help those type of individuals - do you bring in paranormal teams?

Jock Brocas: Firstly, let me explain something here and this is my own opinion. There are few paranormal teams that i would trust and i mean few, most are based around overzealous ego and often lead a trail of destruction to families that perhaps need serious help as i mentioned previously. I prefer to work alone at times and when the need arises,i will bring in other professionals whom i trust such as doctors, psychologists, parapsychologists and maybe an Investigator. However, one does not seek out problems like investigating known areas or haunted locations and I certainly do not label everything as demonic. I would only respond to an appeal for help and then it would take an inordinate amount of research, due diligence and discernment to move forward and bring on others. I do a great deal of counseling and research as well as using my mediumship abilities to work with a case. I know my limits and I know when those are reached and when i have to seek help.

Interviewer: Do You Make Money From Your Cases

Jock Brocas: Whilst I do charge for private sittings and group sittings because of the time spent and not the actual sitting or workshops, most if not all goes to fund my charity. In terms of if anyone reaches out for serious help of a paranormal nature - absolutely not. The skills and abilities that I have on that aspect of my work are there to anchor the work of a divine force and I give of myself freely. If I have been successful and they want to show appreciation, then I will ask for a charity donation of any amount they wish to bestow, but I never charge and will never charge for spirit Intervention, I am a tool for the Divine Spirit and work to better the suffering of those under negative spirit subjugation.

(Continued On Page 65)

The 'X' Zone Broadcast Network
Paranormal / Parapsychology Radio
www.XZBN.net

An Interview With Jock Brocas

Continued From Page 64

Interviewer: Your new book, Deadly Departed: Do's, Don'ts, and Dangers of Afterlife Communication, is about to be published. Tell us about the book.

Jock Brocas: This book is about the realities of mediumship and its associated dangers. Too many individuals chase mediumship and afterlife connections looking for fame and fortune or the desire to feel needed and revered. Standards have dropped and ignorance often goes before the eyes of truth, thus opening oneself to a plethora of problems. The book is simply a tool to help professionals and those involved in the vocation to understand, develop and serve in the right way. It goes against the grain of many proclaimed spiritualistic beliefs and challenges one to consider the reality of the demonic and evil pervading the world and the minds of the innocent.

It won't teach you to be a medium, exorcist or demonologist. It will give you knowledge and understanding that you can refer to time and time again. The book is not finished, it never will be and there will be more and more versions coming out. Part of the proceeds of the book go to the ASSMPI.

Interviewer: You are a cofounder of the American Society for Standards in Mediumship and Psychical Investigation. What is the organization's mission?

Jock Brocas: To raise standards in mediumship and to research mediumistic afterlife practices from a balanced perspective. We support and help educate mediums as well as being able to support and help a community that is heavily grieving. We have also recently begun a Parapsychological Intervention Division that has two directives.

- To research and answer a need within medical and psychological practice.
- To offer guidance, support and intervention to those plagued with what seems to be issues of a paranormal nature.

Interviewer: What else should our readers know about your work in the paranormal field?

Jock Brocas: I am a fiercely private person, I understand the dangers of the afterlife and the grief those suffer from. I am nothing but a mere tool in spirits tool box that is willing to be used.

Interviewer: What would our readers be surprised to find out about you?

Jock Brocas: I am a trained classical singer.

Interviewer: What projects do you have planned for the future?

Jock Brocas: I have so many projects, from publishing more books to helping support others with their education about the afterlife. I would like to lecture more in Universities to give students a potential glimpse into a balanced view of afterlife research, dangers and its place in our educational system.

Interviewer: List websites and social media here:

**Jockbrocas.com
Extrememedium.com
Assmpi.org
theothersidepress.com**

Big Fight Over Bigfoot in British Columbia

Forget Cohen. Forget Manafort. The real court action has been taking place in British Columbia, where a battle is being waged over a decision that could change the entire course of human history: The acknowledgement of the existence of Bigfoot.

by Richard Binder

Forget Cohen. Forget Manafort. The real court action has been taking place in British Columbia, where a battle is being waged over a decision that could change the entire course of human history: The acknowledgement of the existence of Bigfoot.

The Vancouver Sun reports that documentarian and "sasquatch tracker" Todd Standing filed a lawsuit in October 2017 against the provincial government of British Columbia, accusing the province of "dereliction of duty" for "non-recognition of sasquatch." Standing told the B.C. Supreme Court that he has evidence "way beyond a reasonable doubt" that sasquatch exist, and he asked that a government biologist be appointed to accompany him into "known sasquatch habitat" for three months to prove it.

According to CTV News, Standing was a Bigfoot doubter nearly a decade ago, and searched forests initially to disprove its existence. "Obviously, I was completely wrong," he said. Although he has no living or dead samples among his evidence, he says he has captured sasquatch on film, including his 2017 documentary "Discovering Bigfoot."

Lawyers for the province and other government officials are not convinced. The Ministry of Forests, Lands, Natural Resource Operations and Rural Development responded to Standing's suit with a denial of his claims. Marina Goodwin of the Ministry of the Attorney General asked for a dismissal of Standing's suit, saying "the claim lacks an air of reality."

Justice Kenneth Ball has reserved his decision on the application to dismiss, and will provide it in writing at a later date. During the hearing, Ball suggested the matter was an issue for the executive branch, not the court, to decide.

Troy Hunter, Standing's lawyer, told the Sun that although wildlife protection is at the heart of the case, it also raises the constitutional issue of discrimination based on political or other beliefs. "There is a substantial question to be tried, and there is a serious purpose involved," he said.

In an interview with My Comox Valley Now, Blaine McMillan, author of "Wood Knocks & Tossed Rocks: Searching for Sasquatch with the Bigfoot Field Researchers Organization," casts some doubt on Standing's filmed evidence. "A lot of the photos, I wouldn't say that they're good evidence. They're kind of shaky, and if you look real close on two of the faces that are in there, it looks a lot like a human covered in hair. But it doesn't look like a 'squatch, at all. I'm not saying he fabricated it, because I don't know, but it doesn't look real enough." But McMillan doesn't rule out the existence of sasquatch: "Somebody said there were white grizzly bears. Nobody believed it until they actually saw one!"

Standing remains committed to his cause. Outside court, he said, "We'll see what happens, what the court thinks. But, I mean, come on, is it not the discovery of the millennium to find a primate species in North America? If I'm right, this is the discovery of the millennium and it's not wasting anyone's time. This is an extremely important issue." []

Gluten-Free Isn't Enough, Here's What's Missing
(Plus a Tip on Halting Autoimmune Issues)

by Kristin Grayce McGary

Gluten-Free has certainly entered the mainstream. Even your local conventional grocery store carries gluten-free food options. I'm committed to a gluten-free lifestyle, no matter what. If you're gluten-free, then you likely understand how gluten is "goo" food, indigestible, inflammatory, autoimmune triggering, gut damaging and therefore also horrible for your brain (hence that foggy thinking and distractibility). I understand that changing your diet and lifestyle can be scary, challenging, and even frustrating. However, if you're committed to your health, the information below may change your life and health picture forever, so please keep reading. One thing you may NOT know is that being gluten-free isn't always enough. No one really talks about this, so I believe it's time. You deserve to know the truth.

First of all, let's define gluten-free (GF). Gluten-free means you are truly "gluten-free." If you're eating gluten once a week or once a month, technically this isn't gluten-free. It takes about 1/8 of the size of your pinky nail amount of gluten to cause an inflammatory cascade of imbalances and tissue damage that can last 9 or more months. So, having gluten once a month may still be causing inflammation and health problems that you aren't aware of yet. I believe in strictly following a gluten-free diet – no cheating. There is no moderation when it comes to a poison to your body. This may seem extreme, but you'll understand if you keep reading. Of course, consuming less gluten is always ideal, but please consider really going entirely gluten-free. It just may help you alleviate future suffering.

I was having severe but random gut pain, constipation, and brain fog on a gluten-free diet. Going gluten-free did help reduce my abdominal bloat, but it still occurred, just less frequently. It also reduced the razor blades in my gut, but not completely. I couldn't figure out what was causing these seemingly random symptoms. I thought maybe I'd just have to live with it. I had tried everything, even a "gut-repair program" without much change. And then I learned about cross-reactivity. I learned that my body was acting as if millet, quinoa, sesame, corn, eggs, and coffee (never drink it but had been doing coffee enemas with disastrous effects) were like gluten in my system. It was as if I was taking one step forward with gut repair, and then one stop back by creating more damage with gluten-free cross-reactive foods. The valuable, life changing information I'm speaking about has to do with cross-reactivity. In short, this means your body reacts to foods as if they are gluten. There are foods that are similar enough to the proteins in gluten that your body mistakes them for gluten proteins like gliadin, and reacts, creating inflammation, tissue damage, low level autoimmunity (the precursor to autoimmune diseases), and gut damage. Even if you don't have full blown Celiac (autoimmune reactions to gluten that can occur anywhere in the body, not only the gut), or you've been told you have Non-Celiac Gluten Sensitivity, or you just notice you're a bit more sluggish or bloated after gluten, you will greatly benefit from this information.

I don't agree with a deprivation approach to nutrition, that you should remove all of your favorite foods without healthy substitutions. This just plays into cravings, subconscious patterns of sabotage, and often frustrated failures. So, don't be afraid of the following information. There are tons of delicious substitutions that will leave you feeling satisfied (physically and emotionally). What I do believe in, is commitment to make healthy food choices based on your individual body and its metabolic, hormonal, nervous, and immune systems. You may not have any cross-reactivity to foods, or you may only have a few. You won't know unless we do the test.

You may be wondering, "How do I know if I cross-react to a food?" First, this kind of reaction is NEVER tested on any standard food sensitivity test. IF you've had food testing by other labs, they don't test for this, and I don't trust most food testing because they simply aren't accurate. There is only one test specific to this kind of reaction and it's performed by Cyrex labs – Array #4 Gluten Associate Cross Reactive Foods and Food Sensitivity. The reason it's so valuable is because many "health" foods are on this list.

Cyrex Array #4 Gluten Associated, Cross Reactive Food and Food Sensitivity Screening Test list:

Rye, barley, spelt, polish wheat
millet
quinoa
sesame
potatoes
egg
Casein (alpha, beta), Casomorphin dairy
Milk butyrophilin
whey proteins
soy
yeast
coffee
buckwheat
sorghum
hemp
amaranth
teff
oats
tapioca
rice
chocolate (milk)

Wow, wouldn't it be great to know if you cross-react to eggs, coffee, hemp, or other gluten-free grains and foods?

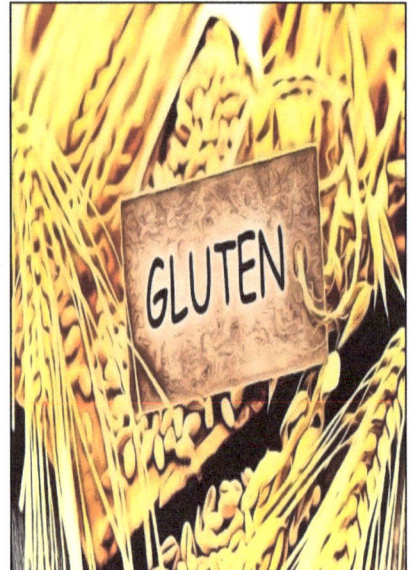

You will know that you cross-react by doing this test, but you must prepare yourself in order to receive accurate results. If you don't have diagnosed Celiac disease, then eat everything on the Array #4 list of foods for 7 days in a row (this includes gluten), wait 26 days and get your blood drawn for the test on that 26th day. This ensures that your immune system has made the antibodies to the food antigens and we will get accurate results.

If you or someone you know has gut issues, autoimmune issues (Hoshimotos Thyroiditis, Rheumatoid arthritis, Lupus, Multiple Sclerosis MS, psoriasis, eczema, or Crohn's disease, to name but a few), then this test is vital to you being able to fully heal. If you eat foods to which you cross-react, or even a speck of gluten, then it will likely flair your autoimmune condition and cause multiple future autoimmune diseases. These issues become compounded. You never just get one autoimmune disease. Unless you properly halt it, you will likely get two, three, or even four of them at a time. And this seriously impacts the quality and length of your life.

It's clear going gluten-free isn't always enough, and taking the next step on your health journey to identify and eliminate cross-reactive foods is necessary for you to maintain or regain vibrant health. Please use this information to become empowered to take back your health, and check out healthy alternative recipes on my website here: http://kristinmcgary.com/eat/

Blessings of Vibrant Health,
Kristin Grayce

About the Author
Kristin Grayce

Kristin Grayce McGary LAc., MAc., CFMP®, CSTcert, CLP is a highly sought-after health and lifestyle alchemist. She is renowned for reversing annoying and debilitating health conditions and helping people to live with clarity and vitality. Kristin Grayce is also a speaker and author of Ketogenic Cure; Heal Your Gut, Heal Your Life. www.KristinMcGary.com

Scar Tissue Locks in Trauma & Lost Souls

by Maureen Higgins

We are living in intense times! The vibration on the planet is incrementally rising to a higher level of consciousness more aligned with love. This last Summer Solstice jumped up the frequency quite a bit higher!! The rise in frequency brings up all our unresolved issues and patterns that are at a lower vibration. This is ultimately good, since it brings more love, happiness and freedom.

Your body has likely been keeping your mental, emotional and physical challenges in an unconscious state until you're ready to deal with them. You're likely finding that now is the time to resolve these challenges!

We are all called to let go of our past issues and patterns, which isn't always easy. This can be especially challenging since sometimes the past doesn't want to release. I've gone through this stuck state many times myself. These stuck states keep me searching for better ways to let go of the past more effectively for myself and the clients I work with, so we feel happier and lighter.

I discovered, a couple years ago, that old physical and energetic scar tissue can keep people stuck. This discovery changed the way I work with others.

My first encounter with scar tissue was when a friend's relative had a large mass on her chest that medical doctors couldn't figure out. They finally decided it must be scar tissue from a car accident a year before. My friend got permission to have me look at it.

When I energetically looked at it, I saw a male lost soul woven into her field a number of feet away from her physical body. This lost soul directly connected into the chest area where the scar tissue was located. The physical scar tissue was at her chest, but the lost soul was caught in a corresponding energetic scar tissue. It was as though his connection was pulling on her scar area and making it very pronounced.

My take on it is that, when she got in the car accident, she dissociated/partly left her body. This opened up her energy field, leaving a void of sorts. Dissociation is common with trauma. It is also called post traumatic stress disorder (PTSD). As the dissociation lessened, her energy field started closing up, going to a new normal. As her energy field closed up, it "trapped" this lost soul.

I asked to energetically unweave the lost soul from her field and then crossed him over through a tunnel of light to his next highest level destination. I asked him to go wherever his

Spirit deemed optimal for him with his Spirit Guides assisting. I then asked to repair her energy field, since it was broken due to the lost soul being there. I also asked that her spirit was brought back in, since it had partly left her body. This is called a soul retrieval.

My friend talked to her relative the next day and found that she had been hearing a man's voice and knew there was a lost soul around. She tried repeatedly to cross him but couldn't get him to go. It made sense to her that he was woven into her field due to the car accident. Over time, her chest scar tissue disappeared since the lost soul was no longer "pulling on" her scar tissue, causing it to bulge out.

I went through a stuck state, connected to scar tissue, with a slightly different slant than my friend's relative. I could tell my body was holding onto a difficult memory. The clue was the strong emotions and flashbacks/old scenes that showed me at age 5. Something was keeping it hooked in and it just wouldn't move.

I tried to let go of the memory for a couple weeks or more without success. I then remembered how old physical injuries can lock things in. I was physically injured in this past scenario I couldn't let go of. A light bulb went off. This must be the reason why things won't let go!

Instead of the scar tissue trapping a lost soul, the scar tissue was trapping an old memory. As soon as I asked to unweave this memory from my old injury site (where there was scar tissue), I felt the old emotions and scenes instantly go away. I felt renewed!

How do you know if you have an old scar tissue locking memories, emotions and/or lost souls into your energy field?

You may feel old emotions and have flashbacks like I did. You may know that there's a lost soul around you like my friend's relative did. More likely, you may feel something is off, but not sure why. You may not notice anything at all, but get a knowing that something is stuck. You can try the exercise I described above and also seek help from a professional, such as a counselor or psychologist, who uses alternative techniques.

This is the era to transform the past. The more you heal yourself, the more others heal as well! We are all interconnected through a giant matrix – the Oneness field. Healing yourself does heal others!

About the Author
Maureen Higgins

Maureen Higgins has her Master of Arts in Human Development with a focus on societal and religious belief systems, trauma and recovery, and alternative healing options. She has been in private practice for 20 years and has workshops, healing audios and a service called "3 Questions." You can see her website at www.wingsoffreedom1.com for more information.

Fact*oids

- India has the most cattle, Australia has the most sheep.
- Pandas spend most of their lives alone, only meeting other pandas in order to mate.
- A species is counted as extinct if it is not found in the wild for 50 years.
- Food spends three to five hours in the stomach and six to 20 hours in the large intestine.
- Melanin is the pigment that gives skin its color; an uneven production of it causes freckles.
- Your fingerprint patterns are formed months before your birth.
- The top of the index finger is one of the body's most sensitive parts.
- Ninety percent of all volcanic activity occurs in the oceans.
- The oceans cover 71% of the Earth's surface.
- The oceans contain 97% of the Earth's water, but less than 1% is fresh water.
- Eighty percent of all life on earth is found under the ocean's surface.
- The longest cave system is Mammoth Caves in Kentucky - 348 miles (560 km),
- Butterflies don't spin cocoons: moths spin cocoons.

Fact*oids - Gluten Free Brain Food!

THE RESOURCE CENTER
FOR THE EVLOVING HUMAN BEING

SHAMANISM FOR AN EVOLVING WORLD

Based on sound principles employed by shaman worldwide, this ancient practice can support us through the current unprecedented transitions.

PATH HOME offers: online shamanic classes, books, workbooks and music for personal growth and development, national and international long distance shamanic healing sessions performed by Gwilda Wiyaka and her Path Home certified shamanic practitioners, and our new radio show library, MISSION: EVOLUTION Radio Show where host Gwilda Wiyaka brings together today's leading experts to uncover ever deepening spiritual truths and the latest scientific developments in support of the evolution of humankind.

www.findyourpathhome.com

The Amazing Brain Music Adventure: Click Your Amygdala

by Neil Slade

I want you to think of the best time you have ever had in your life........Got it?

Now, multiply that experience, that feeling, times ten. Multiply it times a hundred, or a thousand. Or ten thousand. Or even more.

You can turn on increased creativity, intelligence, pleasure, even ESP and other paranormal abilities as easily as clicking on a light switch. You can have "the best day of your life" over and over, each time better than the last. You may even be able to move clouds and change the weather using the incredible power of your own human infinity machine- your brain.

That is exactly what you will experience – no exaggeration in the least – when you learn how to self-stimulate a part of your brain known as the amygdala. This is not wishful thinking or new-age hocus-pocus. This is what the latest brain and behavior research is now showing us is possible........for anyone. The method for amygdala self-stimulation is easy, and has been learned by persons ages 6 to 86. The basic method can be learned and taught by anyone, for free. It is democratic in the extreme. You are getting started by reading this article. Results are often immediate, and are accumulative – it gets better the more you do it. Unlike stage magic, this is no illusion. This is real brain magic.

Popping Your Frontals

No surprise that these things are actually possible once you realize that the three pounds of solid neurocircuitry between every person's ears is the most complex structure we know of in the entire universe. You have more connections in your brain than there are literally grains of sand on all the beaches on Earth. Carl Sagan has pointed out that in every brain, your fantastic one included, there are more combinations of connections than there are protons and neutrons in the universe. Heck, telepathy is nothing for your infinity brain calculator. Provided you know what buttons to push.

Brain Science

New research in the field of brain and behavior now allows any ordinary person to learn how to control and self-stimulate their own brain for such results as mentioned above. Numerous studies in the field of brain research pinpoint this area of the brain which seems to be responsible for releasing enormous levels of untapped intelligence, creativity and pleasure. Additionally, and remarkably so, self-amygdala stimulation frequently additionally turns on such "hidden" sub-conscious functions that might be ascribed to normal-paranormal function.

Direct self-controlled amygdala stimulation can produce an intensely positive peak experience emotional state, akin to the states referred historically throughout world cultures and religions by various names: nirvana, satori, samadhi, born again, peak experience, cosmic consciousness, one-with-the-universe rapture. Among brain laboratory subjects, this has been affectionately nicknamed "Popping your frontal lobes."

Now science understands the actual neuro-pathways and brain physiology responsible for this "mystical" state, and makes it available to anyone, from bus drivers to short-order cooks, as well as fasting monks. Only now, you don't have to meditate for twenty years to experience it.

Self-amygdala stimulation increases activity of the brain's most advanced and evolutionarily most complex structure of the brain – the frontal lobes. Hold your forehead with one hand. Everything under your palm is your frontal lobes, the front 1/3 of your brain. The frontal lobes are further developed in humans beyond all other mammals, save dolphins and whales (Who is to say they are not more intelligent than we? Different perhaps...). The human frontal lobes are exactly what allow us to plan and devise actions far beyond the capability of lower mammals and apes. The frontal lobes allow the most advanced behavior.

Creativity-Imagination-Cooperation-Intuition-Logic

By deliberately focusing mental energy and activity – a simple thought process – on the anterior amygdala, this causes an increase in frontal lobes processes, which instantly causes increased and measurable levels of intelligence, creativity, pleasure, and often various "normal-paranormal" experiences. The method can be as simple as "imaging" a feather tickling the amygdala, which automatically shunts neurochemical activity forward into the previously "dormant" frontal lobes. The amygdala can be seen as a gateway click switch, somewhat like the light switch on your wall. But in your brain, you "click" on the big light bulb in your frontal lobes.

Russian neurosurgeon Alexandre Luria, along with many other distinguished researchers, have repeatedly shown us that the frontal lobes are at least 90% dormant, "untapped", unused. Although some may object to this description of the brain, it is one effective way of describing the infinite potential of the human brain. We normally don't live up to even a fraction of what is available or possible. It is the great cosmic joke.

Self-amygdala stimulation without electrodes can be performed by using the brain's capacity for guided imagery.

In this day and age, when 6-year-old kids are learning to use complex computers, nearly all of us have failed to properly learn about the most complex machine in the universe – our own brain. We are taught how to drive sophisticated cars, operate complicated tools and appliances, but nobody ever taught us how our own brain works. We are driving blind.

Nevertheless, when an individual learns some very basic things about their brain, and thus learns some basic brain self-control and amygdala/frontal lobes control, then one begins to access radical and overwhelmingly positive changes in function, behavior, and activity. We start to access more and more of that enormous untapped infinite potential. We give our brain wings. As one subject stated, "This feels like flying."

In a 1998 national radio broadcast on Art Bell's Coast to Coast radio show, Slade guided exercise elicited thousands of responses from persons "tickling" their amygdala forward as brain basics and directions were given over the air, including the simple "feather tickling" visualization. For many, this caused immediate dramatic auditory, visual, and physical sensations.

(Continued on Page 70)

The Amazing Brain Music Adventure: Click Your Amygdala

Continued From Page 69

Mind Music Metamorphosis

In 1987, Slade wrote:

"A wild mountain man screaming… he started me on this brain stuff.

"I write this sitting at an old weather beaten redwood desk looking out a large picture window facing east. I am 10,200 feet up in a mountain log cabin, aspen and spruce trees everywhere as far as the eye can see. I look down on gray and white clouds enveloping the tall rolling green valley in front of me.

"To one side of the cabin is a huge 300-foot tall granite cliff. Across the valley, off in the distance, looms 14,000-foot high Mount Evans.

One hundred miles downrange, Pikes Peak.

The scenery from this vantage point in the Colorado Rockies, is stupendous! I am at the Colorado Brain Research and Development Laboratory near Blackhawk, Colorado. My journey here began in 1981. I was watching TV late one Saturday night in Denver, half-asleep and flipping through the channels. On a local progressive educational PBS channel, I stopped to watch a group of people talking about their brain(s) and their experiences while in the mountains at a unique wilderness laboratory.

"The leader of the group was a wild looking guy wearing faded blue jeans, with long hair and a beard. Only later would I learn that he had had attended four universities, and was anything but a 'hippie.' What especially got my immediate attention, and what woke me up, was the frank and logical manner in which they described some fairly outrageous and unusual experiences they were having. They described fantastic and intensely pleasurable daily events. They found creativity and invention pouring from them effortlessly, like water from a faucet.

"They all agreed that the key to all of this was having learned how to turn on previously 'uncharted' regions of their brain. If what they were saying was true, my own brain must have been on hold for most of my life. After the show ended, the leader of the group appeared with an interviewer from the station for a live segment. This time the 'brain man' wore a conventional city suit. He spoke with a great deal of enthusiasm and animation, joking more than occasionally.

"Being intrigued by this combination of science, nature, and non-convention, I wrote in and received typewritten information about the 'Brain In Nature' course held every summer in the pristine wilderness forest, forty miles west of Denver. I also learned that, according to the latest neurological opinion, the human brain's potential was infinite – and in a manner, our potential is vastly unused. After all, what is any percentage of infinity?! The main purpose of the program was to discover exactly why human neurons remained so unused, and what methods would additionally activate them.

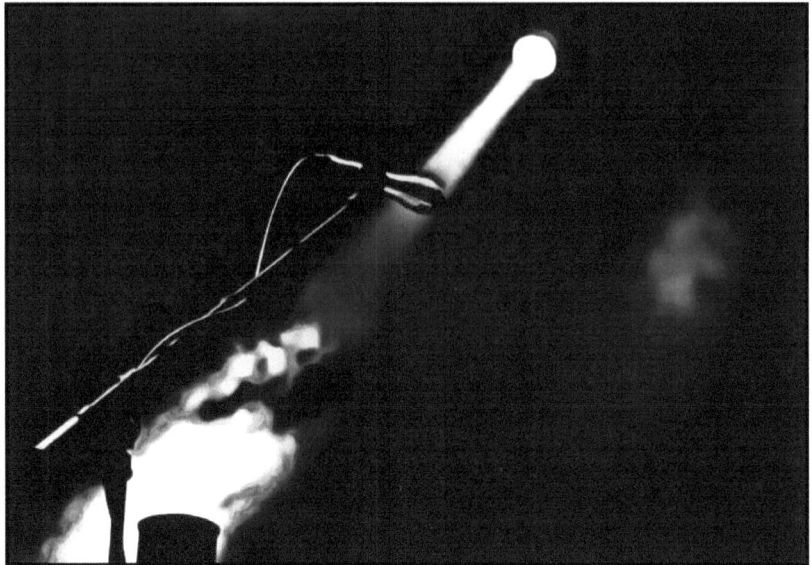

"Directions were enclosed for visiting, and so the next weekend I drove up. It sounded like fun, and an adventure. My first experience at the lab was unforgettable. Mainly, because the first thing that happened was that I was scolded severely by the director, like some dumb kid, for not reading the directions carefully. I expected to be welcomed with open arms and instead had the director yelling at me for coming up on the wrong day.

"'You didn't read the instructions,' he insisted. 'Visitors are allowed on Sunday, NOT SATURDAY. The first thing you'll learn up here is to read the instructions.'

"Embarrassed, and maybe insulted, I was nonetheless encouraged to stay put. As long as I was already there, I might as well see what the place was all about. The history and the evolution of the facility turned out to be quite amazing, and like nothing I imagined it would be."

The story unfolds with the "DAT Stingo" as a spearhead infantry scout for General Patton's army in World War II. He experienced the horrors of war from the front lines, and was one of the soldiers to first to arrive at Hitler's death camps to liberate the remaining survivors. On his return home after the end of the war, the director attended the University of Chicago earning his bachelor's and master's degrees in behavioral science and nearing completion of his Ph.D. His horrific experiences during the war drove him to ask but one question: "Why must I kill my brother?"

To this, his school and his professors had no answer. But one professor's advice was, "If there is an answer to this question, it's up here," pointing to his own gray head. "The answer has got to be in human brain… but the research hasn't been done yet in academe. If you want to go slow, work here. If you want to go fast, you're going to have to build your own research center to solve that riddle."

So, Stingo dropped out of his Ph.D. program, and started to scheme how to put together his own research facility. Unfortunately, to do that, one had to have money, and he had none. But he could tell a good story! He decided if there was a fortune to be made in a hurry, he might just be able to do it in show business. Twenty five years later, he would wink, "Yep, I bought this mountain and built this place with just a guitar, three chords, and nine folk songs." And he was right.

He started out playing the local joints around Denver and eventually landed a spot on Groucho Marx's "You Bet Your Life" television show from Hollywood. He wore buckskins and played the part of a backwoods mountain man to perfection. It was during that appearance on the Marx show that a New York City producer spotted him. "I know a good phony when I see one," the mogul observed, "and that son of a bitch is a great one!"

So, Stingo was quickly summoned out to New York City and was immediately signed to do a summer replacement show on NBC network television. He hosted a weekly program in which the "new" fad of folk singing (back in 1955) was featured. People like Burl Ives and Woody Guthrie made guest appearances and performed with him. The network paid him $2,000 an hour for this lucrative play. On the last show, he looked right into the camera an asked the million viewers watching, "If anybody out there has a mountain to sell, call me!" And sure enough, once he got off camera, somebody did.

At the end of the summer, he took two grocery sacks full of money and ran! He gave one to the IRS, and he bought "Laughing Coyote Mountain" with the other. He began to axe timber and build log cabins. That was in 1957. For the next thirty years, Stingo dedicated himself totally to explore behavior from the perspective of the human brain. He and his staff examined every bit of available scientific research and philosophic literature they could get their hands on. They ran their own short and long term studies and experiments. The environment of rugged mountain wilderness provided a total focus into the self that could never be replicated in any city or sterile clinical hospital. There was no electricity (as Carl Jung had insisted in his own Swiss study retreat), no TV, no movie entertainment. There were no four-lane highways to get away from it all. You were away from it all – to face only yourself, your mind, and your brain.

(Continued On Page 71)

The Amazing Brain Music Adventure: Click Your Amygdala

Continued From Page 70

To the end of the lab's operations in 1993, it remained remarkably free of electrical power lines or even running water. It was just you, the hand water pump, a wood stove, and your own central nervous system.

The brain lab's records grew and grew. The log buildings became crammed full of file cabinets. The books lined the walls from the stone floors to the ceiling rafters eighteen feet up. In the end, he and his group discovered the mechanisms to release startling new intelligence, creativity, and pleasure inside the human brain. His conclusions were original and unmatched by any other research establishment at the time. Then, and since, his findings are supported and corroborated with foundation findings by scientists everywhere.

My Own Brain

After my first visit to the lab in 1981, I spent the next eleven years running back and forth between my own home in Denver and the forest field station. My own personal "experiments," with my own brain, was guided by the work done at the Dormant Brain Lab. This took the form of "brain exercises," journal keeping, analysis of activity, and periodic consultation with the director, and other staff members and participants. Before long, I was assisting the director in various assignments he gave me, organizing city group sessions, information gathering, organizing lectures, and eventually writing my own books on the subject.

The results of my work were breathtaking on many occasions – sitting on the peak of Laughing Coyote Mountain, with the clearest possible perception of everything around me – a fifty thousand square mile view of the earth circle, with incredibly heightened senses and awareness. I learned how to go far beyond my own limitations, mental and physical, tested by pulling hundreds of thirty foot tall firewood logs down the labs steep wooded slopes. I ecstatically felt on many occasions the most powerful emotional experiences of my life. This might take the form of fantastic waves of internal energy, or indescribable and spectacular feelings of unity and balance. Strangely enough, these were more often than not triggered by simple daily activities – hearing a piece of music, walking among the trees, discarding a useless notion, or just sitting on my sofa at home.

When I began my investigations into the work at the lab and into how my own brain worked, my creativity and emotional state might be compared to a plugged up toilet (even with my degree, magna cum laude) – not to mention what I observed in most everybody else at the time. Since learning the basic bio-mechanics of my own human thought motor – utilizing the discoveries of general neuroscience as well as the brain lab's own methods and discoveries, I have written, arranged, performed and recorded eight albums of original music, some of which

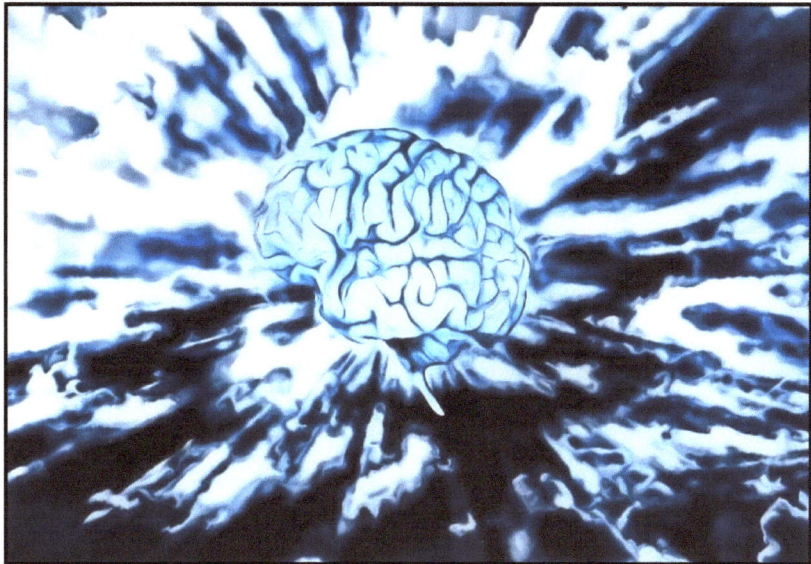

has received national public television and radio airplay. I have written several books, and I have established and run my own successful musical teaching and publishing business, sidestepping the 9 to 5 minimum wage-slave labor syndrome. My social relationships have gone from amazingly disastrous in pre-brain days, to harmonious and highly entertaining. The simple ABC's of "how the human brain works" has had nothing short of a miraculous effect on my daily life. And as for the miracles of paranormal telepathy and pre-cognition – they have become rather commonplace for me after many years of clicking my amygdala forward and turning on magical frontal lobes circuits.

The crux of the program at the brain lab hinged on voluntary self-control of one particular section of the human brain, a trigger site or neuro-gateway for intelligence, pleasure, and creativity: the anterior amygdala. The brain has two of these organs, one for the right hemisphere of the brain, the other for the left side. Each amygdala is about the size of an almond, a small knobby protuberance about one inch inside each temple in the brain – a part of the brain's limbic system. Various research has found that stimulation of this part of the brain results in automatic responses of pain or pleasure – depending which part of the amygdala is stimulated. Simple electrical anterior amygdala stimulation shuts off the "killer instinct" and results in automatic responses of cooperative and pleasurable behavior.

Self-amygdala stimulation without electrodes can be performed by using the brain's capacity for guided imagery.

For example, by simply imagining that you are tickling the front part of each amygdala with a feather, you change the flow of electro-chemical activity in the brain – and voila! This clicks the amygdala forward, if only temporarily.

This imaging alone increases frontal lobes activity and begins increases in creativity, intelligence, and so on. The more frequently you tickle, the more you click, the more pronounced the results. These changes are measurable by modern brain scanning medical instruments such as PET and MRI machines.

(Continued on Page 72)

The Amazing Brain Music Adventure: Click Your Amygdala

Continued From Page 71

The brain is a thought machine – and thus, one controls the brain and it's electro-chemical circuitry with simple thought. (No surprise there!) This simple exercise properly done often brings immediate results, with sometimes very pronounced effects. The brain lab developed hundreds of methods that further refined, accelerated, supercharged, and make permanent the results.

When a person learns how to internally stimulate the amygdala and voluntarily increase frontal lobes processes at will, it can eventually result in a very intense peak phenomenon known as "frontal lobes transcendence" or "popping your frontal lobes." This occurred regularly at the brain lab where all the distractions of a typically hectic or neurotic life were minimized, or where subjects and students received sufficient training. For myself, this first occurred on September 11, 1987 while sitting in the control room at a recording studio. It was just about the last thing on my mind. Generally, this phenomenon can't be predicted exactly – more like when a soap bubble is ready to pop.

What is it like to pop your frontals? Imagine you are sailing in a rickety wooden boat in 1492, looking for India, lost in the middle of an endless ocean for what seems like an eternity. Everybody, including yourself, is just waiting for you to fall off the edge of the planet into oblivion. Then all of a sudden, out of nowhere…

YOU SEE LAND! HOLY COW!!!!!!!!!

That's something like what popping your frontal lobes feels like. Only, it's really happening, and it's happening to YOU. NOW.

Some persons have compared popping their frontal lobes to feeling as though they were flying through the cosmos at the speed of light, or feeling the power of a train blasting through their head (pleasurably so) at 120 miles an hour. Or as one adult student put it, "a million times better than the best sex." It all depends on your personality and your preferences. After your first (they keep happening) frontal lobes "big bang," things are never quite the same again. You begin looking through a mental windshield that is clean for the first time since you were a little kid. My college education and ten years of meditation and yoga practice never prepared me for this.

Why has nature provided the human brain with this emotional fireworks rocketship blast? Nature is smart. Your brain wants you to survive. When you use more of your brain and access more of your brain's potential specifically located in the most advanced part of your brain – your frontal lobes – your chances of survival in this rough world skyrocket. Sustained and intense pleasure is exactly how neurocircuits in various sites within the brain motivate and reward the individual for frontal lobes advanced survival thought production. Free and legal. Use enough frontal lobes- and you hit the jackpot.

The True Face of Woman
by Gwilda Wiyaka

For at least the last 15,000 years, the ambient galactic frequencies bathing the planet supported a patriarchal society. That is not to say that all the societies during this period have been patriarchal. There have been many successful matriarchal societies, like those found among the native tribes in the Americas before the influence of patriarchal societies arrived on the scene.

However, it does mean that all of our structures, social, economic, government and religious, to name but a few, have been shaped by an overlording masculine frequency. Our roles as men and women, and even our personal identities, have been forged by the predominantly masculine frequency.

Now, as we enter into the Age of Aquarius characterized by unity and enlightenment, the frequencies are shifting from one predominantly masculine, to one that supports balanced masculine and feminine expression. It is a time when a deeper level of the feminine is awakening within both men and women.

While men and women are designed to be equal but opposite, they are by no means the same. Men have XY chromosomes, and Women XX, leaving men with only three quarters the genetic material as women.

Women are more genetically prepared to channel the female frequencies, and men the masculine. In order to regain a male/female balance as we come out of a predominantly masculine era, it is necessary to channel more feminine energy into the human world. Women are genetically better set up to do this.

My old Lakota teacher spoke of these times when the feminine would return. He told me it would be up to the women to lead us back into balance. At the time, it was the early 1970s and woman's lib and bra burning were hot items – no pun intended. When I asked him if the return of the feminine was what the women's movement was about, he said that while the increase in feminine energy may be prompting women to act out, they were still acting as warriors which was a masculine expression , not a feminine one.

"The true face of woman has not been on the earth for many years. So many years, that no one remembers what it looks like," he went on to say.

Now, some forty-odd years later, I am starting to see what he was talking about. None of us know what it is to be in masculine/feminine balance.

There is much talk of equality in the workplace, but the workplace itself was structured under the old patriarchal format. What we view as woman's equality is really equal involvement in masculine structures that are rapidly falling apart as, increasingly, they are no longer energetically supported.

In regards to male/female conflict and misunderstanding, so many wonderful men I have worked with over the years in my private practice, have indicated that they just want to be told what to do to make things right. They just want to make their women happy – provide for them and keep them safe.

Well, at this point, it's not about doing. It's about being. It's about being present to channel the new frequency into our human situation, so that as the old structures dissolve and crumble, new ones can be forged, supported by the frequency of the Aquarian age.

A drastic shift is upon us. One that will impact us on all levels – physical, emotional, mental and spiritual – within our beings and in the world around us.

The light is only as clear as the window through which it shines. The largest complications we face are the old imbalanced masculine/feminine frequencies and resulting structures within us.

This is an inside job.

As we are exposed to the more feminine frequencies, they will unearth these internal imbalances. We are left with the choice of facing our shadow and processing it, or pushing it further into denial, where it will continue to fester and impinge our ability to channel the new light. This is true for both men and women.

Yet, as bearers of the genetic material designed to channel the feminine, it is women's dubious honor to energetically lead the way. As the women change around the new balanced frequencies, the men will naturally follow. After all, the imbalance has persisted long beyond its shelf life and is serving no one. The old ways are rapidly failing in the new light of day.

So, as women, how do we become something we have never seen before? How do we move beyond imbalances that, over the ages, have become forged in our very bones?

Fortunately, the increase of balanced energy is not only bringing up all the imbalances to be faced and cleared, but also bringing inspiration and insight for a new way of being.

Many scholars, scientists, mystics, authors, bards and poets, inspired by the increasing light of the times, are bringing forth leading edge information that can assist us on our journey.

I am personally dedicated to finding these gifted individuals of service and helping them spread their wisdom through the spoken and written word. It is my hope that, through this service, I can support our path to unity and enlightenment.

Gwilda Wiyaka is the award winning author of So, We're Still Here. Now What? Spiritual Evolution and Personal Empowerment in a New Era, and her latest book, The Science of Magic Book of Mysteries Volume 1. Considered to be an expert on the modern day application of ancient shamanic principles, Gwilda is a shamanic instructor, the founder/director of Path Home Shamanic Arts School, and has a long distance international shamanic healing practice. Gwilda has studied shamanism for over forty years, been a shamanic practitioner for more than thirty years, and a teacher of the shamanic arts since 1996. As host of Empowered Woman With Gwilda Wiyaka Radio Show, broadcast through All Women's Radio Network, Mission: Evolution Radio Show, broadcast through The 'X' Zone Broadcast Network, and Editor-In-Chief of The New Age Chronicles, Gwilda dedicates her life and career to supporting her readers, listeners, students and clients on their path to spiritual evolution and personal empowerment. For more information on Gwilda and all she offers, visit: findyourpathhome.com, missionevolution.org and ewwgw.com

How Important is Your Name?

by Sharón Lynn Wyeth

Author Malcolm Gladwell stated, "I wrote Blink because I began to get obsessed, with the way that all of us seem to make up our minds about other people in an instant - without doing any real thinking." Do we make up our minds about others because of first impressions, or does it go deeper than that? Are we subconsciously picking up something held in a person's name, which is not recognized consciously, such that we have an immediate impression of who the person is?

Currently, there is a new science on how to interpret names, which studies the placement of the letters in a name and how the letters interact with each other to reveal hidden secrets about one's character. The ability to analyze any name originated from coupling acute observation skills with a mathematically trained mind which excelled in identifying patterns.

Name interpretations, based simply on how a name was spelled, was researched and developed over a 35-year period. The science was created utilizing the fields of psychology, sociology, philosophy, statistics, and a myriad of other areas of study and disciplines. Its initial start in 1980 includes a period of fifteen years spent consciously searching for the patterns in the letter combinations in names and then matching those patterns with their corresponding vibrations. Also, three years of further testing the research was conducted in over seventy countries (including India, Russia, and China), spanning 6 continents.

Vibrations indicated behaviors, and behind those behaviors were thoughts and feelings. Lists of all observed traits that could be expressed as an adjective or adverb that could describe people with the same first name, but who had different middle and last names, were made. Commonalities were attributed to the first name and other qualities to their other names. Eventually attributes were broken down within a name and assigned to a specific letter, and later to the placement of the letter within the name. Ultimately, letter combinations were also observed to have their own qualities and characteristics.

Over time, it became apparent that the first name represented the essence of who a person was, the middle name indicated behaviors that would come into fruition when the person was under stress, and the last name indicated the environmental influence.

Other patterns soon emerged, such as procrastination occurred when the middle name was a stronger name than the first name. Some letters tended to ground a person, while others caused a person to be considered somewhat scatter brained. Other letters indicated humor, while others, discernment. When different letters were missing from a name, it indicated that those qualities, represented in the missing letters, were also missing in the personality.

Once the system was tried and tested on thousands of willing people, with a high accuracy rate based on an individual's responses, the system was shared in over seventy countries over a three year period of time. The question was, can this system of interpreting names work in languages other than English?

The answer was yes, with a few tweaks for some languages. Accent marks, umlauts, and other diacritic marks used with names needed to be interpreted. In English, the first vowel is the one heard when there is a vowel diphthong. In German, the second vowel is heard in a diphthong. Thus, the interpretation needed to have the vowels reversed to be accurate. Name interpretations were accurate in other languages with a few minor adjustments.

Name interpretations that are based on deciphering the placement of the letters in the name, and the patterns formed by combining different letters together, can determine someone's personality predispositions. In other words, what we think, feel, and how we behave can all be revealed in one's name.

The behaviors represented in the first letter of the first name are what give us our first impression. An example of this is the letter 'S' which implies the person is smart. The last letter in the first name is our lasting impression, or the first thing we will say when asked to describe an individual. When the last letter is 'Y' it indicates that the person is a chameleon and can get along with anyone that s/he wants. The key here is the desire to get along with others and to find common ground.

The first vowel in the first name reveals our communication style, what types of gifts we like to receive, how we show love for another, and our learning style. For example, people with a first vowel of 'A' show their love by doing things for another person, usually by helping them with their work. Thus, the task is either completed faster as two people were doing the work, or the quality of the completed task is better since 'two brains are better than one.'

There are multiple ways of achieving similar qualities. For example, the letters 'J', 'S' and 'W' in the first letter position of the first name, all indicate that continual learning is important to the individual. Yet, how they learn is different.

People whose first name begins with 'J' are intuitive and they just know things. Others consider these people brilliant. While people whose name begins with 'S' are school smart. They can learn anything once someone shows them the basics. However, 'S's prefer not to be micromanaged, so once s/he has caught onto an idea, s/he prefers not to be told anymore, instead wishing to discover the rest on their own. In contrast to both the 'J' and the 'S', people whose first name begins with 'W' learn through experiences. They dislike making the same mistake twice, believing in the age-old adage that wise men learn from others' mistakes, while fools learn from their own.

Interpreting a name can indicate why some individuals require clutter around them, who will be the better athletes, and who will be better at math, music or mechanics. Names also indicate who is more mentally oriented and who comes more from their heart.

Knowing how to interpret a name helps us communicate more clearly with other people in order to rapidly establish rapport. Interpreting a name involves studying the placement of the letters and how the letters interact with each other.

Names give us clues about the other person, which in turn, saves time and energy in the complicated task of getting to understand another individual. Compatibility between two people can be determined by comparing two people's names. Points of common interest are indicated, as are points of possible stress. The best part of interpreting a name is that the solutions to our challenges are there along with our potential problems.

The name a person uses indicates their personality traits, while within the birth name is their contract with the Divine which indicates one's purpose, and why one is here. We are here for many reasons, most importantly to learn to be of service to others by sharing our knowledge and to grow in consciousness. Once one knows how to read one's name, one's true purpose can be revealed.

In summary, each individual is born into this life with both talents and challenges. These gifts and challenges are indicated in one's birth name, while the personality is indicated in the name the person uses on a daily basis. Talents help the person grow, which can help provide gifts for the rest of the world. Challenges can provide a testing ground in order for the person to become strong and resilient. This can lead to having more empathy and compassion for others, as after experiencing hardships, one realizes that life may not have been easy for others as well. Every person born has something innately special to contribute to our world by sharing his or her natural born gifts.

So, when someone asks, "Who are you?" we reply with our name, as if that says it all. Indeed it does, once you know how to interpret a name.

Sharón Lynn Wyeth is the creator of Neimology® Science, the study of the placement of the letters in a name and what the letters reveal. This system is explained in detail in her bestselling book, Know the Name; Know the Person. You may contact her through her website: www.KnowTheName.com

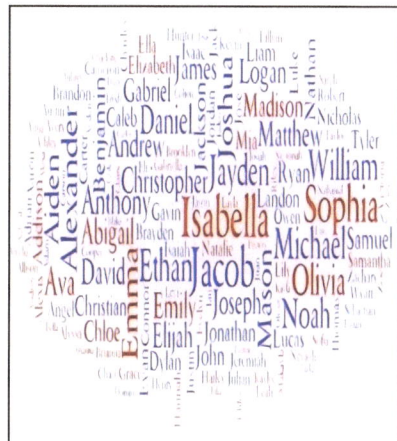

Of Earth and Sky
A Disturbance in the Force

by Cody Alexander

"I felt a great disturbance in the Force . . ."

The famous quote from Star Wars Jedi master, Obi-Wan Kenobi, raises the interesting subject of ripples in the energetic field of the universe. The "disturbance in the Force" was the death of a planet and its inhabitants, light years away. In order to have felt it, there would have to have been some sort of energetic wave created as a result of the cataclysm, moving through space, strong enough to register on the Jedi's senses.

Granted, this is science fiction. However, this particular work of science fiction refers to the concept of a universal field of energy – oneness – that we can tap into and read; that events create a kind of imprint upon/within this universal field of oneness/awareness.

This is not a new idea. Spiritual masters have long recognized the energetic connection between all of creation.

So here's the question: even if we are not spiritual masters, do all humans resonate in reaction to significant happenings on the planet, even from a great distance? Are we sensitive to solar and Earth geophysical events? Are we affected by waves of group emotion resulting from polarization and trauma?

As a shamanic practitioner, I know of clients and friends who strongly reacted to the tragedy of 9-11 without knowing what had happened. In another instance, the massive destruction caused by the 2004 tsunami in Indonesia was similarly felt by people thousands of miles away, long before it was reported on the news.

Many of us are familiar with the instant repulsion we can feel in proximity to negative energy (low frequency) in people, places or things, whether or not we know the stories behind them. Does this, too, affect us even at a distance?

What about the low frequency energies resulting from rising pollution, political upheaval, climate shifts and environmental changes? Do we have to be physically present for our body, mind, emotions and spirit to register distress, or is pain referred to another part of the world resulting from events a continent away? Are we linked more deeply to the planet and each other than we realize?

Then we have the constant exposure to sensationalist stories in the media. Does this create a general malaise we might mistakenly assume is our own?

If we accept the concept that we are all related, that everything is one, then by extension, is it possible to feel (consciously or not) everything around us, regardless of proximity?

For example, let's look at news reports. A general tendency is to believe what is presented on television or social media as truth. If we do not question the motivations or agenda behind what is reported, it is easy to react in a predictable fashion. Emotional reactions shared by those in agreement give birth to an amplified group frequency, broadcast as an aligned wave, impacting us whether we are privy to the initial information (trigger) or not. Like dominoes, we stand or fall depending on our availability or susceptibility to the frequency broadcast.

It can be easy to assume that negative group input, broadcasting as a general malaise, is our own, without necessarily realizing that it is coming from without and not within. Hence, general feelings of a negative nature can be difficult, if not overwhelming, when we do not have the reference points to determine their source.

Long story short, because of the global challenges humanity is facing, and the common denominator frequencies they generate, there can be a tendency to identify with the negativity and throw up our hands in overwhelm.

Yet if we make the effort to look beyond popular media, we can find multitudes of proactive individuals creating viable solutions to current problems, and a different picture emerges. Miracles happen every day, resulting from the determined efforts of undaunted souls who see our global challenges as an opportunity to create something new. Positive action and uplifting stories also emit a frequency, carrying the potential to counteract the all too prevalent negative overlays so pervasive today.

Japanese author, researcher and entrepreneur Masaru Emoto "published several volumes of a work entitled Messages from Water, which contain photographs of ice crystals and their accompanying experiments" as to his theory "that human consciousness has an effect on the molecular structure of water." The photographs reveal elegant crystalline structures of water exposed to positive influence, and the misshapen structures resulting from the opposite.

We are water beings, living on a mostly water planet. What kind of effect can we have if we focus the group frequency of love on our polluted waters, individual and global? The possibilities are staggeringly hopeful. Energetically, when humans are aligned through our intention and focus, we can accomplish the seeming impossible. Energetically, when we allow for possibilities outside of the norm, then space is created for alternatives heretofore unimaginable. Our belief that we can find answers to hard questions opens the space for solutions to appear. This is the frequency of possibility.

Case in point:

18 year old Boyan Slat presented at a Ted Talk in 2012. Boyan, a Dutch inventor and entrepreneur, is also an Aerospace Engineering dropout. Boyan addressed the Great Pacific Garbage Patch – a natural vortex in the ocean which has gathered plastic waste in an area the size of Texas. Many see this problem as insurmountable. But maybe not so much. Boyan introduced a radical yet viable device he designed to clean it up. Slat outlined the concept of solar powered floating booms using the natural movement of the water to gather garbage at various depths without harming marine life. The plastic could then be pulled out of the water and recycled.

As founder and CEO of the nonprofit company Ocean Cleanup, Slat "raised $2.2 million in a crowdfunding campaign, and other investors . . . brought in millions more to fund research and development. By the end of 2018, the nonprofit says it will bring back its first harvest of ocean plastic . . . from the North Pacific Gyre, along with concrete proof that the design works. The organization expects to bring 5,000 kilograms of plastic ashore per month with its first system. With a full fleet of systems deployed, it believes that it can collect half of the plastic trash in the Great Pacific Garbage Patch – around 40,000 metric tons – within five years."

In another example, Japanese inventor Akinori Ito has successfully created a household appliance (seriously) that turns plastic into fuel. "A video shows Ito placing plastic bags, styrofoam containers, and other random bits of trash into a tabletop machine that melts them and condenses the gas released to produce usable oil. The highly efficient, non-polluting machine can process polyethylene, polystyrene and polypropylene (but not PET bottles), and it can convert 2 lbs. of plastic into a quart of oil using just 1 kilowatt of power." The appliance is available through his company, Blest Corporation. How cool is that?

Recently I met a remarkable pastor who had emigrated from South America to the USA after having survived a civil war and countless challenges, in order to build a spiritual community in Colorado. His church was mobile as there was no money for a building. He had nothing to go on except his faith in the Divine, that somehow, his hard work and dedication would be supported, that things would work out in a good way.

Enter stage left, the "For Sale" property he was prompted to investigate on the remote chance he might be able to raise the necessary funds for purchase. After a discussion, the current minister at the property informed the pastor he would sell the property for the price at which it was originally purchased.

Thinking this must still be tens of thousands more than he could afford, the pastor inquired as to the amount. Ready for this? The chapel, offices and extending property, worth millions today, was sold to the pastor for $1.

I was deeply affected by his story and the simple beauty of the parish chapel and surrounds. This property and its steward is a living tale, broadcasting a frequency wave of manifested trust and faith.

Ambient frequencies are powerful. It behooves us to be discerning as to the nature of the frequencies with which we engage.

What and whom do we invite into our space? With what do we align? Are we helping or hindering? What are we amplifying through our agreement?

Generous acts of the heart, remarkable inventions, transformative and revolutionary thinking, the indomitable spirit of proactive, adventurous individuals, create beacons of hope. This generates a frequency, amplified by like-minded individuals – lights in the darkness; the possibility that together, we can make a difference in record time. []

Gran's Garden Part 2
A Children's Story

by Gwilda Wiyaka

When Thea and Tim visited Gran for Mother's Day weekend, she informed them it was time to move the seedlings they had started in pots, out into the garden. The children ran onto Grans closed porch to see how their little plants were doing.

"Gran!" Tim wailed, "My tomato plants are so long and skinny, they are about to fall over!"

"Mine too!" Thea exclaimed. "And the peppers aren't much better. Look, they are all leaning to one side."

"Not to worry, little ones," Grand assured. "They are growing tall and leaning to the window to get more sun. That's how you know it is time to put them outside. Now that it's Mother's Day weekend, the danger of frost has passed and we can put them out in the garden where they can get what they need."

"What do they need?" Tim wanted to know.

"They need direct sunshine, water, more soil, and the wind blowing on them to help strengthen their stems."

"Well, let's plant them," Thea suggested.

"We can plant them in a couple of days. First, we have to harden them off so they get used to being outside and don't go into shock when we transplant them," Gran instructed. "Let's take them out to your special raised bed garden where we planned on putting them. We will let them sit out during the day and bring them in at night to get them used to being outside."

The kids were amazed at the size of their lettuce, spinach, and snow peas they had planted in the spring. Gran promised them a fresh salad to fix with dinner. She showed them how to tell which lettuce heads, spinach plants and peas were ready to pick, and instructed them on how to carefully harvest them. You had to be careful when you picked the peas so you didn't hurt the plant and it could continue to make more. The lettuce and spinach had to be pulled up carefully so as not to disturb the roots of their neighbors. But the most important thing, Gran instructed, was to give gratitude and thank each plant for its sacrifice.

After a couple of days, Gran announced at breakfast that they could transplant the little tomatoes and peppers. Tim was so excited to get started, he wolfed down his homemade pancake so fast, he almost choked on it.

Gran helped the kids gather all they needed; garden gloves, small hand shovels and rakes, buckets of her special soil and compost mixture, complete with alpaca poo, and a watering can full of water. They took their little plants back out to their garden and set them next to the supplies. Gran showed them how to plant each plant, how far apart to put them, and where they belonged in the raised bed.

"You see, if we put the tomato plants on the west side of the spinach, they will grow tall and shade the spinach plants from the hot afternoon sun. This will help the spinach last longer, as they don't do well in the heat, but tomatoes love it."

Once the tomatoes were planted, Gran brought out wire cones from the garden shed. She called them "tomato cages" and helped the kids put one over each little tomato plant.

"Why do we have to cage them up? Will they run away?" Tim wanted to know.

"No, sweetie, they need the wire to climb on so they are supported when they get big."

"Kinda like a jungle gym?"

"Yes, just so," Gran answered with a smile.

Gran took Thea and Tim out to the chicken coop to see their little chicks, except they were not so little any more. The little fuzzy yellow chicks had done what Gran called "feathering out," and were like tall, gangly teenagers. Though they were all yellow balls of fuzz when they got them now some were red, some golden and some brown.

Gran showed the kids how to add wood shavings to the floor, and throw the scraps from the lettuce they had harvested on top. The chickens ran to the lettuce and pecked and scratched until it was mostly eaten. What they didn't eat was all shredded up with the wood shavings.

"What do we do with that mess now?" Thea asked, nose scrunched up in disgust.

"We leave it there until we clean the coop next week. That way, the chickens continue to scratch at it and make compost to add to the composter. You see, on a farm, if you do it right, everything works together," Gran shared.

"Now let's put the pea pods in the composter, add water and stir it. Then we can go inside and wash up to fix Mother's Day supper. Your mom and dad should be here soon. Aren't you excited to give your mom her gifts?"

"Yeah!" Thea and Tim exclaimed in unison, jumping up and down.

After supper, it was time to go back home with their folks. Thea and Tim tearfully hugged their beloved Gran goodbye. Gran promised to take good care of their chickens and garden until they could come back and take care of it themselves when school was out.

Finally, summer break arrived. Thea and Tim were excited to spend more time with Gran on her farm and see how their little garden and chickens were doing. Their parents' car had barely come to a stop when both children unbuckled and ran into Gran's house, the screen door slamming behind them.

"How are the chickens? Is the garden still growing?" Thea and Tim shouted in unison. "Go see for yourself while your mom, dad and I catch up," Gran instructed.

The first stop was the garden. To the

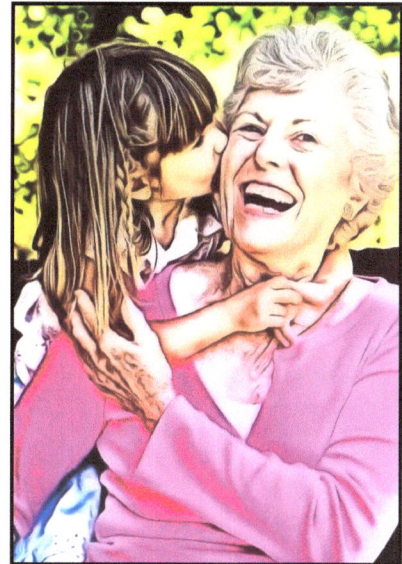

kids' amazement, it looked like a jungle. The pepper and tomato plants had flowered and were putting on little green peppers and tomatoes. The squash seeds they planted over Mother's Day weekend were huge plants, with giant leaves and big yellow flowers. The base of the flowers were becoming little squash.

"Let's go see our chickens," Tim enthused.

Both children set off at a run to the chicken coop. When they went inside, full grown chickens greeted them like old friends, clucking happily. Gran had put straw in the little boxes that were stacked up one wall. When Thea looked inside one of the boxes, she was amazed to see a little brown egg. Tim looked into another box and found a tiny green one. They carefully picked up the eggs to examine them. Something was clearly wrong. Eggs were supposed to be white and much larger. They ran back to the farm house, eggs in hand.

"I think something is wrong with our chickens," Thea sobbed to Gran. "Look, their eggs are tiny and all the wrong color!"

"How exciting, children!" Gran exclaimed. "You got to find their very first eggs! Don't worry, they always start out small. They will get larger soon. Your chickens are Buffys, Rhode Island Reds and Anacondas. Buffys and Reds lay brown eggs, and Anacondas lay pretty green ones."

Sure enough, as summer wore on, the eggs got bigger and more plentiful. Though the strange colored shells took some getting used to, the eggs inside were the same as any others, except better. They were delicious on top of their pancakes with breakfast, or scrambled with ham. The children faithfully took vegetable scraps to the chickens, cleaned the chicken coop, and put the compost the busy little birds had made into the composter for next spring. They also ground up the egg shells from breakfast and added them to the composter. They watered and weeded the garden. It continued to grow, and soon they were eating fresh summer squash, cherry tomatoes and cucumbers.

Thea decided right then and there that summer was her favorite time of year.

To be continued in the next edition of The New Age Chronicles.

In the Mirror of Nonviolence

by Michael Nagler

Anandamayi Ma, one of the greatest mystics of our time, or any time, gave us a warning we have been ignoring, at our peril:

Man appears to be the embodiment of want. Want is what he thinks about and want indeed is what he obtains. Contemplate your true being or else there will be want, wrong action, helplessness, distress and death.

The results of not being able to "contemplate our true being" are mounting now on all sides. The BBC documentary, *Century of the Self (2002)* describes how Freud's nephew, Edward Bernays, took his uncle's discoveries about the unconscious forces in the human mind and gifted them to industry and government for the twin (and closely related) purposes of advertising and propaganda. Ironically, one of the major groups to seize on this new way of manipulating human beings was the Nazi party (Freud and Bernays were of course Jewish). The film cites Paul Mazur, a leading Wall Street banker working for Lehman Brothers in 1927: "We must shift America from a needs- to a desires-culture. People must be trained to desire, to want new things, even before the old have been entirely consumed... Man's desires must overshadow his needs." We are reaching a crisis now where this distortion of human nature must be reversed. In fact, it's overdue. As Gandhi said a bit over a century ago:

A time is coming when those, who are in the mad rush today of multiplying their wants, vainly thinking that they add to the real substance, real knowledge of the world, will retrace their steps and say: 'What have we done?'

That Gandhi was concerned with this distortion is not a coincidence (for those who still believe in them). By multiplying our insatiable wants instead of gratifying our real needs, life becomes an endless conflict. One of the most successful models of conflict resolution worldwide is Marshal Rosenberg's Nonviolent Communication, and the core of his method is learning to see and bring out the real needs one is seeking to fulfill and not confusing them with the *strategies* by which we are seeking to fill them, i.e. what we or our opponent thinks we want.

Human needs are actually easily met (relatively speaking); wants, even when met, leave one unsatisfied because they are not really what one was after. Human needs are actually few in number – dignity, community, meaning and of course, the classic three physical needs for food, clothing, and shelter. In fact, the resources to meet some of these needs actually grow with use: when I respect you, my dignity increases. Wants, by contrast, multiply endlessly and the resources we think we require to fill them are exhaustible, as we are realizing now to our great distress.

Thus the key to resolving conflict and to building a sustainable economy that truly satisfies people and planet is substantially the same. In fact, to keep our eyes on our real needs as beings of mind, body, and spirit, in other words, to "contemplate our true being," as Anandamayi Ma put it, brings us to the heart of every problem of our time – and their solution.

The explosive growth of scientific thought in the West that led to industrialism on a global scale, the seductive benefits of which are now being swamped by mounting problems rising on every side, from personal to environmental, was correlated with a wrong image of ourselves – who we are, why we are here and how we are to relate, ideally, to one another and the natural world. The "story" that accompanies and made industrialism possible – the underlying narrative implicit in textbooks, newspapers and films – has us as physical beings compelled to seek satisfaction in consuming increasingly scarce resources, which of course puts us into perpetual conflict with one another and the resilience of the planet.

A shift in emphasis across many fields of modern science, aided by remarkable breakthroughs in physics at the start of the last century, has brought to light a far more hopeful picture of our nature, along with the inspiring possibility of a meaning and destiny that was concealed by the mechanistic, reductionist view of what is now called "classical science." To quote just one of the many voices heralding this change, that of quantum physicist Henry Stapp:

*The quantum conception of man resemble . . . the image set forth in various religious systems. Hence it may be able to tap the powerful resonances evoked in humans by such beliefs. . . .The assimilation of this quantum conception of man into the cultural environment of the 21st century **must inevitably produce a shift in values conducive to human survival.***

The quantum conception gives an enlarged sense of self as architect of the universe. From such a self-image must flow lofty values that extend far beyond the confines of narrow self interest. . . . With the diffusion of this quantum conception of man science will have fulfilled itself by adding to the material benefits it has already provided to man a philosophical insight of perhaps even greater value.

A little over twenty years have passed since Dr. Stapp wrote these words. That is not much time for a change of this magnitude – the remarriage of religion and science (at least mysticism and "new" science) and the complete revision of the human image! But the fact is, we don't have much time.

I want to propose that a final discovery remains to be made by those working on the "new story" liberated by these scientific breakthroughs in quantum theory and many other fields ("new" in quotes because it is actually a perennial story we're seeking to rediscover). It is the discovery of the vast potential for nonviolence in the heart of human nature. As Gandhi said, "Nonviolence is the law of our species, as violence is of the brute." We now know that violence is far from being the law of even subhuman nature; but we are still not fully aware that nonviolence is the law of our own. We are not aware of its extent, its power, its many applications – or its fundamental role in our being.

In a way, what's required is that two communities join forces, that of those developing the new story – working out the merger of science and what's called the "wisdom tradition" of all ages and its applications to our lifestyles and institutions – and those, daily increasing in number, who are exploring nonviolence on the streets and in the classroom. My own intellectual Odyssey began more on the nonviolence side. I had always been interested in the new story and began to see the ways that the scientific side of its development was weighing in as a strong support for the ways nonviolent action affect opponents and observers.

(Continued on Page 78)

KAL'S KORNER with KAL KORFF: Kal Korff has been an Analyst, Broadcaster, Commentator and Investigative Journalist on or for such popular TV networks as ABC, CNN, Discovery Channel, FOX, History Channel, MSNBC, NBC, National Geographic and has appeared on countless radio shows and in the newspapers, including National Public Radio's Science Fridays, Art Bell's Coast-to-Coast AM, Dr. Seth Shostak of SETI, Jeff Rense's Sightings, Laura Lee Show, San Francisco Examiner, Prague Post, Metropolitni Expres, Washington Post, U.S. News and World Report, Phoenix New Times, Daily Review, Argus, Huffington Post, Stanford Daily, San Jose Mercury News, Oakland Tribune, Ohlone Monitor, Omni, Skeptical Inquirer, Skepsis, True, Saga UFO Report, Beyond Reality, Fortean Times, San Francisco Chronicle, Frontiers of Science, LBC Radio, Daily World TV, RTL, DW2, TV Nova, Radio Praha, Radio Free Europe, YouTube, Scribd, Facebook, Twitter, 'X' Zone Radio Show and others. To contact Kal Korff - Email - kalkorff@xzbn.net

www.XZBN.net

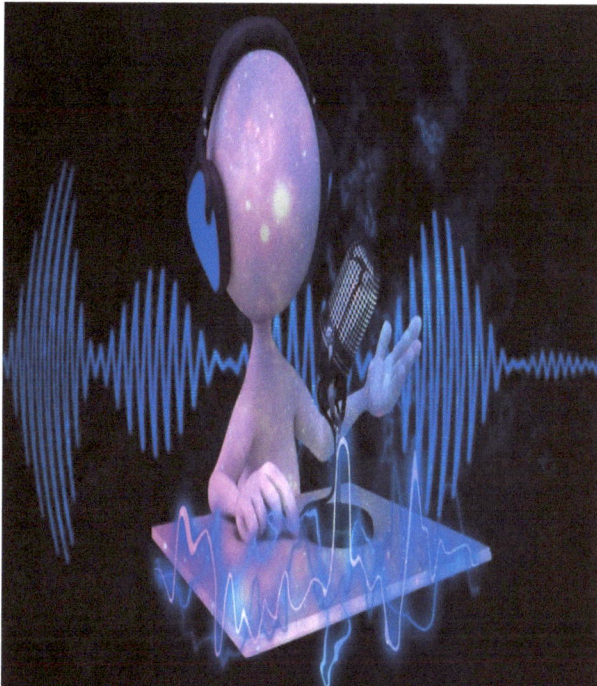

SimulRadio

Songs and Stories for Soldiers is a 501(c)(3) non-profit corporation dedicated to providing free, customizable electronic entertainment for members of the American Military, both active and retired. We will be providing MP3 players, with headsets and USB connection cable or the most recent technology, free to American Military. We will start with active duty wounded, and as their needs are met we will branch out to Veterans and VA hospitals across the United States.

songsandstoriesforsoldiers.us

In the Mirror of Nonviolence

Continued From Page 76

For example, through the discovery, in 1982, of "mirror neurons;" the network of special motor nerve cells in the central nervous system of higher primates (and possibly earlier evolutionary life forms, which await further experimentation). These cells reflect precisely the actions and attitudes of those we observe in others, so that if I respond with calm and awareness of the deeper mental state beneath an opponent's hostility, I actually evoke that deeper state through its physical representation in the other's nervous system. You don't have to be "mister nice guy" to respond to another's courage and respect; you just have to have a brain.

Generalizing from discoveries like this, it becomes clear that nonviolence is as native to the new story of humanity as violence is the besetting sin of our own – the industrial age story of separateness and materialism. The new story, conversely, must focus more centrally on what is a human being, and discover that nonviolence lies at the heart of our identity. But there is another side to all this. As Prof. Sally Goerner of the University of North Carolina has clearly said:

Since transformative change is a matter of when (not if), the real question becomes whether such change will be smooth or catastrophic. Pressure is building, and "stuckness" is everywhere (think of education).

Now, for a change of this magnitude to be effected in a way that is "smooth" rather than "catastrophic," we need a kind of power that is sufficiently strong but gentle – in other words, nonviolence. To take just one example, the Civil Rights movement. As the Montgomery bus boycott swept to its successful conclusion with the revoking of the discriminatory laws in 1955, everyone, segregationists and activists alike, braced themselves for a strong kickback. Nothing happened. Within days, as Martin Luther King describes in Stride Toward Freedom, people were acting as though segregated seating had never existed. The dictum that what seems impossible before a revolutionary change seems inevitable after it is reliably true, is that change is nonviolent.

As one writer put it, "You don't counter a myth with a pile of facts and statistics. You have to counter it with a more powerful story." For many centuries, the sages of all nations and religions have been telling us that story; that we are not these mere bodies, marvelous as they are. Swami Ramdas, who visited the U.S. in the 1950s, bore witness to this from his own realization:

On the physical plane man [sic] is but an animal. On the intellectual plane he is a rational being. On the moral plane he is a power for good. On the spiritual plane he is a radiant being full of divine light, love and bliss. Humanity's ascent from one plane to another is its natural movement.

Despite appearances, then, we are passing through a time of great possibility. Yes, problems are mounting. Yes, the institutions we might have expected to deal with them seem to be paralyzed and people at large are not yet mobilized to deal with issues of this magnitude. But the problems we face can be the occasion for a great renewal if we realize what's ultimately wrong and how we can address it. We are passing through a spiritual crisis. We've forgotten who we are and what we are meant to do here on this earth. Now, however, modern science and ancient wisdom are converging, giving us the affirmation we need from two great inquiring systems.

They are telling us why we can never be fulfilled by consuming material goods; why we can never become secure by punishing "criminals" and defeating "enemies," but only by rehabilitating those who offend and turning enemies into friends. They are telling us that the infinite differences among us are not loci of separation but manifestations of the normal diversity of life. Society, like nature, can be organized along lines of "unity in diversity" rather than those of uniformity or separation. As the Koran puts it, God has "made you into tribes and peoples so that you could discover one another," not fight against one another's welfare. In all these dimensions of the needed shift, and in the methodology needed to create that shift without invoking catastrophic ruptures, nonviolence is the key that is waiting to be discovered and practiced in every walk of life.

About the Author
Michael Nagler

Michael Nagler is Professor emeritus of Classics and Comparative Literature at UC, Berkeley, where he founded the Peace and Conflict Studies Program; Founder and President of the Metta Center for Nonviolence (www.mettacenter.org); author of Our Spiritual Crisis, The Nonviolence Handbook, and The Search for a Nonviolent Future (2002 American Book Award). Both have been translated into Arabic, Italian, Spanish, Korean, Croatian, and other languages. Other writings have appeared in the Wall Street Journal among other venues. He has spoken and written about nonviolence, meditation, and world peace for more than thirty years at campuses, public venues, and the UN, and co-hosts Nonviolence Radio bi-weekly with Metta's Executive Director, Stephanie Van Hook at KWMR, out of Point Reyes Station, CA.

Fact*oids:

- Seven out of 10 of the first domain names registered went to universities.
- The next full moon on Halloween will occur in 2020.
- The first Space Shuttle astronauts selected M&Ms as part of their food supply.
- The tongue is your strongest muscle.
- Your hair will grow almost 600 inches in your lifetime.
- The hardest substance made by your body is tooth enamel.
- A human's eye iris provides better identification than a fingerprint.
- When you sleep your brain is more active than when you are watching TV.
- There are 3 fruits native to North America: blueberries, Concord grapes, and cranberries.
- The ocean's plant life makes up 85% of all of Earth's greenery.
- Polecats are nocturnal European weasels, not cats.
- There are over 6 billion dust mites in an average bed.
- The roar of an adult lion can be heard up to five miles away.
- The average beard grows five inches (140 mm)
- Earth's automobiles are multiplying three times faster than the human population.
- A gallon of seawater contains about 1/4 pound (110g) of salt.
- Up to 50% of the world's population has neither placed or received a phone call.
- Phosphenes are the colors and stars you see when you rub your eyes.
- If you live to age 75, it is estimated you will have slept about 23 years.
- Blood travels 60,000 miles (96,540 km) a day as it circulates through the human body.
- On average you inhale 75 million gallons of air in your lifetime.
- *Jiffy* is an actual time unit: 1/100th of a second.
- Mosquitoes prefer blondes to brunettes.
- Over 99.9% of all animal species on Earth were extinct before man's arrival.

Fact*oids - Gluten Free Brain Food!

Soul Nutrients:
A Love Letter

by Kirsten Pagacz

Dear OCD,

Although you have given me quite a lot of protection over the years, you have also given me a lot of pain and suffering. When I am with you, I no longer feel good about myself. Even though our time together has been very intimate, I cannot say that it has been very healthy.

I remember one of the many times when I was a young child and I was left in the care of my dad. Frequently he was high on weed, or tripping on LSD, his distant pink pinwheel eyes provided no sense of safety or love. You were there to give me something to hold onto when the ground beneath me felt unstable. You gave me my own world to escape into. A private world where nothing except you and I existed. You gave me a real sense of something to do with myself and my manifested unbridled anxiety. On days where no one else was around, you were there, always.

One of the things that you provided for me was taking away any boredom that I could have experienced. For instance, on an airplane ride, rather than being in the moment of a long and tiresome flight, you gave me so many things to think about that I really didn't experience boredom, ever.

But you gave me unsolvable riddles and that really wasn't fair. You captured my attention tens of thousands of times, and even when I wanted to look away more than anything else in the world, I was frozen. YOU decided when the next minute of my life could begin. I no longer want to give you that power.

Hundreds of times when I wanted to be available and present with my family or friends, you stole away my mind and my time. You left my spirit to feel just like a ragged sheet blowing in the wind. I was only a small percentage of myself, just hanging on, faking it, and trying to get by. I always felt undernourished. You took away my shine and I am going to get it back, come hell or high water.

I guess what I am saying OCD, is that it is time to break up. I can't dodge my life anymore. I am done living in fear. I am done responding to a false reality that you have methodically crafted so perfectly just for me. You are too all consuming and I have other things to do than run back to you again and again and again to your empty arms that used to control me.

What used to seem like some sort of haven, is no longer healthy for me and it can be argued that it never was. I am determined to find new things to do with my life and my time. My goal is to feel uninterrupted joy and find a way to love myself even when I feel misshapen.

I want real peace of mind, not just an empty prize that you promise after demanding my attention and making me do weird stuff in such a shameful way.

I want to access my creative brain juice and live within the spirit that God gave me and put my energies towards good things now, things that I value. This IS the fork in the road where I say good bye. Thanks for all you have done, thanks for trying to protect me, even in your very strange and controlling way.

Good luck and goodbye and, in an incredibly twisted way, thanks for being my friend all these years. My most distracting friend that manipulated me and injected me with daily terror. You have beaten me down and I want to be built up and not so damn fearful all the time. I want to feel available, feel good about myself and worth something.

I am built for love and I am built for purpose and I am finding my way. Yes, I am certain that it will get lonely sometimes without you, but I would rather stand naked and vulnerable by myself than in your jurisdiction of maddening illusions a minute longer.

I must go, because I know you won't.

Wishing you progress and peace of mind. As always, if you wish to communicate with me further, after any of these "Soul Nutrients," my email is ocdrelief@retroagogo.com.

Thanks for being on this journey with me.

Warmly,
Kirsten Pagacz

About the Author: Kirsten Pagacz is the author of Leaving the OCD Circus and the founder of Retro-A-Go-Go, an online seller of retro kitsch. She suffered from OCD for two decades before discovering that it had a name (and a cure). Leaving the OCD Circus reveals the raw story of Pagacz's traumatic Childhood and the escalation of her disorder – demonstrating how OCD works to misshape a life from a very young age – and explains the various tools she used for healing, including meditation, cognitive behavioral therapy, yoga, exposure therapy, and medication.

Website: www.kirstenpagacz.com

The Born Aware Phenomenon

by Diane Brandon

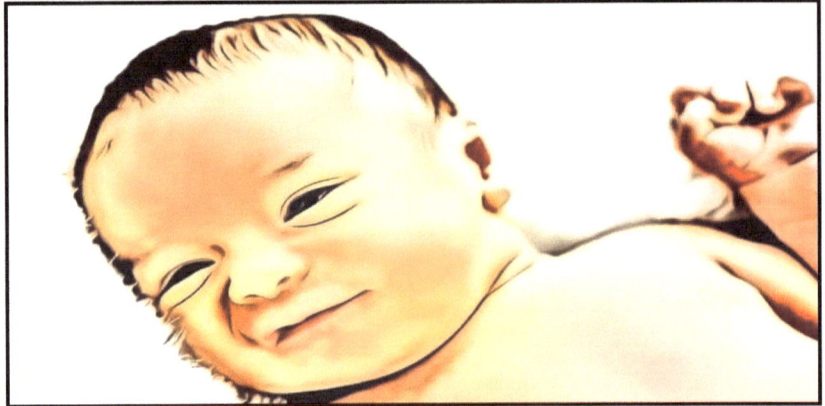

What is your earliest memory? Do you remember anything before the age of 1 – or 2 – or 3 – or 4? Most people don't. However, some of us do.

I have always remembered what I thought when I was born. I kept these thoughts to myself and never knew that this was unusual. This was my norm and I never even wondered whether others had similar memories or not.

What I thought when I was born was spiritual in nature (for example remembering being with God before coming here) and the knowledge that being here was both temporary and necessary. In other words, I was spiritually aware from the moment I was born, in a clear manner and with a mature awareness and consciousness. This is the Born Aware phenomenon.

It wasn't until much later in life that I began to realize that my at-birth memories were unusual. I later encountered two other people who, independently of each other, spontaneously shared their own at-birth memories with me in a short period of time. I knew that I was being given a message to write about this phenomenon and began to embark upon a journey of investigation into this phenomenon.

This was the seed for my book, Born Aware: Stories & Insights from Those Spiritually Aware Since Birth. I have found several other people with memories like this and know that there are more of us out there.

So what is "The Born Aware Phenomenon"? And why should we pay attention to it?

The Born Aware Phenomenon refers to people who have literally been spiritually aware from the moment they were born. We remember what we thought when we were born and our thoughts were typically spiritual ones: knowing that we're here on this planet temporarily and that it's not our true home; remembering the other side to varying degrees; and a whole range of spiritual, non-earth-bound thoughts and perceptions.

Our memories of our at-birth thoughts have stayed with us. We have never forgotten what we thought when we were born – and we never needed to resort to external or artificial means or modalities in order to uncover our at-birth thoughts. In other words, we didn't need to use regression, rebirthing, hypnotherapy, or any other modality in order to uncover or discover our natal awareness. We have simply never forgotten that awareness and those thoughts.

Some people may confuse being born aware with being psychic or intuitive, because they may assume that if one is highly intuitive or can see or speak to spirits one must have been born aware. This is simply not true. Psychic and intuitive gifts are a faculty or ability of the consciousness and neither depend upon nor a priori include nor spring from a spiritual awareness (or memories of the other side or spiritual advancement).

The same is true of children who remember past lives. A great deal of research has been conducted over the years into children who spontaneously remember their past lives and may, at times, continue to feel that they are still the same person from a recent past life. Children who remember past lives are not necessarily born aware nor necessarily spiritually aware. They simply have a memory of their previous lifetime and may still be in the persona of that lifetime.

The born aware phenomenon is also distinct from the phenomenon of those who are innately spiritually oriented. By spiritually oriented, I am referring to people who have always felt a spiritual orientation and/or awareness that this earthly reality was not the only reality. They tend to have a subtle awareness that this planet is not their true home. There are many, many people who are innately spiritually oriented. They tend to take quite naturally to spiritual topics as soon as they are exposed to them. They tend to feel like outsiders or like strangers in a strange land. They often become spiritual healers or intuitives or spiritual practitioners or work in helping professions as adults. Many also typically feel that they are lightworkers who are here on a mission and/or to heal others.

However, they typically lack the at-birth awareness that those born aware have, as well as some of the attributes that born awares share. The born aware phenomenon refers to those people who have always remembered what they thought when they were born and their spiritual awareness at birth – pure and simple. The awareness we have at birth is clear and mature. It is not at all infantile or undeveloped or whatever one may consider the awareness of a baby to be. It is also devoid of a human personality – which, of course, has not yet developed.

I use the term Higher Soul Awareness to refer to our at-birth consciousness. It's the consciousness that we have as souls when we're not here on this planet – or incarnated elsewhere -- and that we had on the other side before being born. It's distinctly different from our human persona and our human type of consciousness, which it transcends. Those of us born aware flit back and forth throughout our lives between our human side and our Higher Soul Awareness. We're hybrids, neither completely here nor there (on the other side). (I discuss the Higher Soul Awareness more extensively in my book and share some recommendations on how to groom that awareness.)

There are many attributes that those born aware tend to have in common, such as our innate spiritual awareness that is a split awareness, an innate awareness of and trust in spiritual agency and protection, an innate awareness (and memory) of the inter-connectedness of everything and everyone, an implicit awareness that we're here to do or accomplish specific tasks, an innate and deep sense of integrity and ethics – and more. (These are shared and discussed in my book.)

There are also many lessons to be learned from the born aware phenomenon. First of all would be the acknowledgment that there are different types of human consciousness, which don't emanate solely from our physical brains or physiology. Babies can indeed be aware and, at times, may have an awareness that is more mature than that of their parents or adults around them (if the latter are primarily in their human personas).

The phenomenon definitely shows us that this reality on earth is not the only reality and that consciousness does indeed transcend the physical. It teaches us that there is indeed another "side" or "heaven" – a "place" that exists outside of our earthly reality that is quite real, irrespective of the terms we used to refer to it. We indeed don't die when our bodies die. We indeed, as well, existed before we were physically born on earth into a human body.

There are many spiritual lessons and implications from the born aware phenomenon as well, which I detail in my book, Born Aware. This is what the born aware phenomenon is and the benefits that learning about it can bring us.

It's a very real phenomenon, as I well know, and deserving of wider knowledge.

About the Author: Diane Brandon is an Integrative Intuitive Counselor, teacher, former radio host, and coach, as well as the author of Born Aware: Stories & Insights from Those Spiritually Aware Since Birth, Intuition for Beginners: Easy Ways to Awaken Your Natural Abilities, Dream Interpretation for Beginners: Understand the Wisdom of Your Sleeping Mind, and Invisible Blueprints. Born and raised in New Orleans, she has an A.B. from Duke University and did Master's work at University of North Carolina. Her website is www.dianebrandon.com.

How Can We Receive Guiding Visions From the Universe?

by Sara Wiseman

When you start to follow Divine guidance, you begin to experience life differently.

You recognize that all the plans you have made and all the thoughts you are thinking are ways of moving through this reality we call life.

This is the way most of the world moves.

But you also realize that this left brain, rational way of thinking is not the only way you can walk your path.

There is another option.

You can follow your intuition. Or better put: You can allow yourself to be guided.

The path of no path

At first, the idea of following your intuition – really following it as a spiritual practice, even if it makes no sense or goes against the plans you have made – seems like a phenomenally foolish idea.

Why on earth would we walk blind, when we can rely on our rational, logical thinking brain?

Why would we wander in the desert of unknowing, waiting for guidance that is subtle at best, confusing at worst, when we can instead charge forward with certainty, sticking to our plan, sticking to the way that others, the media, our culture, our society, tells us is the right way to go?

Why would we walk the path of no path?

That's when we want to have a clear understanding of how, exactly, to access Divine guidance.

Accepting your soul reality

When we accept that we are souls first, it becomes easy to understand that we are fully able to communicate with the Universe at a soul level, at any time we need.

It is no mystery, it is no great technique!

• We do it when we sleep and dream.
• We do it when we are daydream.
• We do it when we practice lucid dreaming
• We do it when we spend time in nature.
• We do it when we meditate.
• We do it when we pray.
• We do it when we are engaged in c r e a t i v e Flow.
• We do it when we connect deeply with another.
• We do it sometimes, when we are simply being, fully present to the moment.

At all of these times, we move outside of or lift off from our rational, logical, left brained selves, and lock into the hum of Universal vibration.

And, here is the key:

You cannot reach Divine guidance, unless you are able to enter into this state of gentle trance.

You can't get there from your normal mind that is busy with fear and anger and anxiety and panic.

You have to lift out of those states of being, into a state of being where you are aligned with Universal vibration. You have to lock into the hum.

Many doors will open

Having direct connection with the Divine: with all the guides and angelic beings and the visions and messaging that will show you the way, is like walking up to a big house, opening an unlocked door, and walking in.

It's really that easy.

But which door?

Sometimes you want to go in the front door, sometimes the side, sometimes the back, sometimes you might want to climb in through a window!

Each door or window or other opening will have you entering a different area of Divine connection.

You don't need to be concerned about where you'll end up; the Divine will determine that for you.

But if you want a vision, you'll ask for a vision in a certain way. If you want a message, that will come in that way. If you want direct connection with a guide, that will come in another way.

Again, the first way of going up to the house, is always to enter a light trance state. To lift yourself up from this reality, and to raise vibration or shift field so that you inhabit another reality. Relaxation is the key

Sometimes people attempt to do this with breathing techniques; this is great. But breathing a particular way is simply a technique to get you in the door.

• Others use mantra, or music.
• Some use meditation tapes.
• Some gaze at a candle.
• Some access this state when they are drifting to sleep.

Again... these are all ways in...these are all the doors that you can use to help you reach this trance state.

But after a while, when you've been in this light trance state enough times, and by enough times I mean ten times or 100 times, or 1000 times or 10,000 times, you become able to access this state very quickly.

It becomes as easy as closing your eyes, taking a few breaths in through the nose, and allowing yourself to enter in.

Familiarity with the trance state

One of the reasons it becomes easy, is because once you have visited this "house," this particular layer or level of Divine vibration a few times, you recognize what it feels like to have entered in.

You begin to understand when you're in too deep of a trance – in which case you'll probably fall asleep. Or when you in too light of a trance – in which case all your thoughts will bombarded with judgment about what you're doing.

You begin to understand when you have reached a psychic sweet spot: in deep, but not too deep.

One of the ways you will know you are in this sweet spot, is that visions will begin to arrive in your mind's eye, without your creating them.

You may believe you are imagining them, but this is not so. As you follow and allow and watch these imaginings in your mind's eye, you will notice that they begin to take on a power of their own.

Familiarity with the trance state

One of the reasons it becomes easy, is because once you have visited this "house," this particular layer or level of Divine vibration a few times, you recognize what it feels like to have entered in.

You begin to understand when you're in too deep of a trance – in which case you'll probably fall asleep. Or when you in too light of a trance – in which case all your thoughts will bombarded with judgment about what you're doing.

You begin to understand when you have reached a psychic sweet spot: in deep, but not too deep.

One of the ways you will know you are in this sweet spot, is that visions will begin to arrive in your mind's eye, without your creating them.

You may believe you are imagining them, but this is not so. As you follow and allow and watch these imaginings in your mind's eye, you will notice that they begin to take on a power of their own.

How visions will appear

They will, as you wait and relax and stay in trance, begin to show you a truth, or a possibility that you can create, or an outcome in the near future, or an outcome in a longer future.

They may show you the possibility that you are now creating – if you're creating a negative experience, you might see this as a warning. If you're creating a positive experience, you will see this as support.

Or they may show you a higher possibility than you might have imagined; one that fills your heart will love and joy.

By "they," I mean all the ways that they might show up: as guides, as angels, as the departed, as other energy, as message, as knowing and as vision.

Visions are energy universes that arrive as pictures in the mind; sometimes as simple pictures, like you might picture something simple in your mind – an ear of corn, a large beetle, a blue flower.

As you get more adept at holding the visual energy in your mind, these visions become more complex: you may experience as a memory but of the future, or as imagination that you are not creating, or as if you are watching a movie in your mind.

Sometimes, the visions are so clear and real and we are so engaged with them, we enter the visions: we project our energy body or energy Universe into this vision reality, and experience it fully.

The way is yours

As you begin your journey of following Divine guidance, you will move through many levels:

At first, you will access guidance via simple synchronicities, etheric messages, Convergences. As you practice, and as you spend time in this most relaxed state of light trance, you will begin to receive, experience and inhabit visions that are both very simple and very complex.

There is no way to learn, except to try it for yourself. There is no teacher who can teach you, more than you can learn yourself, simply by trying, failing, trying again.

The more you relax and let go, the more you can access this state.

The more often you access this state of "entering in," or locking into the hum, the more you will be able to receive visions.

The more you are able to receive visions, the deeper your understanding of your soul self will become.

Begin today. Close your eyes now. Take a deep breath. Then another. Allow yourself to enter in to Universal vibration. See what information awaits you now. []

The Importance of Shadow Work on the Path of Enlightenment

by Morrighan Lynne

Born perfect, our soul enters this material world with a set of plans, goals, and intentions. With all the excitement the cosmos can muster, we leave our spiritual home for the adventure that only this world can provide. We have things to do and can't wait to get started.

Unfortunately, it doesn't take too long to realize that not everyone supports our trajectory.

Diving head first into a sea of obligations, social requirements, limiting beliefs, and responsibilities, it's a wonder we ever remember the original plan of our soul. We are the proverbial babes in the woods, completely at the mercy of our caregivers and surrounding circumstances. As time beats on, life can beat us down.

Oftentimes, it can feel like we're standing in the ocean trying to get our footing, but those waves just keep coming. The crashing water sucks us under as we fight to catch our breath before the next wave comes. Over time, we become unrecognizable from that little fiery-headed child we once knew ourselves to be. As we struggle to navigate this human life, we eventually begin to forgo the plans of our soul and succumb to the survival of our physicality. This is the typical journey of a human on this planet. We are born with dreams to make come true, with adventures written in our soul. And yet, before we can actualize those dreams and set those plans into motion, we are stripped of our passion and fire. We are domesticated and trained to be consumers, to be a part of the machine. Simply living to get through life.

But then one day, something stirs from deep within. Like the embers of a dying fire, the coals shift and the wind picks up. There is still life in those smoldering remains. The knowing that we are more than an empty shell begins to awaken. The tiny fire that was perhaps extinguished flickers back into existence. And before we know it, we find ourselves asking the bigger questions that enliven our mind and ignites our soul. Instantly, we crave for more. More of what, we aren't sure. But it is more, nonetheless.

But where do we start, how do we give ourselves over to it? How do we trust the inner navigation when it has been mocked and scorned for so many years? How are we ever to rise above the domestication and trust the inner wisdom within? And in that moment, the search begins.

Awareness is funny that way.

We didn't know we were living a small life until we gathered the awareness that we wanted to be more. It's in that contrasting distinction that panic can set in, leading us to the belief that something is missing, that we must find whatever was taken from us. We frantically search the globe for the hidden treasures that will heal our broken hearts and make whole our lacking soul. This is the first response to our awakening.

After a while, we move towards our next course of action in the awakening process: to swing hard in the other direction. We over-exaggerate our positivity, thinking that if we train ourselves to only say loving things that it will counterbalance our negative experiences.

Oftentimes, we get trapped in the game of saying sugary-sweet affirmations and downplaying any instance that does not reflect the language of our newfound spiritual path. This over-acting in the "Love and Light" aspect can cause just as much imbalance within the whole being as when we only focus on the negative aspects of life. Anytime we give too much attention to one side or the other, we are out of alignment with our wholeness.

I see many spiritual practitioners and New Age seekers being afraid to acknowledge the not-so-great aspects of humanity. They close their minds to conversations that are anything but positivity and uplifting messages. It seems that if they acknowledge that such things exist, they believe it will open them up to negative forces, or that they will fall from the "positive pedestal" that has been constructed. And when that pedestal comes tumbling down, it can lead to a loss of faith, igniting the ego with fear of being wrong, and opens us up to being judged by others (and ourselves).

So, if living in victim-mode is too limiting, and jumping over to play with unicorns and slide down rainbows is unrealistic, what are we left with? How can we attain the healing and wholeness we are seeking?

The answer is…shadow work.

This sacred process is the bridge between who we were and who we want to be. It beautifully connects the past with the future in a supportive way, rather than feeling shame for what we've done and pretending that everything is perfect.

If we look into our past and feel ashamed for who we've been, but then try to "create" the person we want to be without healing those wounds, we will end up feeling like a phony representation of our ideal human. It never fully feeds our soul and will further exacerbate the false belief that we are not already whole. Pretending to be the person we think is acceptable never fully aligns us to our true self. So what is shadow work?

Shadow work is the process of sifting through the pieces and parts of ourselves that we have hidden away our whole lives. As children, we learned to hide them for safety. Much like if you broke your mother's favorite vase, but you threw it in the garbage before she found out. You hid the broken pieces for fear of repercussions. Well, we do that in everyday life.

We are so afraid of judgment and rejection, we'll push down anything we fear might "give us away" to the people we admire, respect, and love. We identify these "unacceptable" components and shove them down, deep inside, so that others can't see how ugly we feel about ourselves.

Shadow work is the process of acknowledging those pieces we've hidden away and accepting them as a part of our wholeness. They are the wounds that we have left to fester, because it was just too painful to deal with them at the time. They are the attributes we don't feel we deserve, so we cut them away and denied their beauty.

It is anything and everything we feel shame around and just simply don't have the tools to heal them properly. In order to survive, we have learned this extremely efficient, albeit unhealthy, coping mechanism.

It takes a brave soul to open up those doors and peek into the darkness. We have thrown them away our whole lives for a reason…it was just too difficult to face. But it's in the acknowledgment that they even exist which allows them to begin the healing process.

When we are brave enough to face all that we've been, we can truly step into all that we want to be. By embracing the wounds, giving them a voice, and hearing their stories, they find peace. And in peace, there is freedom.

It can be scary work. We don't always want to see the things that hurt us. But if we can simply be the space for these wounded parts to be acknowledged, let a little light shine down on them, they'll begin to unravel the subconscious beliefs that they are unworthy of love. And when we believe we are worthy of love, we allow love into our lives.

We cannot heal what is wounded by simply being positive and ignoring that the wounds exist. It will not go away if we avert our eyes and deny their existence. And on the flip side, admitting that you have wounds does not make you a negative person.

There is a middle space, where speaking the truth about your situation and yet remaining proactive in your own healing process, that can catapult you to the next level of your life. In this grand quest of enlightenment, truly the way to achieve it is by being in alignment with all that you are.

Embrace the path that got you to this point. Honor the experiences that have molded and shaped you. Be grateful for the bumps and bruises, but do not hold them captive. Only in the acceptance of all you were, will you find out who you can truly be.

About the Author
Morrighan Lynne

Morrighan Lynne is a renowned Spiritual Medium, Psychic Empath, Clairvoyant, Intuitive Coach, Ordained Minister, Paranormal Investigator, and published author. Lately, her focus has been on shadow work and helping fellow empaths embrace their superpowers. Her new book is called The Spirited Human; Proactive Tools for a Reactive World. Filled with personal stories, comedic ah-ha's, and practical spiritual teachings, The Spirited Human is the handbook for us all. Part instruction manual for being human and part road map for navigating the soul, Morrighan Lynne takes you on a journey back to your true self.

Website: www.morrighanlyn.com

'Easy prey': How a massive psychic fraud gained its power

By Blake Ellis and Melanie Hicken, CNN Investigates

CNN journalists Blake Ellis and Melanie Hicken have spent years investigating one of the largest consumer frauds in history -- a case that has stumped global investigators for decades. The scheme, which duped victims out of millions of dollars with letters claiming to be from a famous French psychic named Maria Duval, is the subject of the reporters' new true crime book, "A Deal with the Devil." The following excerpt has been edited for brevity.

Chrissie will never be sure when exactly her mother got her first letter from Maria Duval or how she became a target.

What she does know is that in the months leading up to her mother's eightieth birthday, before Chrissie or even Doreen realized that Alzheimer's disease was slowly and silently infiltrating her once rational mind, Doreen had handwritten at least forty different checks in response to Maria's letters, which Doreen believed were ending up with the psychic.

Chrissie suspects that her mother's obsession with these letters had far more to do with gambling on a cure for her failing mind than with winning a financial jackpot. In fact, Chrissie would later find evidence of an internal battle that Doreen hid from her children for years. She'd kept a Reader's Digest book full of brain games promising to keep her mind sharp. Not a single page was completed. And in her small personal address book was a page where she incorrectly wrote her son's phone number over and over again. On other pages, she furiously wrote her son's name repeatedly, sometimes followed by the words, "I kneed (sic) new shoes," and "Help me."

"You could see the pressure of the pen. Obviously she was angry with herself," Chrissie said. "To have a glimpse into somebody's mind like that -- how difficult it was for her to figure out a phone number that she has phoned for so many years. It's scary."

We leafed through the pages of this small book as we talked to Chrissie. And though we had never met Doreen, it was painful for us to read these outbursts from a woman so trapped in her own mind. But this all came later. The first time Chrissie began to realize how bad things had gotten was in the winter of 2010, when she helped her mother go through all the paperwork that had been building up in the condo where Doreen lived alone.

It was all so out of character. Doreen was once frugal and practical to a fault, owning her own successful business and managing her family's finances at a time when few women did so. Now she seemed to have become an entirely different person. Doreen's children found buried within the piles of coupons, magazines, junk mail, and the occasional misplaced sock a bill from a department store credit card with a shockingly high balance. Concerned, Chrissie dug into the rest of her mother's finances. And when she turned to her mother's bank statements, she saw a disturbing number of payments to two names she didn't recognize: Destiny Research Center (while this name would remain a mystery to Chrissie, it would become very important to us) and Maria Duval. Every check was made for the same precise amount of $59 (in Canadian dollars).

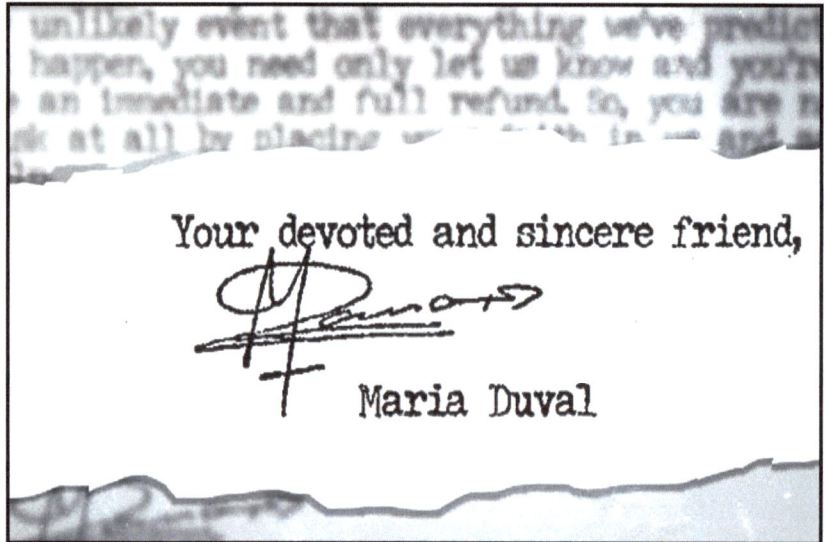

"Who is this? What is this place? What are you getting for this money?" Chrissie asked her mother.

Suddenly, her mother's pleasant demeanor was gone. She turned defensive and secretive, and simply shrugged in response to Chrissie's questions and admonishments. "She was unable -- not unwilling, but unable -- to specify what she was getting in return for this amount of money," Chrissie remembers. "She finally showed me large round metal talismans encased in little velveteen pouches with symbols and some with motivational words or astrological signs on them."

It was soon evident to Chrissie that the cheap trinkets and the mysterious woman from the letters were an inescapable presence in her mother's life.

When Doreen was at her best, Chrissie convinced her that the letters were a terrible scam that was stealing her retirement savings. This realization took a huge toll on Doreen. "She was shocked, dismayed, and ashamed when she realized her stupidity and the financial damage she'd caused herself," Chrissie said. "I gave Mum strict orders to throw away anything from Maria Duval or Destiny Research; she seemed to understand my frustration and anger (at this scam) and readily agreed."

Still, as her memory declined, Doreen returned to her secretive relationship with Maria, almost like a child hiding a secret stash of candy from her parents.

Even after Chrissie and her brothers took away Doreen's checkbooks and assumed legal responsibility for her finances, she would cobble together piles of cash and coins to make up the amount Maria was requesting from her.

From two years' worth of bank statements, Chrissie is certain that Doreen sent at least $2,400 to the psychic. Her total losses were likely much larger.

"These scammers seem to have targeted my mother as easy prey, probably from the very first check she sent to them," Chrissie told us. "Not only was my poor mother quickly losing her mind due to Alzheimer's disease, she was lonely, bored, (and) wanting to be wealthy and well. She didn't have the quality of mind anymore to realize how much money she was losing or how often she was sending money!"

Finally, knowing that the painful tug-of-war with her mother wasn't going to get her anywhere, Chrissie turned her anger and frustration to Maria. She reported the crime to the police, but they told her there was little they could do to help recover any of the money Doreen had given away. So she sent letter after letter to the address on the solicitations, tersely demanding a refund ("of any amount -- even just $59.00 to show good faith") and for Doreen's name to be stripped from the mailing list. Her efforts proved fruitless. So Chrissie's brother finally resorted to forwarding Doreen's mail to his own home, where he could sort through all the junk mail and scam letters, keeping only the bills and other important documents. At one point, he received thirty-six scam letters in a single day, all addressed to Doreen.

As Chrissie's brother handled all the mail, Chrissie turned into an armchair detective, scouring the internet in an attempt to uncover which heartless criminals had gotten their hands on her mother's hard-earned money.

"It was painful. Then it was frustrating. Then I just grew angry," Chrissie said. "I'm not an angry person by any means. It takes a lot to get me mad but, boy oh boy, to find out how long they had taken advantage of this woman who believed that she was getting something for her money."

Chrissie spent months trying to get to the bottom of the fraud.

When her mother passed away a few years later, roughly a year before we began our own hunt for answers, Chrissie still had no idea who was behind the Maria Duval letters.

(Continued on Page 88)

THE
FUN
OF DYING
FIND OUT WHAT REALLY HAPPENS NEXT

Foreword by
Victor Zammit, Ph.D

ROBERTA GRIMES

THE
FUN
OF GROWING FOREVER
WE CAN'T TRANSFORM THE WORLD UNTIL WE TRANSFORM OURSELVES

Foreword by
Jack Canfield

ROBERTA GRIMES

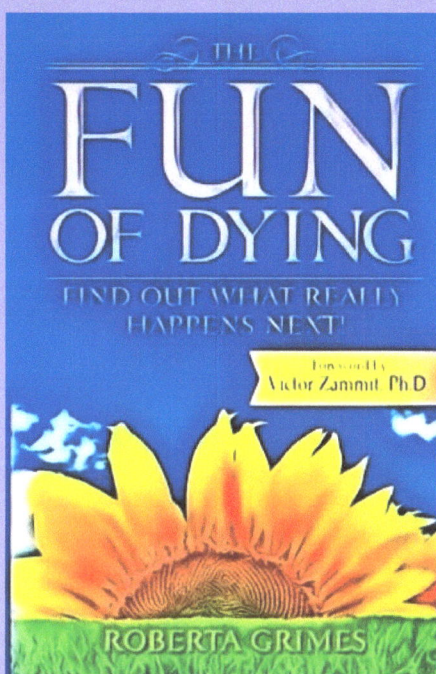

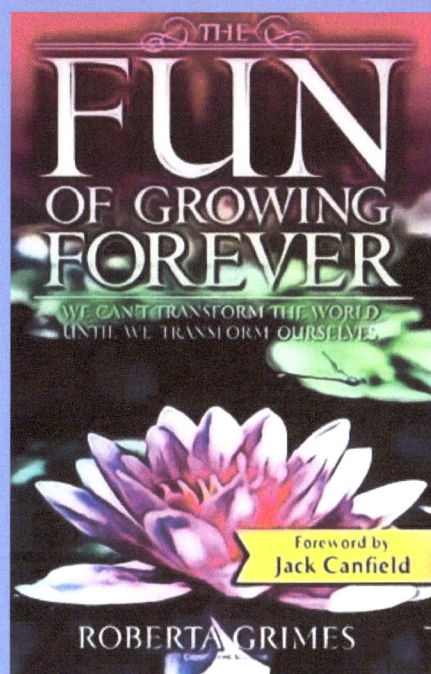

www.RobertaGrimes.com

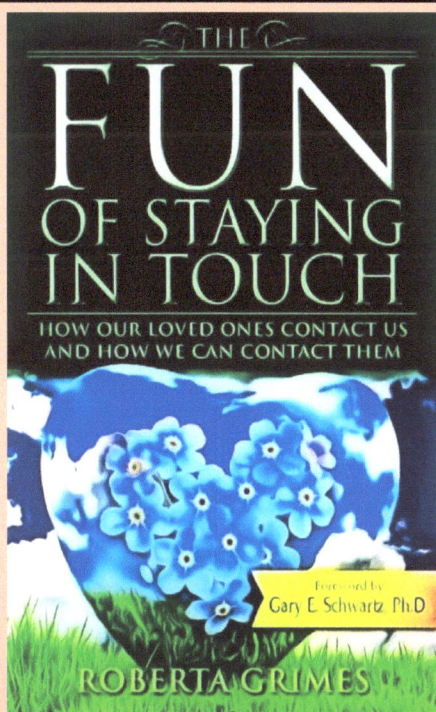

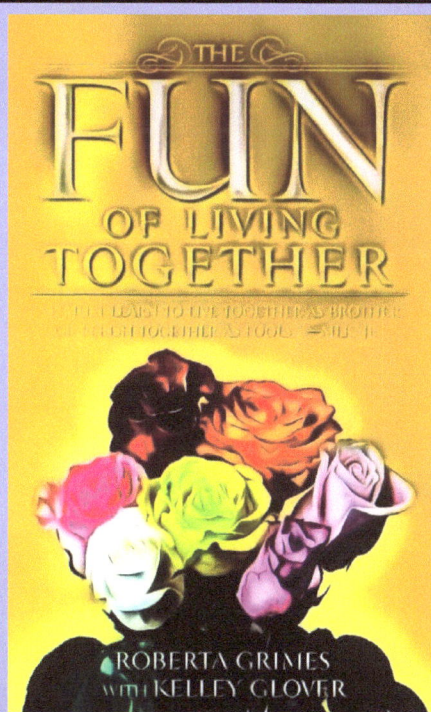

www.RobertaGrimes.com

THE
FUN
OF STAYING IN TOUCH
HOW OUR LOVED ONES CONTACT US AND HOW WE CAN CONTACT THEM

Foreword by
Gary E. Schwartz, Ph.D

ROBERTA GRIMES

THE
FUN
OF LIVING TOGETHER
WE'LL LEARN TO LIVE TOGETHER AS BROTHERS OR PERISH TOGETHER AS FOOLS —M.L.K.

ROBERTA GRIMES
with KELLEY GLOVER

www.RobertaGrimes.com

www.RobertaGrimes.com

'Easy prey': How a massive psychic fraud gained its power

Continued From Page 86

Maria's victims are all over the world, but they have one thing in common: desperation. We found stories from her victims everywhere we looked -- online, in old newspaper clippings, and in the many government documents detailing the scam.

Many of the victims reminded us of Doreen: Suffering from illnesses that were chipping away at their brains. Lonely after spouses and friends had passed away. Living on a fixed income and worried about everyday bills or the money they were going to be able to leave behind.

"He is so desperate for money that he pins all his hopes on this," one person wrote online about their 96-year-old father-in-law, who refused to believe that the letters were a scam and even tried to send a cash payment after his family closed his bank account.

In a letter to Maria that was found by US authorities, another victim wrote that she was in such serious financial straits that she was struggling to afford new glasses or a dentist appointment. She apologized to Maria for not writing more often, telling her that she was "in distress" with back problems. "I am getting more broke every day. I can't send what I don't have." We wanted to understand why these people were the perfect targets. So we called Dr. Peter Lichtenberg, a clinical psychologist and the director of Wayne State University's Institute of Gerontology, who has studied the financial exploitation of the elderly and the underlying psychology of scams for years.

"It's a combination of loneliness, depression, and a real sense of invisibility," he told us when we asked him what made people fall for a scam like the Maria Duval letters. This isolation and psychological vulnerability creates the perfect setting for a scammer to enter people's lives. As they are feeling invisible to society and even to their own families, suddenly someone out there -- in this case, a woman who looks so trustworthy and kind from her photo alone -- has chosen them and is giving them the attention they have been missing.

For those who feel like they have lost their sense of self, this scam makes them feel important. The promises of financial windfalls also tap into the overwhelming desire at this stage in people's lives to be able to create a legacy for future generations.

To make matters worse, many people suffering from dementia are more likely to become secretive or suspicious of their own family members, especially if those individuals are attempting to pry into their finances or personal lives. This makes someone like Maria, whose letters profess love for who they are and an understanding of everything they're going through, that much more attractive. And it makes it even harder for families to break through.

The Maria Duval scam reminds Dr. Lichtenberg of a cult in the way that it creates a special relationship with its victims that is entirely resistant to logic. "The key is almost cult indoctrination. ... They're so far in, you have to cut the contact off in order for them to come back to reality, he said. "It's the leader, the belief in this person, in this woman and her magical gifts and her specialness."

Hearing this, we thought about how family members told us about letters warning victims to keep their relationship with Maria a secret, one that outsiders simply wouldn't understand. Dr. Lichtenberg said that even mild symptoms of aging can affect someone's ability to reason -- a person doesn't need to have severe cognitive impairment.

Deteriorating memories can also play a role in an individual's susceptibility to such a scam, as many victims are unable to estimate just how much money they've been sending. Some of Maria's victims weren't elderly or cognitively impaired at all. Rather, they were simply lonely. And others just seemed more easily persuadable, trusting to a fault.

"I have sent this woman lots of my money where I could not pay my bills," a mother of five wrote in an online consumer complaint forum in 2014, saying that she was living on a fixed income and thought that sending money to Maria would help bring about a better life for her children. "Yes I feel like a fool, but when you receive (these) letters over and over you feel like a failure if you did not send it in to get a better life for your children." In another online complaint, a woman from Michigan recounted how Maria's letters had come to her in some of her darkest days -- soon after she separated from her husband, lost her job, and said a hard goodbye to her son, who had joined the military. "This scam crushed the last bit of hope I had in any kindness or miracle that could be, and pushed me over the edge," she wrote. "Congrats! You got another weak one."

It wasn't surprising for Dr. Lichtenberg to hear that it wasn't just the elderly who were being duped by this scam. The same desperation can attack anyone's judgment, he told us, whether someone is dealing with a death in the family, job loss, financial misfortune, or depression. "The human condition is not all that different throughout life," he said. "People get the feeling of invisibility and think, 'This is not what life should be, this is not what I expected life to be.'"

In some cases, Maria's letters have taken a more sinister tone, suggesting that misfortune awaited those who ignored her. In 1997, one woman told the Scottish Sunday Mail newspaper that she was terrified of what would happen if she didn't send money. "When I wrote to say I didn't have that kind of cash, the letters got even more frightening," she said at the time. "I was so scared I couldn't eat or sleep, worrying whether I'd be hit by more bad luck."

Dr. Lichtenberg said that scare tactics like this can be incredibly effective, and in many cases they are employed as a last resort to get a victim's money. "It's all sweet and nice as long as the cash is coming, and if that stops it can get very dark," he told us. "The path of least resistance is to just send more money."

Listening to Dr. Lichtenberg talk, we realized that this scam truly used every tool in the book. Other popular schemes seemed to rely on one main emotion. Schemes promising lottery wins rely on hope. Romance scams, in which fraudsters develop fake relationship with victims, rely on loneliness. And so-called grandparent scams that convince family members to wire money to a loved one they claim is in crisis rely on fear. But Maria's letters use a combination of all these emotions.

This is what made the scam so powerful. The letters appealed to the most base emotions of fear, loneliness, and hope -- making it nearly impossible for victims to resist. []

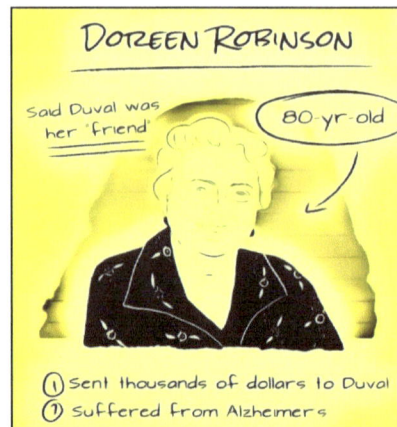

DOREEN ROBINSON

Said Duval was her 'friend'

80-yr-old

① Sent thousands of dollars to Duval
② Suffered from Alzheimers

Maria Duval Psychic Scam Costs Americans $180,000,000.00 USD

Injunction halts Maria Duval scam

Scambusters

A scam based on the name of Italian psychic Maria Duval has taken an estimated $180 million from U.S. victims, plus lots more from abroad.

Now a permanent injunction has stopped the scammers in their tracks but the money they took may not be recoverable.

In this week's issue we'll explain the scam and how it has preyed on the most vulnerable victims.

Are you under the spell of "Maria Duval"?

More than a million Americans allegedly have been.

And, like them, do you believe in fortunetellers and psychics like Ms. Duval who claim to be able to read and guide your future?

Lots of people do. But then again, plenty of people don't.

We're not planning to enter into that debate but what we do know is that many people who claim to be psychics have been exposed as frauds.

As we've previously reported in "Psychic" Scammers See Money Troubles in Your Future, that doesn't stop gullible members of the public from handing over large sums of money to bogus clairvoyants.

Probably one of the biggest psychic scams of all time revolves around the name of Italian clairvoyant Ms. Duval (also known as Maria Gamba).

Over a couple of decades, victims have received letters, often sent out in random mass mailings, claiming Ms. Duval could read their future, identify their problems, and provide them with solutions to transform their lives.

The letters were often personalized with names of the recipients. In other cases, victims responded to newspaper and magazine advertisements.

All they had to do was send money. Investigators reckon the scam has netted its operators as much as $180 million in the U.S. and considerably more than that worldwide.

The trouble is, no one is quite sure where and to whom the money has gone, though it seems likely much of it has ended up in China.

Ms. Duval, who is believed to be still alive as of this writing, supposedly sold her successful astrological prediction company to another firm back in the '90s but her name is still being used as the source of this firm's psychic predictions.

The long, rambling letters make unsubstantiated claims in Ms. Duval's name about her psychic skills and then go on to say she has, in the words of online information site Wikipedia, "telepathically received an important and urgent message" for the recipient.

"A special constellation of the stars …

means that an important time period has begun in the life of the recipient," Wikipedia adds.

"The most important wishes of the recipient can become reality now but only with the assistance of Maria Duval."

The letters and ads then offer some sort of talisman, such as a crystal or a secret document that supposedly can be used for a psychic or telepathic connection with the clairvoyant.

"These letters seem to be written by professional marketers using several well-known marketing methods," Wikipedia notes.

Victims are often asked to send in samples of their handwriting and other personal items to convince them that the personal service aspect is genuine.

Needless to say, there is no verifiable evidence that any part of this service — which costs between $20 to $100 at a time — has ever produced any beneficial results.

By its very nature, the scam has often attracted victims who are already in dire straits, perhaps through illness, financial loss, family troubles, and other misfortunes — in other words, the most vulnerable who can least afford to be conned.

Earlier this year, an investigation by broadcaster CNN identified a "huge business network" as being behind the scam.

There even seems to be some doubt about whether Ms. Duval really exists and whether, in fact, she is the person in a video supposedly of her on YouTube.

However, CNN claims to have interviewed Ms. Duval's son who told them she had lost control of her name and that she herself was a victim of the scam.

According to the broadcaster, the U.S. Postal Inspection Service has labeled the scam as one of the largest consumer fraud cases it has ever encountered "with more than a million Americans misled into believing they are purchasing personalized advice and unique artifacts."

CNN adds: "In reality, postal inspectors say the Duval letters are mass produced and the trinkets are worthless pieces of plastic from China."

In May of this year, a Department of Justice injunction barring certain named people, including Ms. Duval, from sending letters to people on U.S. soil was made permanent.

Criminal investigations into the scam are ongoing and stretch across the entire globe. As with the U.S., many countries have now taken legal action to halt the solicitations, although some people are still receiving them.

As for whether victims can hope to get any of their money back, that seems like a long shot, since no one knows where the cash has ended up and who the real masterminds behind the scam really are.

Announcing the injunction, U.S. Attorney Robert L. Capers for the Eastern District of New York said: "To line their own pockets, the defendants preyed upon the superstition and desperation of millions of vulnerable Americans. We will use every means at our disposal to protect our citizens from fraudulent schemes like this, that target the lonely, the ill, and the elderly."

If you're interested in seeing the five-

part CNN investigation into the Maria Duval scam, start here:

Who is behind one of the biggest scams in history?

It's one of the world's longest-running cons. Hundreds of millions of dollars stolen from some of the world's most vulnerable people -- the sick, the elderly and the poor -- who all thought they had found a savior in a mysterious woman named Maria Duval.

It has claimed more than 60 times the number of victims of Madoff's Ponzi scheme. With millions of people affected from the United States to Japan, federal investigators say it would be hard to find another case of consumer fraud that has hurt more people.

Since the alleged mail fraud started around 20 years ago, a laundry list of government agencies across the globe -- including the U.S. Department of Justice, British authorities, Canadian fraud investigators and Australian consumer protection officials -- have attempted to put an end to the scheme.

But somehow, it has raged on for decades.

It all centers around a mysterious French psychic named Maria Duval. In letters, interviews and Internet videos seen around the globe, Duval says she has had visions of the world exploding and humans living in space. She claims to have successfully predicted election results, forecast winning lottery numbers and helped police investigate crimes. She says she even found the missing dog of movie star Brigitte Bardot.

And millions of people have been convinced by her "personalized" letters that she can help them, too.

In what appear to be handwritten notes signed by Duval, she tells them they could win the lottery, recover from ailments or avoid terrible misfortune. All they need to do is pay a small sum -- often around $40 -- to receive her guidance, lucky numbers and special talismans like a Five Forces Stone or a Vibratory Crystal.

While many recipients would simply dismiss these letters, the scheme's massive success stems from its ability to take advantage of emotionally and financially vulnerable people. Many of its victims are elderly, often suffering from dementia or Alzheimer's. Others are lonely or depressed and are touched that someone is thinking of them.

"Not only was my poor mother quickly losing her mind due to Alzheimer's disease, she was lonely, bored, wanting to be wealthy and well," said Chrissie Stevens of her late mother Doreen Robinson, who fell prey to this scheme.

As her health and mental capacities diminished, Robinson sent more and more money to Duval -- sometimes as often as twice a day -- eventually adding up to more than $2,400 in a single year. (Other victims have lost even more.)

And Duval was just one of the schemes Stevens discovered her mother, 80 years old at the time, had fallen victim to. She ultimately realized her mother was tens of thousands of dollars in debt and had been sending much of her monthly fixed-income payments straight to Duval and other scammers. *(Cont's on Page 90)*

Maria Duval Psychic Scam Costs Americans $180,000,000.00 USD

Continued from Page 89

Robinson passed away in September of 2014, and Stevens is still brought to tears remembering her months-long battle to try to rip her mother free of Duval's grasp. Even after her mother promised to stop sending in more payments, Stevens found an envelope stuffed with cash and change that she had been hiding, hoping to send to her "friend" Maria.

Elderly, broke and homeless: The victims of a $200 million psychic scam

"She didn't have the quality of mind anymore to realize how much money she was losing or how often she was sending money," said Stevens. "She put value on silly, worthless, two-cent amulets she'd paid a fortune for and received nothing of value in return."

Learn about her until late September, when we were combing through piles of solicitations sent to seniors. Several readers had sent us this junk mail urging us to look into the many unscrupulous nonprofits, political groups and flat-out scammers that prey on the elderly by mail.

Among the mailings, we found a letter from a psychic named Patrick Guerin and were intrigued by its many details and promises -- of lottery winnings, luck and happiness.

In a quick Google search, it became clear that all sorts of psychics are targeting seniors. But one name kept coming up: Maria Duval.

Duval's own website showcased glowing testimonials from happy customers, international press clippings and links to media appearances and video clips where a French-speaking woman claiming to be Duval speaks about her psychic "gift."

But the search also revealed website upon website filled with emotional complaints from people who had been scammed out of their savings. Through our research, we learned of an 88-year-old U.S. military veteran who sent Duval $4,000 hoping to win the lottery so he could afford assisted living. And a young British girl who reportedly drowned with one of Duval's letters in her pocket after becoming obsessed with the psychic.

While there is no way to know just how many people have been duped by the scheme, the U.S. Postal Inspection Service alleges that the operation (which has included additional letters sent out by Guerin, her psychic sidekick) has claimed more than 1.4 million victims in the United States alone.

"It's remarkable," said Postal Inspector Clayton Gerber. "Maria Duval's name comes up in almost every major country."

How have Duval's letters been able to reel in so many victims?

It starts with so-called sucker lists. Federal court documents claim Duval's network zeroed in on potential victims by purchasing personal details, like names and addresses from data brokers that typically sell this information to marketers or retailers.

Advertisements placed in newspapers around the world have solicited this data too. These ads sometimes don't mention Duval's name at all. Instead they ask readers to send in everything from their zodiac sign and time of birth to their marital status -- all under the guise of a research study where they could end up winning large amounts of money.

By using this valuable information, Duval's letters can seem shockingly prescient.

"You are mainly under the influence of Venus. In addition to being born on May 22, 1927 in Kansas City at 12:00, I can already see some aspects of your personality," Duval wrote to one of her victims.

Tens of thousands of these letters have been sent out per month, allegedly adding up to millions of mailings in a single year in the U.S. alone. We've seen some as long as sixteen pages, and others that include coffee cup stains and little notes scrawled in the margins to make them look more realistic.

Many letters then ask victims for more personal information along with their payments -- sometimes even requesting mementos like photos or locks of hair.

"As soon as I have your photo (or the strands of hair from your head) in my possession, I am going to be able to concentrate all my psychic strengths further," Duval wrote in one of her letters. "I will keep the photo with me for the months and years to come so my contact as a medium can be with you permanently."

Once victims responded, Duval would reply offering additional help -- again for a price. In some replies, she would introduce victims to her psychic friend Guerin, who would then send his own letters offering even more good fortune and seeking even more money.

We reviewed a handful of the 1,500 letters written by victims in response to Duval that were recovered by U.S. officials in a matter of weeks. These letters tell a story of desperation -- detailing large debts, illnesses and worries about Social Security and Medicare benefits.

For some victims, their correspondence with Duval turns into their most cherished relationship -- one that can distance them from their family and friends. Some even send Duval holiday cards.

And many people have sent so many small payments to Duval that they have ended up giving thousands of dollars to her over the course of a few years.

All of this money adds up to millions. In the U.S. and Canada alone, investigators estimate that the scheme has raked in more than $200 million since 1999.

Although there's no estimate of how much money has been lost worldwide, we found traces of Duval's letters in more than a dozen countries -- most recently in Russia.

But Duval herself remains a mystery. Even though her name is on all of the letters, international investigators can't figure out who she really is -- prompting people around the world to come up with their own theories.

Some say she is actually the brainchild of an elderly Argentinean man, or cooked up by someone in Singapore. Many are adamant she's a real person enjoying a luxurious retirement in the South of France, while others are convinced she is the creation of criminal cartels.

"It is unclear whether Maria Duval is a real person or a fictitious character," U.S. prosecutors said in court filings.

But if Duval doesn't exist, who is the blonde woman in the YouTube videos? And if she's not in charge, who is really pulling the strings? And how have they evaded authorities for so long?

The investigation into Maria Duval will continue and reported here in The 'X' Chronicles.

Thanks to CNN and Scambusters for their great investigating and reporting in the Maria Duval case.

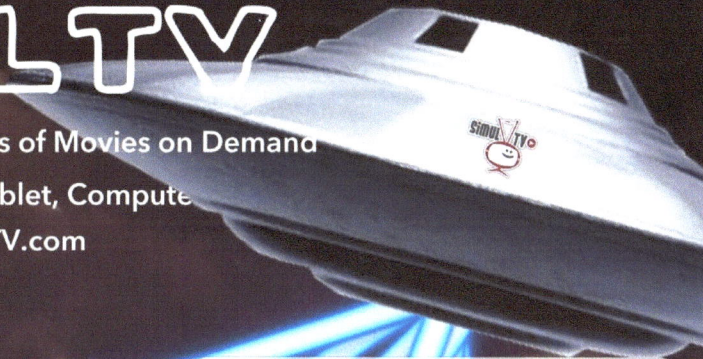

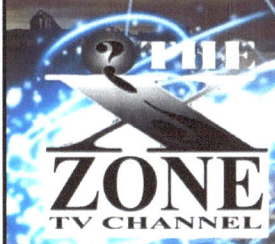

MY THOMAS
by
Roberta Grimes

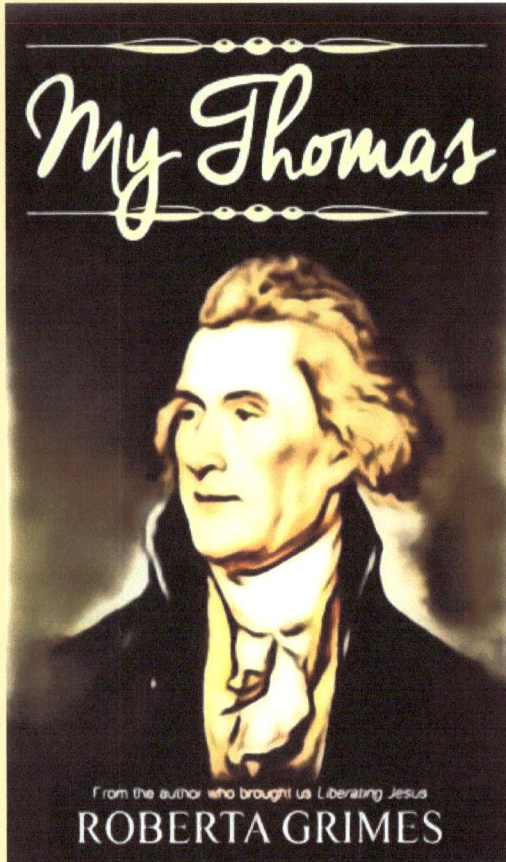

When Martha Skelton finds herself falling in love with a shy young burgess named Thomas Jefferson, it feels like an inconvenience. Widowed at twenty-two, Martha has no desire to lose the independence she has gained in the wake of her husband's death. But she cannot deny her feelings indefinitely. Despite her intentions, her friendship with Thomas develops into an intense and all-consuming love.

History casts a shadow on Martha's newfound joy. Through her father's slave and mistress, Betty Hemings, she comes to understand the true nature of slavery, an institution she has always taken for granted. As Betty's revelations tear down the walls of her ignorance, Martha begins to work with her husband to end the despicable practice forever.

This story is essentially true. Thomas Jefferson was such an obsessive record-keeper that we know what he was doing nearly every day of his adult life, and all the public things he is quoted as saying in My Thomas come from his contemporary writings. Martha's marriage to Thomas spanned the decade from 1772 to 1782, so it put her at the center of the audacious grab at freedom that was the American Revolution. Jefferson's writings suggest that if he had not been widowed, he would have retired from politics following the war and devoted himself to finding a way to end slavery that could have truly and forever healed the separations between the races. It is hard to read Martha's story now and not think about what might have been.

ROBERTA GRIMES is a business attorney who had two experiences of light in childhood. She then spent decades studying nearly 200 years of abundant and consistent communications from the dead, quantum mechanics, and the nature of consciousness to learn in detail what happens at and after death. She shares her discoveries in The Fun of Dying – Find Out What Really Happens Next (Greater Reality, 2010, 2014). Her sequel, The Fun of Staying in Touch (Greater Reality, 2014), details the many ways in which the dead give us signs of their survival and the exciting new ways that we can contact them. Roberta has been a guest on more than 100 radio programs during the past year, recently including The 'X' Zone Radio Show with Rob McConnell. She delivers weekly podcasts on WebTalkRadio.net that feature interviews with prominent experts. Her iTunes podcast archive has hundreds of thousands of subscribers. Visit Robert Grimes Online at www.RobertaGrimes.com. *MY THOMAS* is NOW Available at bookstores everywhere including:
Barnes & Noble, Costco, Target, Books-A-Million, Hudson Booksellers, Walmart, Kmart, Sam's Club, Walgreen's, CVS & Amazon.com.

www.ingramcontent.com/pod-product-compliance
Lightning Source LLC
Chambersburg PA
CBHW042008080426

42733CB00004B/42